Erik Bruhn

JOHN GRUEN

Erik Bruhn
DANSEUR NOBLE

〖 THE VIKING PRESS   NEW YORK 〗

Acknowledgment is made to Lucia Chase, for the
quote from her letter to Erik Bruhn; to *Dance Magazine*,
for two articles, July 1969 and July 1973; to the
Library & Museum of the Performing Arts, for a letter
from Ted Shawn; and to *The New York Times*, for permission
to use material from letters and reviews, ©1959,
1961, 1967, 1971, 1972, 1974 by The New York
Times Company. Reprinted by permission.

First published in 1979 by The Viking Press
625 Madison Avenue, New York, N.Y. 10022
Published simultaneously in Canada by
Penguin Books Canada Limited

LIBRARY OF CONGRESS CATALOGING IN PUBLICATION DATA
Gruen, John.
Erik Bruhn, danseur noble.
Includes index.
1. Bruhn, Erik. 2. Dancers—Denmark—Biography.
3. Choreographers—Denmark—Biography. I. Title.
GV1785.B78G78 792.8'092'4 [B] 79-12719
ISBN 0-670-29771-2

Printed in the United States of America
Designed by Ann Gold
Set in CRT Electra

[Foreword by Erik Bruhn]

SINCE MY retirement from dancing in classical ballets in 1971, I have often been asked, sometimes insistently so, to write my autobiography. For various personal reasons, this idea has never really appealed to me. For one thing, my nature much preferred to explore everyday possibilities, which eventually become the past, rather than to waste important time concentrating on what was already past. Also I have read several autobiographies that left me with few insights about the author. I suppose I also feared that I easily could lose the sense of what actually did happen by becoming so conscious of how I would like to appear in such a book.

When John Gruen first suggested that he write a book about me, I had every intention of saying no. But my vanity must have been in a state of nonresistance, because I did not refuse the offer; frankly, I was flattered. I found myself asking John what kind of a book he had in mind and how he would approach it. To my delight, he was willing to take on the heavy job of enduring endless hours of research, tracing old newspapers, ballet magazines, etc., for dates and events in my past.

I merely had to answer his questions in taped sessions. I agreed that he would be free to ask any questions about my work and about me as a dancer, as well as about any stories he might have heard about me as a person. (I am glad to say that throughout his work on the book, John asked no questions that ever embarrassed me. There were a few I personally found of less interest than others, but the only "danger" in these questions was the fact that I have a tendency to lose control of my imagination. Nevertheless, John always managed to get me straight back on the road.)

I had met John only once before, for an interview that he used in his book *The Private World of Ballet*. At the time I did not know John's writing style and was unfamiliar with his work, but when he later presented me with *The Private World*, it eliminated any doubts I might have had.

Eventually John and I met with his publisher and editor and an agreement was signed. Everyone seemed pretty excited, except me. At that point I could not believe that any questions John might ask, nor that any of my answers, would be of the slightest interest or excitement to anyone. I merely felt relieved that I had not agreed to write the book myself.

In the summer of 1978 American Ballet Theatre was preparing for a tour of Europe which would take us to Austria, Greece, Rumania, Italy, Germany, Denmark, England, and France. I was signed to make my debut as the Moor in José Limón's masterpiece *The Moor's Pavane* and to appear in Germany, Denmark, and France. Since I did not know the ballet at all, I was to rehearse the role while on tour.

John planned a visit to Vienna at the time ABT was performing there. As I was busy only with rehearsals, I had plenty of free time to meet with him to plan the book. It also gave us the opportunity to get to know each other a little and I gradually gained more confidence in John as a person and in the work we would concentrate on in Copenhagen, where I would have a week off from the tour.

Meantime, I had six Moors to face. Due to conflicting schedules during the tour, the full cast of four dancers in *The Moor's Pavane* was never really assembled in rehearsals until the evening before my first Moor in Munich. I really did not know on opening night whether I was doing the correct steps or was in the right place at the right time; God knows what kind of character I must have portrayed that evening. As it happened, we had the first four Moors to dance within seven days in Munich, Copenhagen, and Hamburg. Only in the performance in Hamburg did I feel the four of us got together and I returned to Copenhagen to work with John, tired but in a much better mood after the tension and doubts I had had about myself as the Moor. John and I planned to meet daily for lunch or dinner, allowing for four to six straight hours of work each day.

If I had thought in the beginning (which I did) that my part of the job would be an easy ride, I soon realized the emotional strain the sessions would create when I recalled certain periods and situations in my life. I am sure that no one in his right mind ever forgets the important moments in his life—whether they are of a happy, sad, or tragic character—but we don't go around remembering those times every day and I find myself far better equipped to cope with a present situation than with sentiments of the past.

Looking back from this distance, certain times and people are bound to appear to me in a different light. With luck, we mature into having a better understanding of what actually happened and, as we grow up and sometimes away from certain situations, we all see those same times again, but from where we are at this point.

Since that first week in Copenhagen, the following sessions we had, whether in Toronto or New York or simply on the telephone, seemed to become a lot easier for me. And now that the book is finished and ready for the audience we hope exists for it, I would like to thank the Gruen family for the warm and friendly atmosphere with which they surrounded me and for the always delicious meals and drinks afterward. I would also like to thank Rosemary Winckley for her extensive research and enthusiastic interest.

To all my friends and those people who took time out to contribute to what constitutes their part in the book, I also give special thanks. There are other people, indeed some very close to me to this day, who are not in this book. But dancing was just one part of my life and they would relate only to aspects of me not included here. However, I would like to thank them, too, for helping me become a fuller person, if not necessarily a better one.

My contribution to the dance so far (and I hope there will be more to come) has only been achieved through the fact that I have never tried to neglect my natural need to enrich my life as a person through and with other people first and foremost. Only in that way could dance become a natural expression and a true extension of me as a person.

Appendix, Filmography, and Selected Bibliography begin on page 227.

Illustrations follow pages 40, 82, 124, 188.

〚 Acknowledgments 〛

MANY individuals have given of their time, thoughts, and feelings in connection with this portrait of the great Danish dancer Erik Bruhn. Of them all, I owe my deepest gratitude to Erik Bruhn himself, who gave me the privilege of sharing part of his life over a period of some fifteen months in such disparate places as Copenhagen, Vienna, Toronto, New York, and Fort Worth. His patience during the endless hours of taping and talking has been as remarkable as it has been generous. His honesty and candor have turned an exciting project into a memorable experience.

I am equally indebted to the many dancers who have shared the stage with Erik Bruhn and who have unstintingly provided me with invaluable insights on Bruhn as an artist and a friend. My gratitude goes also to those who have known him outside the realm of his profession.

I owe thanks to Genevieve Oswald, Curator of the Dance Collection, The New York Public Library, for her own time and for the cooperation of her staff. Also of invaluable help has been Andrew Mark Wentink.

My special gratitude to the Trojaborg family in Copenhagen—Werner, Ruth, Steen, Ulrik, and Nanna—all of whom extended to me the kindness of sharing their home during my visit in Denmark. Since I am unfamiliar with the Danish language, the Trojaborgs were of immense help during my interviews with Erik Bruhn's Danish friends and in translating numerous articles and reviews.

I wish further to thank Steven Bradley, who spent many weeks with me in researching material on Erik Bruhn's career. His thoroughness in transcribing dozens upon dozens of tapes and his goodwill throughout our association are deeply appreciated.

Of very particular help in the preparation of the manuscript was Rosemary Winckley, whose knowledge of Bruhn's career and of ballet in general, and whose sensitive suggestions and great dedication to this project provided me with added inspiration.

For her enthusiasm, encouragement, and unfailing support I give heartfelt thanks to my editor, Barbara Burn.

J.G.

OCTOBER 1978

Erik Bruhn

〖 CHAPTER 1 〗

I T HAS BEEN said that "There is good dancing, there is great dancing, and then there is Erik Bruhn."
This phrase means, of course, that in the world of dance Erik Bruhn stands alone, but it is also true in a deeper, more personal sense. Throughout his life, both as artist and as private individual, Erik Bruhn has been surrounded by the myth of solitude—the aura of aloneness. As one of the twentieth century's greatest classical male dancers, he has unwittingly created a legend that has placed him outside the general public's realm. In the eyes and minds of those who follow the dance, Bruhn has stood as god, idol, ideal—the essence of perfection. They have looked upon him as a man of mystery, an enigmatic being whose presence on the stage evokes wonder and awe. Ballet critics the world over have been forced to alter their perception of dance at the sight of Bruhn's performances. In a way, critics have learned about dance by the example of Bruhn's art. No matter how knowledgeable or astute, the ballet critic sharpens his or her vision of male dancing with the advent of an artist possessed of the purest classical technique, the most astonishing clarity of line, and the widest possible dramatic range.

Having to live up to such a wealth of talent has not been easy for Erik Bruhn, though lavish, and burdensome, praise has never been denied him.

He recalls how members of the Royal Danish Ballet would stand amazed at his feats in the Royal Danish Ballet School classroom. "People

〖 1 〗

from the professional company would come and watch me do certain things," says Bruhn. "Of course we were all trained in the Bournonville technique, but I had a facility for turning and I could do certain things within the framework of the music that somehow intensified my movements. This all came very naturally to me, and I had no idea why. At any rate, the press got wind of my ability and someone came to interview me. For some reason I told the interviewer that I planned to stop dancing— right then, at fifteen. You see, I became frightened of my capacities, and frightened of the responsibility of the talent I was apparently born with. Of course, I continued dancing, but that initial fear has never left me."

The phenomenal gifts belonging to Erik Bruhn have haunted him throughout his career, and have deeply colored his private and personal life. Not only did Bruhn become the greatest male dancer of his generation but he was additionally blessed by an extraordinary physical appearance. Superbly proportioned, his trim five-foot-eight frame is at once delicate and tensile, elegant and supple. Most startling is his face of quite breathtaking symmetry. The perfect composition of his features, Nordic in character, gives an image of nobility. With light-blue eyes set beneath a strong brow, an aquiline nose, a sensitive mouth, and firm if not stubborn chin, the face projects lofty coolness. By the same token, it is a face that can mirror many moods: icy imperturbability, impassivity, aloofness, deep anger, and even cruelty. It can also reflect tenderness, passion, and, as it breaks into a smile, an altogether infectious warmth. When Bruhn performs, the beauty and mobility of his face are invariably brought into play. But then, onstage, Bruhn makes use of everything he has. Not only a great dancer but a superb actor as well, he immerses himself totally in whatever role he undertakes and brings to light and to life whatever character he portrays. In a sense, Bruhn the private person is rendered invisible in the throes of a performance. Part of his power as an artist is his ability to transform personal experience into art without once revealing the source of that experience. It becomes transmuted into pure characterization.

To try to explain Erik Bruhn's genius is extremely difficult. Objectivity blurs because of the overwhelming and relentless acclaim that has come to him. Writers on the dance have written endless words in praise of Bruhn's art. They have analyzed, dissected, and theorized. They have attempted to translate the ephemeral into the permanence of the written word but have only succeeded in conveying verbal images that merely approximate the reality of any Bruhn performance.

What was always easy to describe, from a critical point of view, were the technical underpinnings that are the foundation of any dancer's equipment. The trained eye is quick to judge if a pirouette is well executed, if a jump is negotiated with ease, if the line of the body in an adagio variation is correctly placed. What is more difficult to define is the aesthetic intonation that these technical accomplishments have the power to reveal. In Bruhn's case, technique has always been subservient to aesthetic inevitability and fluency. At the peak of his career, Bruhn's body in motion gave the odd illusion of fleetness and repose. Even the most strenuous technical demands gave the appearance of quiet refinement and effortlessness, and control and discipline seemed a matter of instinct. One was never aware of strain, of the body pushing itself beyond its limits. No gesture was ever superfluous, no movement ever overinflated.

Bruhn has had the capacity to offer a vision of true classicism through economy, simplicity, and taste. But it was not only the aristocratic line of his body that brought forth these qualities. In a way, it was Bruhn's intellect that provided the impulse behind the clarity and depth of his artistry.

A thinking man's dancer, Erik Bruhn has never allowed his performances to be devoid of some sort of intellectual focus. He has never been a dancer to simply go out and "sell it." He has never been known to set foot on a stage without first satisfying his own needs for complete understanding of what he was about to perform. Whether a ballet contained a story line or whether it was a purely abstract work, this dancer needed to be motivated in order to give full rein to his interpretation. This is not to say that Bruhn offered studied or calculated performances: passion and fire were as much a part of his dance equipment as nobility and refinement. A true man of the theater, he never lost sight of the fact that to be a dancer was also to be an entertainer—a performer whose job it was to satisfy a paying audience. Bruhn's consummate artistry did not deter him from frequently bringing down houses with breathtaking pyrotechnics in such a classic warhorse as, say, the *Don Quixote* pas de deux or in the bravura passages of the great classics. Bruhn could soar in the air, slash through space, turn and jump with thrilling speed and élan, and rivet his audiences with the incredible daring of dangerous technical feats.

What has often been remarked about Bruhn is the magic he wielded the moment he stepped on the stage. Countless dancers, critics, and fans have agreed that the moment Bruhn appeared, one could never take one's eyes off him. He had merely to stand or sit still to capture the total attention of any audience. In his quietest moments he brought with him a near-mystical circumference that could mesmerize even the least knowledgeable balletgoer. Without dancing a single step, and on a stage brimming with dancing activity, the eye invariably moved toward Bruhn and just as invariably stayed there. It may have been his look of self-containment, which promised some sudden release. Audiences did not wish to miss the moment when Bruhn would propel himself into action. But even as he stood or perhaps quietly walked across the stage, he projected an intensity of feeling that in itself contained a magical power.

Indeed, some of the mystery connected with Erik Bruhn's greatness as a dancer has eluded him. To this day Bruhn is at a loss to explain just why or how the mantle of supreme artistry fell upon his shoulders. This is not a matter of modesty but one of genuine surprise. His acclaim at a very young age did not give him a sense of elation. In truth, the dance came slowly to Erik Bruhn.

As a young child he was neither goaded into dancing nor was his family theatrically or artistically inclined. In a sense the will to dance assailed Erik Bruhn out of a need for escape. To begin with, it was an obscure desire to find an identity that he barely understood. Young Erik grew up with four sisters, a strong, willful mother, and an ever-present, comforting aunt—an overwhelmingly female family. The boy rarely saw his father, who frequently absented himself from a household dominated by his wife, who provided the principal support of the family because Ernst Bruhn's penchant for gambling and travel was stronger than his need to be a paterfamilias. Thus, Erik Bruhn, young as he was, was looked upon as the man of the house—a role he neither wanted nor relished. He was loved and spoiled, but he was also deeply affected by what seemed to him the strange and conflicting personalities of the family members. Still, it was the complexity of his early life that shaped him. Bruhn's tenacity, independence, lifelong introversion, his sense of aloneness, and, to a strong degree, his stubbornness became the steel that ultimately provided him with psychological armor, which would eventually shield and protect him from the outside world and finally give him the strength to forge ahead in a profession that has always demanded superhuman discipline and total dedication.

Indeed, when the struggle of work produced technical ease, refinement, and control and when Erik Bruhn emerged as the personification of a classical dancer, the outside world would bestow on him rewards with which no human being, no matter how gifted, could easily come to terms. The burden of greatness would too often prove unbearable to an artist whose destiny it was to represent the ultimate vision of classical perfection in the imperfect, turbulent, and often treacherous world of the dance.

〖 CHAPTER 2 〗

ONE MORNING in October 1928 Ellen Evers Bruhn rose from her
bed feeling unusually tired. She was heavy with child, but this did
not deter her from going to the center of Copenhagen, where she
owned and operated an exclusive hairdressing salon. She knew that her
fourth child was due to be born, but there was a string of appointments
awaiting her at the shop—women of means and long-standing clients, who
would allow only Ellen to dress their hair.

Ellen Bruhn was a stocky, highly energetic woman, not conventionally
beautiful but radiating a great sense of vitality. She was a person who liked
to fend for herself. She had left home at the age of fifteen for Norway,
where she was given a job as an assistant to a well-known hairdresser. Two
years later she had mastered her craft and resolved to continue in her profession in her native Copenhagen. At seventeen she obtained work in the
city's most fashionable hairdressing establishment and became so adept at
her métier that she resolved to open her own shop, taking with her any
number of customers from her previous place of employment. The Evers
Hairdressing Salon at Kobmagergade 16 thrived. Ellen Evers, as she was
known to her clients, was brilliant at her work, and her liveliness and
charm brought in more and more customers.

But on this particular morning she felt weak and exhausted. Oddly
enough, there were no birth pangs—no pains announcing the imminent
arrival of a new child. Still, her overwhelming sense of fatigue troubled

her, and she thought it best to go to the hospital. The doctors knew immediately that the baby was about to arrive. They kept saying, "Push, push! You must push or the child will die." Drained to the utmost, Ellen could not help, and the doctors had to pull the baby out of her womb. It was a healthy boy and as he was being washed and laid in his mother's arms, the nurses and doctors noted with smiles the perfect shape of the baby's body. His tiny legs were slim and long and his torso perfectly molded. Ellen Evers was happy that, at last, she had given birth to a son. After three daughters, it would be splendid to have a boy in the house.

Erik Belton Evers Bruhn was born on October 3, 1928, in Copenhagen. When mother and son returned to their house, the family gathered around to admire the new arrival. There was Erik's father, Ernst. There was his half sister, Else, and his sisters, Birthe and Aase. Also on hand was Minna Evers, Ellen's sister, who would soon be moving in to be in charge of the children while their mother continued working. Everyone admired the blond, curly-headed baby—everyone, that is, except his half sister, Else. She was a big girl for her thirteen years, the offspring of a father she had never known. Being the eldest and unusually attached to her mother, she became increasingly jealous of each subsequent child. She hated sharing the attention that had been exclusively hers for several years. With the arrival of yet another sibling she felt a strong twinge of resentment. Else looked disdainfully down at the angelic, sleeping creature.

When Ellen Evers had blossomed into a young, high-spirited girl, she had kept her own counsel regarding her morals and her principles. Erratically educated and highly independent, she did not follow in the accepted mores of society. A free spirit and always unconventional, she would live with the men she loved and bear their children without the benefit of a marriage certificate. A born provider, she was invariably drawn to men who were somewhat passive and given to letting Ellen run their lives. It was not anything she really minded. She could never, in fact, relish the idea of simply sitting at home and being a housewife. She enjoyed the company of people and took pleasure in working and in earning money. When she met Ernst Bruhn she found him enormously attractive—a handsome Dane of aristocratic bearing and beguiling manners. She was drawn to his cosmopolitan ways, for he had spent some twelve years in Russia and had traveled in foreign lands. She noted also that he was a pliable man, someone who would not be didactic or dominating. She observed, perhaps happily, perhaps not, that Ernst Bruhn lacked ambition. Unlike herself, he did not evince the drive to succeed in any given profession. But then, there were reasons.

The meeting between Ellen Evers and Ernst Bruhn came about circuitously. One of her clients was a pretty, somewhat restless woman whose name was Mrs. Bruhn. In time, the two women developed a friendship. Ellen learned that Mrs. Bruhn was Polish and was married to a Dane whom she had met in Russia, an irrigation engineer who had been working successfully in his profession for twelve years. When the Russian Revolution broke out in 1917, Bruhn managed to escape and he returned to Denmark, much to his wife's regret. Mrs. Bruhn recounted that on their way out of Russia her husband had contracted malaria. Indeed, he was so weakened by the disease that he was unable to work steadily.

On several occasions Ernst Bruhn would appear at Ellen's salon to pick up his wife. Ellen looked at her client's husband and found him pleasant and attractive. He too had found Ellen congenial—a person he could talk to. One day Ernst Bruhn appeared at the shop specifically to see Ellen herself, and he told Ellen that his wife had left him. She had, in fact, left Denmark and gone to live in Switzerland. It appeared she could no longer bear her life in Copenhagen, did not like its people, could barely speak its language, and apparently had had her fill of Ernst Bruhn, who seemed unable to find work. Ellen commiserated with Ernst and the two began to see each other. After many subsequent meetings, Ellen Evers suggested that Ernst move in with her. Happily, he agreed. Ernst Bruhn took kindly to little Else, Ellen's daughter by a previous lover. Ellen bore him two daughters, Birthe and Aase. Although Ernst and Ellen eventually learned that his wife had settled in Switzerland and had asked for a divorce, which Bruhn granted her, they did not bother to get married.

The couple was happy, Ellen's shop thrived, and the children were cared for by Minna Evers. But problems began to develop when Ernst Bruhn found it increasingly difficult to earn a living on his own. Though now recovered from his illness—the malaria that had plagued him for many months at a time—he seemed unable to stick to a job for any length of time. Finally Ellen decided to take matters into her own hands. She bought Ernst an antique shop in Copenhagen which, under his supervision, floundered—he would continually undersell the fine objects in the shop and, at times, would even give away antiques out of the goodness of his heart. Unsurprisingly, the venture failed. Ellen bought him a flower shop, but it too was doomed in Ernst's hands. Totally devoid of business sense, Ernst Bruhn made a shambles of every venture that came his way.

The children were growing, Ellen was constantly at the shop, and Ernst Bruhn felt lost in the face of his own inadequacies. He sought consolation in gambling. He was certain that with any luck he could make a fortune playing roulette, cards, or betting on horses and thus relieve his depression and anxiety over his lack of business acumen. Ellen Evers was earning a good deal of money, most of which she carefully hid from Ernst. But Ernst knew the hiding places, took the money, and gambled it away. When Ernst lost he took to the bottle and sheepishly returned home to face Ellen's chastisements. At first Ellen Evers loved Ernst enough not to vent her wrath on him too harshly. She understood him and sympathized with his unhappiness. She closed her eyes to Ernst's newly acquired habits and in the end simply accepted his way of life.

When Ellen Evers found herself pregnant with her fourth child she and Ernst were officially married in Copenhagen. No sooner had she given birth to Erik than Ellen resumed her duties at her hairdressing salon. Business continued to flourish, and in time she became particularly adept at beautifying the gifted actresses who were giving performances at Copenhagen's Royal Opera House. Indeed, some of them insisted that Ellen do their hair in their own dressing rooms. This talent brought Ellen further prestige, but it found her working both day and night.

When Erik was a year old, the Bruhns decided to purchase a pretty, two-story house in a suburb of Copenhagen. It stood on a quiet, tree-lined street—Violvej—in the village of Gentofte, a twenty-minute car ride from the city. Ellen Bruhn had also converted the rear of her shop into a small apartment—a place where she might spend time when she was too exhausted to make the trip back to Gentofte. The household had literally been taken over by the constant comings and goings of the Bruhn children. By this time Ellen's sister Minna had moved in to keep some semblance of family life going for the three rambunctious girls and the little boy, who was dominated by his sisters, particularly by Else, who continued to vent an irrational jealousy on him. Erik had become his mother's favorite child and Else would take pleasure in tormenting him, at times beating him or playing cruel games. Else had for several years been subject to severe fits of depression and violence; she would do strange things, such as stringing up a dog by its neck and beating it. At other times she would herd each of her siblings under her parents' bed and command them to remain there for hours. If anyone dared to move, she would be ready with a whip. In point of fact, Else was showing signs of what amounted to a deeply neurotic personality. She would fly into violent rages and furiously berate her mother or any member of the family. At these times Ellen Bruhn would take Else with her into town and allow her to live for weeks in the apartment behind the shop, away from her brother and sisters.

But Else noticed that her mother was once again pregnant, and that there would be yet another child to divert attention. And in due course the family was increased by the Bruhnses' last child—another daughter, whom they named Benthe. But the Bruhn marriage had become intolerable and when Erik turned five the couple decided to separate. Ernst Bruhn moved out of the Gentofte household, yet the constant quarrels would continue throughout the couple's lifetime, for Ernst Bruhn would pay weekly visits to his children and Ellen would continue to help him financially whenever the need arose. Although every meeting ended in an argument, the attachment between them was deep enough to make total separation impossible. In later years, when Ernst contracted cancer, Ellen was constantly at his side. She saw him through a series of difficult operations and cared for him until his death in 1958.

Erik Bruhn's memories of his father are a mixture of admiration and dismay. In a sense his father was his only ally in a house full of women. He was handsome and something of a romantic figure, with his seemingly carefree way of life. But the more vivid memories centered on the long and violent quarrels. He and his sisters would cower and pray that the rows would come to an end and that their parents would get along peaceably. Young Erik also sensed that his father resented him, for the affection that Ellen should have given to her husband was lavished on Erik. It was not only Erik's father who showed this resentment but his sisters as well. Erik remembers begging his mother not to spoil him in front of the others, because when her back was turned his sisters would beat him up. Hearing this, Ellen Bruhn would say: "Well, if you're not strong enough to defend yourself it means you're just as weak as your father!" Being like his father was, Erik knew, the worst thing imaginable in his mother's thoughts.

Because of the turmoil in the Bruhn household, five-year-old Erik retreated into himself. While his mother doted on him, she would also have ways of making him feel unworthy. Besides, she was seldom at home and the boy, harassed by his sisters, had to protect himself continually and fend off the frequent abuse that came his way. The one comfort was his aunt Minna, whom the family affectionately called *Moster*. She was a loving woman, who nursed the children, cleaned them, fed them, and, when they cried, cuddled and comforted them. At times she seemed like the mother they never had, and Erik adored her. His mother was a distant and awesome figure to whom he could never quite open his heart.

Erik was a serious little boy; even the expression on his face was oddly closed. Golden-haired, apple-cheeked, and entirely cherubic, he seldom smiled and seldom spoke. He would spend hours alone in the garden—a large one—and be content to sit in an apple tree, surveying what he might imagine was his paradisical domain. His first conscious encounter with death occurred at five when he saw a three-year-old child hit by a truck. He saw the tiny child run and heard the terrifying screech of the wheels as they ran over the child's chest. Stunned and unable to move, Erik could see the child's face and its open, frightened eyes. He remembers that the truck driver rushed out of his vehicle and asked Erik to describe what had happened, for the driver had not seen the little boy in front of his truck. Erik could tell him nothing, paralyzed with fear and guilt. He thought, If only I could have been walking with that child I might have saved him. A day later the papers reported that the little boy had died. Erik did not know what dying meant and his mother and aunt did not enlighten him. "We don't talk about that," they said. From that moment on, Erik developed something of an obsession with the idea of dying. When his grandmother died, Aunt Minna told him, "To die means that you go away for a long, long time." This strange, unresolved thought stayed in Erik's mind and, as he pondered it, he felt both relieved and yet confused that those who die might eventually return.

Young Erik did not make friends easily, but his sisters did and there was a constant coming and going in the house. Erik did not seem to care for other children; his playmates had always been his sisters and although they might handle him roughly and reduce him to tears, there were times when the games were fun. When Erik was sent to the local public school, he felt lost and unhappy. He had never been regimented before, had never faced a teacher, had never sat at a desk. The experience came as a shock, which made Erik retreat even further into himself. At school he barely spoke. His face remained impassive, and when asked a question, he remained resolutely silent. As time went on his teachers became concerned about him; his mother was called in and told that her son would neither speak nor participate in schoolwork and games. They suggested that Erik might be retarded and wondered whether he ought not to be sent to a special school for afflicted children.

But the silent boy was neither unobservant nor retarded. Far from it! He quietly took in everything that went on around him and, though unresponsive to the questions of his teachers, he was learning constantly. He learned how to read and write. Indeed, his recalcitrance in matters of participation were not based on ignorance but on shyness and, to some degree, fear. Often he would daydream. One persistent daydream was the notion that he was invisible—that he did not physically exist. He knew he was alive and "somewhere," but thought that people didn't really see him. This strange feeling of invisibility would continue to haunt Erik Bruhn. He recalls that as a teenager he accidentally met his mother on a busy street. They were practically face to face, but he claims that she did not see him—that he was invisible to her. Experiences such as these would recur as he grew older, and in some ways they would color the fabric of his personality and view of himself.

To shake her six-year-old boy out of this torpor, Ellen Bruhn decided to send him to a local dancing school that was attended by some of his sisters. If Erik could find some release for his aloneness and pent-up energies it might do him a world of good. Reluctantly he agreed to join the dancing class, and as he entered the small studio he was horrified to see that it was filled with little girls. There wasn't another boy in sight. Once again he was surrounded by the female sex and he felt helpless and overwhelmed. By the same token he was unconsciously attracted to the idea of moving to the sound of the piano. Somehow conquering his fears, he placed himself along the barre with the girls and quite easily followed the instructions of a ballet teacher. This was a new sensation—and a pleasurable one. It became even more pleasurable when the teacher singled him out and paid special attention to him. The ballet teacher had noted how perfectly the boy's body was shaped—how very suitable the slim, straight legs would be for dancing and how very well he carried himself. There was an innate grace in the manner in which he raised his arms, turned his head, and executed his first basic ballet steps. She *did* wish that Erik would manage to put some expression in his face—would occasionally smile. But the boy seemed unable to do this. Even as his body began to move with fluency, the look on his face remained untouched by emotional response. But no matter. It was clear that Erik Bruhn held the promise of a potential dancer. The line of his young body seemed altogether unique and his natural musicality needed only to be nurtured and given the chance to blossom.

Erik Bruhn had never seen a ballet and he was totally unfamiliar with performing. Although he had heard his mother speak of actors and actresses, of singers and ballet dancers, he had no notion of what these people actually did. To be sure, he was intrigued by the theater, since his mother came home with tales of this or that performer when she herself went to the theater, ballet, or opera.

The perceptive ballet teacher resolved to choreograph a special solo for her single male pupil. It was to be a little Russian dance and Erik would be given a colorful costume to perform it in a forthcoming school recital. When his ballet teacher told Erik about it, his eyes lit up. He practiced his short variation diligently and, with the encouragement of his teacher, quickly learned the steps. On the appointed day, Erik Bruhn was told that the family and friends of all the pupils of the ballet school would be coming to watch the recital. This news came as a total shock—Erik had no idea that giving a recital meant dancing before an audience. He was petrified at the idea of dancing in the presence of strangers, even if his own mother and aunt might also be there. When the audience filed into the studio, which had been set up with a sea of chairs, Erik trembled. He didn't want to dance in front of all those people.

When Erik's solo was announced the audience applauded but Erik refused to budge. The teacher tried to cajole him into performing but Erik ran out of the room. The embarrassed teacher announced to everyone that a small emergency had arisen and that Erik had to go to the bathroom. There was good-natured laughter, but Erik, who heard the announcement, was mortified. He rushed back into the studio, placed himself in the center of the floor, and in a clear, piping voice declared that he did *not* have to go to the bathroom. With that, he plunged into his dance and performed it brilliantly.

It became increasingly clear to the ballet teachers at the Gentofte dancing school that Erik Bruhn possessed unusual talent. They worked hard with him, and slowly improved his technique and refined his ballet vocabulary. They were continually amazed by the boy's natural affinity for movement and found it remarkable that so young a child could make something special of even the simplest technical demands. Somehow Erik could intuit the way in which to place his body and limbs and how to execute movements and gestures with special grace.

The boy happily continued his ballet lessons in Gentofte until he reached the age of nine. By this time his teachers were convinced that he would be a suitable candidate for the Royal Danish Ballet School at the Opera House in Copenhagen. They felt certain that he would be accepted and that he would develop into a fine young dancer. Mrs. Bruhn was duly telephoned and told of her son's abilities. It was suggested to her that she take him to an audition at the ballet school and that there his training would be far more professional. In time he might even become a member of the Royal Danish Ballet.

When Erik was told by his mother of his teachers' suggestion, he balked. The Royal Danish Ballet School? It was so big! And there would be all those other children—children he didn't know and didn't care to know. He instantly rejected the idea. His mother, not caring one way or the other, shrugged her shoulders and let the child be. He was only nine and there was plenty of time to think about his future. Aunt Minna, on the other hand, thought otherwise. She did not push Erik into auditioning, but felt that in a year's time Erik might feel differently about it. She realized that if he were accepted at the Royal Danish Ballet School, he would not only be learning a profession but would also be given an academic education that would not cost the family a penny. Of course, even if the child were admitted to the school, he would have to prove himself an apt pupil on all counts. But if he passed his examinations and satisfied his ballet teachers, he would eventually be taken into the Royal Danish Ballet with its system of promotions, graded salaries, and ultimately a lifelong pension after twenty years of service to the company.

And so, a year later, Erik Bruhn was asked by his aunt Minna if he wouldn't like to change his mind and go with her into Copenhagen to audition for admittance into the Royal Danish Ballet School. By this time Erik knew he loved to dance and the prospect of becoming a serious dancer did interest him. But he hesitated. Minna smiled. "I tell you what," she said. "If you take the audition I will give you one whole krone.

And if you pass the audition I will give you another krone!" Erik thought about it. At last he said, "All right, I'll go. Give me my krone."

The next day Erik and his aunt traveled the short distance to Copenhagen, made their way to the Opera House, and within a matter of hours Erik Bruhn had passed his audition at the Royal Danish Ballet School. This was the early summer of 1937. That fall Erik Bruhn would become a pupil at one of the world's most prestigious ballet schools, entering a routine that would change his life completely. Standing proudly next to his aunt, he looked up at her and said, "Now you can give me my other krone!"

[CHAPTER 3]

THE TRADITION of the Danish ballet is a noble one. As elsewhere in Europe, ballet flourished under the aegis of royalty, in Denmark under Frederick II, Christian IV, and Frederick III during the sixteenth and seventeenth centuries. At first, ballet and theater were joint arts, and stage performances were given with the opening of Copenhagen's first theater, the Lille Grønnegade, in 1722. Twenty-six years later, the Royal Theatre was opened and ballet performances began to be a popular form of entertainment. Because Denmark did not boast native choreographers, the royalty of the period imported the best-known Italian masters— choreographers such as Gaetano Orlando, Antonio Sacco, Vincenzo Piattoli, and Domenico Andreani. Later, a number of French choreographers were brought to Denmark, notably Des Larches and Pierre Laurent.

As the distinguished Danish dance critic Svend Kragh-Jacobsen has pointed out, by the middle of the eighteenth century, a teaching curriculum had been set up at the Royal Theatre, but the actual school did not come into existence until 1771, when it was founded by the Frenchman Pierre Laurent. Laurent had come to the Royal Theatre from the Paris Opéra and remained in Denmark until his death in 1807. The flowering of the Danish ballet can be attributed to this French master, who was responsible for training talented Danes, a number that was significantly increased when Vincenzo Galeotti, a Florentine dancer, teacher, and choreographer, became the Royal Theatre's ballet master. Over a period of

thirty years, Galeotti established an international repertoire, producing
ballets choreographed by such international masters as Jean-Georges No-
verre and Gasparo Angiolini. Galeotti himself produced several imagina-
tive works based on novels and plays by Voltaire and Shakespeare. In
addition, he was inspired by Scandinavian subjects, which proved to be a
great success with Danish audiences.

Among the dancers at the Royal Theatre was the French-born Antoine
Bournonville, who had been a star in Stockholm, performing in the Gustav
III Theatre. His dancing proved exemplary in Denmark and upon Galeotti's death in 1816 he was appointed director of the Royal Danish Ballet. As it turned out, Antoine Bournonville proved to be only a passable
choreographer and a terrible administrator. Under his leadership, ballet in
Denmark declined, but would again rise to prominence under the inspired
direction of Bournonville's son August. Indeed, when August Bournonville
succeeded his father as director of the Danish ballet in 1829, the Danish
school, as we know it today, was firmly established.

August Bournonville was born in Copenhagen in 1805 and was his
father's first pupil. His debut at the Royal Theatre took place in 1813 and
the youngster was so remarkable that he was awarded a scholarship for further study in Paris. There he came under the tutelage of internationally
known ballet teachers and choreographers, among them the great Auguste
Vestris and Pierre Gardel. Having imbibed the meticulous lessons of Vestris and other French masters, he returned to Copenhagen and took his
place as one of the Royal Danish Ballet's leading dancers. During his early
career as a dancer, the young Bournonville returned to Paris for four years
and was ultimately accepted into the Paris Opéra. It was in Paris that August Bournonville developed the fleet and airy technique which he would
eventually bring back to Denmark, thus influencing all subsequent genera-
tions of Danish dancing and firmly establishing what has come to be
known as the Bournonville style, which to this day characterizes the singu-
larity of the Royal Danish Ballet.

Upon his return to Copenhagen, Bournonville, a highly gifted, impul-
sive, and ambitious man, signed a contract for eighteen years as director,
solo dancer, and choreographer of the Royal Danish Ballet. During this
long tenure he not only ingrained in his pupils the principles of his technique but also created over fifty ballets, some of which have become standard classics of the twentieth-century ballet repertoire. Works such as

Napoli, Kermesse in Bruges, A Folk Tale, La Ventana, Conservatoriet, The Life Guards on Amager, and his most famous ballet, *La Sylphide,* contain a unique style which may superficially be characterized as light, buoyant, and fleet. Each is possessed of specific technical demands which have been considered difficult to master, but once mastered produce a lyricism and naturalness of very particular joy and charm. Several books on ballet technique have been written on the Bournonville style, the first being Bournonville's own treatise, *Etudes chorégraphiques.* Indeed, Erik Bruhn's own book, *Bournonville and Ballet Technique,* written jointly with the American dance critic and historian Lillian Moore and published in 1961, has become one of the definitive modern studies on the subject.

Suffice it to say here that with the advent of August Bournonville as head of the Royal Danish Ballet, a new, individual style of dancing came into being, one that continued to give all subsequent directors of the company a tradition upon which to build. Bournonville left the Royal Danish Ballet in 1877 and the standards immediately declined. Two ballet masters were appointed to the Royal Theatre following Bournonville's departure, the dancer Hans Beck, who led the company from 1894 to 1915, and his partner Valborg Borchsenius. Beck, who was reputed to be Bournonville's last pupil, kept the Bournonville repertoire alive during his period as dancer and ballet master of the company, but neither Beck nor Borchsenius were choreographers, and the company lost its glorious reputation.

At that time, an enthralling ballet company had invaded the West from Russia—Sergei Diaghilev's Ballets Russes. Founded in Paris in 1909 and made up of dancers such as Nijinsky, Pavlova, Karsavina, and Adolf Bolm, among others, the company took Europe by storm and brought Russian ballet to worldwide prominence. One of its chief choreographers was Michel Fokine, who had created a series of masterpieces for Diaghilev, including such works as *Firebird, Petrouchka, Les Sylphides, Prince Igor,* and *Le Spectre de la Rose.* Following a quarrel with the famed impresario, Fokine broke with the Ballets Russes and settled in Sweden in 1918, where he worked with the Stockholm Ballet re-creating many of his works. During this period he was also invited to come to Denmark to stage various ballets for the Royal Danish Ballet. It was the first time that the Danish company was put in touch with a new stylistic outlook that would give its dancers inspiration and newfound creative expression. But Fokine did not remain in Denmark, nor in Scandinavia, choosing instead to emigrate to the United States.

Another of Diaghilev's major choreographers was George Balanchine, who worked with the company during the last four years of its existence—from 1925 to 1929. When the Ballets Russes disbanded following Diaghilev's death, Balanchine was invited to stage a number of his works for the Royal Danish Ballet—works that remain in the repertoire to this day. Like Fokine, Balanchine did not remain in Denmark but returned to Paris, working with the Ballet Russe de Monte Carlo and, in 1933, forming his own company, Les Ballets 1933. One year later, at the invitation of Lincoln Kirstein, a wealthy American writer and ballet aficionado, Balanchine came to New York, where he opened The School of American Ballet. With Kirstein, he eventually formed the American Ballet and, later, Ballet Caravan, which, in 1948, became the New York City Ballet.

During the 1930s the Danish ballet counted among its ranks a dancer by the name of Harald Lander, who had been a pupil of Hans Beck. Trained in the Bournonville style, Lander continued his training in Russia and in the United States. Upon his return to Copenhagen, he was appointed director of the Royal Theatre, a post he held during the 1940s and 1950s and under his leadership, the Royal Danish Ballet once more assumed a position of stature. In addition to reviving many Bournonville works, Lander created more than twenty-five ballets for the company, such as *Bolero*, *La Valse*, *The Sorcerer's Apprentice*, and, perhaps his best-known work, *Etudes*. Lander also created his own version of classics such as *Coppélia* and *Swan Lake*.

It was during Harald Lander's tenure as director of the Royal Danish Ballet that several important dancers began to emerge. The company already boasted such brilliant soloists as Margot Lander and Børge Ralov. In their wake came other outstanding dancers, such as the ballerinas Mona Vangsaa, Kirsten Ralov, and Margrethe Schanne, the latter proving herself to be an artist of exceptional quality. Two other ballerinas came to prominence under Lander's guidance: Inge Sand and Toni Lander (his second wife), and the young Kirsten Simone. Lander produced even greater talent among the men: dancers such as Niels Bjørn Larsen, Frank Schaufuss, Stanley Williams, Poul Gnatt, Fredbjørn Bjørnsson, Henning Kronstam, Flemming Flindt, and, most outstandingly, Erik Bruhn.

[CHAPTER 4]

WHEN THE ten-year-old Erik Bruhn appeared at the Royal Danish Opera House in Copenhagen as one of its young ballet students, he entered its doors with loathing in his heart. "For some reason I looked at the theater and suddenly developed a tremendous hatred for it. I couldn't believe I could experience this feeling with such passion. I couldn't bear the idea of facing all those new kids and that alien environment. It was probably my sense of insecurity that prompted this horrible feeling. I was unnerved by the thought of leaving the protection of my home and my garden. But I couldn't talk to anyone about my unhappiness. I just lived with it."

The first two years at the Royal Danish Ballet School were unhappy for Erik Bruhn. The report cards sent home invariably stated that Erik was too quiet, too passive, and too withdrawn; still, as with his ballet schooling in Gentofte, his dancing lessons found him progressing with unusual speed. Although he hated being the focus of attention, his teachers would often call upon him to demonstrate steps for the other pupils. Rather than being proud of this, Bruhn recalls wanting to disappear into the walls at such moments. The boy's one solace was the fact that he did not have to live at the school. He continued to live in Gentofte, traveling into Copenhagen, and remaining at the Opera House from nine to five. As time progressed, Erik came to realize that in order to find some semblance of happiness, he would have to participate more actively in the school. He would have to join the other youngsters in their rest periods and be more outgoing. Like all young pupils studying at the ballet school, Erik had to take part in various opera and ballet productions requiring the presence of children. This presented him with the opportunity of becoming more gregarious, more open, and, of course, acquainted him with a feeling for the stage and for performing in front of an audience. Still, inwardly, he suffered great pangs of alienation and pain, which caused him to become somewhat arrogant and seemingly unmanageable.

Among his teachers at the ballet school was Karl Merilt, for whom the boy developed a particular dislike. "I hated and loathed that teacher. Although I studied with him for five or six years, I just couldn't bear him. I was so miserable in his classes that I thought of killing myself just so that I wouldn't have to see him or be near him. Well, instead of doing that, I resisted him at every turn. I made him so angry that he nearly had a nervous breakdown! When I turned fourteen I remember not obeying him in any way. I suppose one of the reasons I felt so strongly about him was that he used to beat us with a stick in order to make us jump. Naturally, sensing my feelings, Karl Merilt made me the special object of his venom. I remember his pushing me in front of the mirror and saying, 'Look at that face! No expression! Why can't you smile?!' I would just stare coldly. He was furious. When he told me to do a particular step over and over and over again, I would suddenly stop and leave the class without permission and come back when it suited me. This teacher *couldn't* figure me out. There was no way in which he could control me. The upshot was that I was given a warning from the school about my behavior. Oddly enough, when this happened, I stopped being a problem—not out of fear but because I felt satisfied to have made my feelings known to the teacher; now I didn't have to continue. Actually Merilt was not a bad teacher. It was his personality that grated on me. Anyway, things went a little more smoothly from then on."

Erik Bruhn's behavior toward Karl Merilt foreshadowed an independence that would eventually precipitate other acts of rebelliousness. It was not that Bruhn deliberately went out of his way to make problems for himself or for others, but that he felt a necessity to preserve his own identity and integrity in the face of certain classroom excesses or demands that he could not easily accept. Still, there was no question that as a young ballet student Bruhn was not particularly accessible. He had difficulty making

friends and was not given to showing any great interest in the general so-
cial activities of the rest of the students. Bruhn was not particularly brilliant at his academic courses, although he managed to become proficient
in English and German. Nevertheless, he kept up with his grades and
managed to fulfill all the school's academic requirements, although his
teachers considered him to be a below-average student.

If his regular schoolwork was far from impressive, his progress in the
ballet classroom was exceptional. By 1943 his technical abilities far sur-
passed those of other boys his age. It was at this period that his ballet
teachers pointed to him with pride as having virtually mastered the Bournonville technique, which was the basis of the school's syllabus.

To understand Erik Bruhn's mastery both as pupil and mature dancer,
it is necessary to examine certain precepts of his Bournonville training,
which lies at the core of his art. To that end it is useful to listen to Bournonville himself, who, in the foreword of his own brief treatise explained
the general principles that lie behind a style uniquely different from that
handed down from the so-called Russian school of Petipa, Ivanov, and
Cecchetti. Bournonville wrote:

> Dance is an art, because it demands vocation, knowledge, and ability. It is a
> fine art, because it aims toward an ideal, not only of plastic beauty but also of
> lyric and dramatic expressiveness.
>
> The art of mime encompasses all the changes of the soul; the dance is es-
> sentially fitted to express joy and to follow the rhythm of the music.
>
> Joy is strength; intoxication is weakness. Noble simplicity will always be
> beautiful. The astonishing, on the contrary, soon becomes boring. The dance
> can, with the aid of music, raise itself to the heights of poetry, but on the other
> hand it can equally, through excess of acrobatics, descend to the stunts of the
> mountebank. So-called difficulties are executed by numerous adepts, but the
> appearance of ease is achieved only by the chosen few. The summit of talent is
> to know how to conceal the mechanism through the calm harmony which is
> the foundation of true grace.
>
> To maintain this easy grace, in the midst of the most fatiguing movements,
> is the great problem of the dance, and such virtuosity cannot be acquired with-
> out good exercises, designed to develop the qualities and eliminate the imper-
> fections which everyone, not even excepting the greatest talents, is obliged to
> combat. It is such exercises which I present here to my dear pupils as well as to

my worthy colleagues, reminding them of the oft-repeated saying: that it is not so much on the number of exercises, as on the care with which they are executed, that progress and skill depend.

Elucidating further on Bournonville's thoughts and making clear how they applied to him personally, Bruhn explains how he found ways to give even greater technical credence to the Bournonville aesthetic. "What had repeatedly been brought home to us at the Royal Danish School was that Bournonville detested the virtuoso style of dancing—the tricks, the acrobatics. He saw dance as an art form in which one expressed the joy of life. From a technical point of view, he trained his dancers to cover up any so-called 'preparation.' No one was allowed to see any preparation . . . *how* you turn, *how* you jump, *how* you landed. In the Russian style, the audience was always made aware that you were about to do something spectacular, and it could come off looking like a circus act. Well, Bournonville created a school where dancers were trained to hide these preparations cleverly. There is an easy flow to his style. He wanted the audience to feel that they *too* could get up and dance. He said that a dancer should not be on the stage and vulgarize himself. That was the essence.

"As for myself, the facility I acquired was both simple and not so simple. I was trained to become a dancer. I could just as easily have become a product, because even in Denmark, the school does produce products. What happened to me was that I knew I wanted to move, but I resisted the discipline of the school. Of course, I attended classes—you can't just dance without training. The fact is, I didn't have to fight as much for certain things. Things just came to me very easily, and as the years progressed I was able to let myself come through the mask of training that covers you.

"If you don't have the confidence to show what you feel through technique, then you remain a product. Well, I learned to show more and more of my inner self, and not be introspective. In that way it seemed I became a bit more special in my relationship to the audience. I concentrated and I said, 'I'm not afraid of showing my feelings.' Of course, I *was* terrified, but I made myself come through—at least that human part of me that had a desire to dance. I felt that if you allowed *yourself* to come through, even within the form and discipline that was part of dancing, then you appealed to the imagination of the audience. And I allowed *my* imagination to take over—to inhabit what might just be a routine dance or set of dances that you get through like a job. The audience is then aware that you are letting go and that can become very stimulating.

"In the school, when the administration and the principal dancers would come and watch me as a fourteen- and fifteen-year-old, they admired my ability to do more turns than others within a given amount of musical time. Also, I seemed to be able to jump higher than what had been the set standard. Apparently it didn't look like a trick, but very natural. Of course, they all said, 'Yes, that's very nice, but it's not Bournonville.' I felt that to stick rigidly to the standards of Bournonville would be to settle for comfort. I mean, their idea was that where two pirouettes were called for, then that's what you must do for the rest of your life. And they felt that if you did three pirouettes, then it was non-Bournonville. But, you see, when I dared to do three pirouettes instead of two, I never abused the music. I always finished on time.

"Also, I had a facility for musical phrasing. Dancers who are just 'square' will never squeeze the dynamics out of the music and build up to any sort of climax. My fun in having survived the same daily classes for ten years at the school was that I could play with the phrasing of any given step. I knew the steps would be different each day. Of course, some would not be right, but I was never told *not* to do this. In fact, they would stare and ask me to repeat a step or demonstrate it. And yet, they would never say that it was right. It was like a game. Later on I had a vocabulary I could choose from when doing a certain role. I would experiment with the musical phrasing and, in that way, I could color the steps as well as the character I was portraying. I could actually make the steps fit the character."

Later, when Bruhn had to master the great Russian repertoire and fit his Bournonville technique to the more muscularly rigorous demands of the Russian school, the adjustment was so difficult that it nearly caused him to give up dancing. "You see, the strength you develop with Bournonville is in the feet, ankles, and calves. Less in the thighs, which accounts for the fact that Danish dancers never have bulging muscles, the way most Russian male dancers have. The Danes never overworked the thighs, because Bournonville's choreography stressed lightness. We danced with ballon— the ability to pause while jumping in mid-air—which the Russians also have, but which is achieved somewhat differently. The Russians have elevation. We never seemed to touch the floor, but floated, and that came from the ankles and the feet. Another big difference is lifting a partner.

Bournonville didn't have one lift! Well, in the Russian male repertoire—
from *Sleeping Beauty*, to *Swan Lake*, to *Nutcracker*—there are endless
lifts. When I had to begin doing lifts it nearly destroyed me. I would hurt
my back because of the required lifts. And I nearly destroyed my knees because of the tremendous pressure.

"What I had to do was to develop a stronger plié—a stronger knee
bend. I tried to keep my heels longer on the floor, which again put tremendous pressure on my knees. Finally, after a few years, in my mid-twen-
ties, I was accepted as being able to do those things *along* with
Bournonville. Although I later acquired some of the Russian technique,
and was able to perform the same technical feats, it would always look different because I had a Bournonville background. Oddly enough, I seem to
have influenced some of the Russian dancers in terms of style. What is
even stranger is that despite my so-called non-Bournonville ways, I seem to
have influenced a whole future generation of male dancers in Denmark. It
was because I was successful abroad, and made the Danes realize that one
could 'play' with the Bournonville style without losing its essential purity.
I believe that today, Bournonville is even taught differently because of
what I had achieved."

If Bruhn brought his technical gifts to bear upon both the Danish and
Russian schools, he did so through an innate capacity for intuiting and
then executing movements which heightened any given choreographic demand. But this capacity, great as it was and is, would not possess such
beauty or inevitability were it not for Bruhn's extraordinary response to
music. It is Bruhn's uncanny musicality that gives his performances that
particular dimension of finesse—a freedom that makes the act of dancing a
complete musical statement.

Commenting on his very particular response to music, Bruhn says it is a
response that must be felt individually. "You've got to hear the music for
the first time every time you dance to it. If you hear the same thing every
time, then you never feel the need to go back for *more*. The idea is that if
you hear more, then you find more of yourself *in* the music. For me, music
is a constant rediscovery. Once I know a role technically and know the
outline of the character, then I always go back to the music, because that's
my guide. That's when I know how much I can stretch a certain set of
steps within so many bars. Of course, you must begin and finish in time
with the music, but within that span you must literally 'walk' on the

music. You must breathe it and live it and make it a part of your very being. Without that, all is lost!"

It would seem that Erik Bruhn, even at the age of fifteen, understood that dancing was a matter of fullest involvement—technical, psychological, and musical. At the Royal Danish Ballet School, recalcitrant as he may have been, he astonished his superiors by this early commitment, and his ten years at the ballet school virtually brought forth a finished artist.

〖 CHAPTER 5 〗

URING Erik Bruhn's childhood years at the Royal Danish Ballet
School, Denmark found itself caught in World War II. On April 9,
1940, Germany invaded both Denmark and Norway, an invasion
that found the Scandinavians totally unprepared. Heretofore, Norway,
Sweden, and Denmark had been in a state of long neutrality. Although
Finland had recently experienced the three-month Russo-Finnish war
(from 1939 to 1940), Sweden and Norway had not waged war for 125
years, and Denmark had been devoid of conflict for 76 years. Their armies
had been kept to a peacetime minimum and were ill-prepared for
aggression.

At the time of Germany's invasion of Denmark, the country was ruled
by King Christian X, a monarch deeply dedicated to his country's neutrality and a man loath to drag his land into serious conflict. He rejected mobi-
lization and believed that Germany's takeover was a form of protection
rather than conquest. Indeed, during the early days of the invasion, few
government officials took a stand against the obvious, and only later did
the Danes organize an effective resistance movement.

Unlike Denmark, Norway, under the rule of King Haakon VII, actively
defended its neutrality, its geographic borders with its mountainous re-
gions and fjords serving as at least a temporary buffer. Nevertheless, Norway was ravaged by Hitler's armies, despite aid by the British fleet. The
country resisted for two months before the Nazis had complete control.

Thousands of its citizens were arrested, thousands more killed, and, toward the end of the war, the country was virtually devastated.

As for Sweden, it had signed the much decried Transit Agreement, admittedly under German pressure. The agreement saw German troops, as well as vast numbers of German weapons, passing through Sweden. In short, the country kept its neutrality and economy while trading with Hitler's Reich. It was only when Russia and the United States entered the war that Sweden altered its political course, ultimately resisting Germany's demands. By 1944 Sweden had joined the Allies. Still, in the eyes of its Scandinavian neighbors, Sweden was looked upon as having benefited from the war and at war's end the country was prosperous while Denmark and Norway were reduced to poverty.

Erik Bruhn, though only eleven at the time of the invasion, has vivid memories of the war years. "No Dane will ever forget the date April 9, 1940. I had been studying at the theater for two years. Of course, we had read that the Germans were invading Poland and Czechoslovakia, but never for a moment thought this could happen to us. Then, quite suddenly, it *did* happen. I remember that one morning on my way to the theater I heard the sound of airplanes above me. I looked up and the sky was literally black with planes. I never in my life saw so many at one time. They certainly weren't Danish, because so far as I knew Denmark did not have a large air force. Within half an hour all those planes had landed and the city was swarming with Germans. That afternoon the government announced that the Germans had come to protect us, *not* to invade us. They told us to be cooperative and that nothing would happen to us. In the following weeks the Germans went around checking our papers and since none of us reacted violently, they left us pretty much alone. Little by little we got used to the Germans being among us. Then, of course, it dawned on everybody that we had indeed been invaded, because we had to follow all kinds of regulations. For example, there were times when we had curfews. No one was allowed on the streets without a pass after eight in the evening. We also experienced a few bombing attacks on the part of the British, who wanted to destroy certain German headquarters that were based in Copenhagen.

"Within a year or so, the Danes formed a large underground, some of whose members were part of my own family. At the time, the Germans had rounded up our entire police force and sent them to a camp, stating that they—the Germans—would now be acting as our police force. A cousin of mine who had been a policeman was interned, but later escaped. I recall that he came to our house and smuggled ammunition for the resistance, hiding it in a dollhouse that my sisters had set up in our garden. It was a terrifying responsibility, because only two streets away from us the Germans had found a basement full of ammunition and blown up the entire house. Everybody in the house was either killed or arrested, and those who were arrested were never heard from again.

"I also remember that my family listened to a radio station which gave reports from London about the progress of the war. It was illegal for us to do this, but a lot of Danish people could tune into this station and in fact the underground printed a small newspaper, carrying the contents of the broadcasts. I myself helped distribute this underground paper, carrying it in my school satchel. I did this for two years and only once was I nearly caught. I had left my mother's shop on my way to the theater, when the German police suddenly blocked off the street and started checking everyone's bags. When I saw this, I managed to throw my schoolbag into a doorway and luckily escaped notice."

Throughout the war years Erik Bruhn continued his studies at the Royal Ballet School and he recalls that the Royal Theatre continued to function, giving performances heavily attended by the German military. "The top people would come to see the ballet, because of course there was no language barrier. As for us kids, we had to be picked up by our parents after performances, rather than going home on our own. By this time, I was already fourteen and felt much too old to be picked up by my mother, so I would often manage by myself. Still, it was quite scary, because this was the period when the underground was out to get the Danish collaborators. I would walk quickly in the pitch-dark of the curfew, following some fluorescent spots on the ground, when suddenly I would hear shooting and the sound of people running. I remember feeling for doorways and pressing myself flat against them so as to escape notice. I would continue walking after the noise and shooting had subsided. The worst time for us all was when the Germans had surrendered, when the war was over, because we had a large number of Danes who had been traitors and the underground continued looking for them. For at least two weeks after the underground movement came out in the open, there was shooting right, left, and center. This was a very dangerous time to be on the streets, because anybody could be hit by bullets destined for collaborators. Finally most of these were rounded up and driven through town in open trucks with people screaming and spitting at them; this lasted for a while. It took about two years for the Danish economy to get back on its feet. I must say that I had a relatively easy time of it during the war and it never really interfered with my work at the ballet school."

Indeed, young Erik's work at the ballet school progressed with ever more remarkable results. Stubborn as he could be, he somehow followed some internal vision of what dancing should be about. As a fairly solitary boy, he developed a strong sense of concentration, giving his attention to the refining of his line, technique, and style. At the time, only one fellow student engaged his interest: the entirely vivacious and charming Inge Sand, who would eventually become one of the company's outstanding ballerinas.

"We were teenagers and we developed a crush on each other," says Bruhn. "We wrote each other letters and I used to walk her home after class. Eventually the crush developed into a friendship, which lasted until she died. Inge matured into a first-rate dancer and, while she was not my first partner, she was certainly the first who meant anything to me. She was a soubrette type and in later years I chose her to dance *Swan Lake*'s Black Swan pas de deux with me, which, in fact, I introduced to the Danish public back in the fifties. We also danced the *Nutcracker* pas de deux and the *Don Quixote* pas de deux, which had also never been done in Denmark. As a human being she meant a great deal to me and our relationship strengthened my belief that to have personal rapport with someone was very important before anything can happen on the stage.

"Eventually, Inge Sand married and had a daughter but she continued dancing. We remained friends throughout our separate careers and then, in 1975, she died of a liver ailment due to improper diet. Horribly enough, Inge was told she was going to die—she was given three months. But she had incredible strength of character and lived for another two years. She proceeded to put her life in order and even went to Russia to organize a Royal Danish Ballet tour. And she continued to dance. As it happened, we both found ourselves in the same hospital in Copenhagen in 1975. I was recovering from an operation and she was entering the final stages of her illness.

"I recall that she was unable to recognize her husband or her daughter, but somehow managed flickers of recognition when I came to see her. The illness had not ravaged her. On the contrary, as she approached death she looked extremely beautiful. Her face became clearer and clearer and the eyes, when she opened them, were like those of a child. Finally, she closed them forever and I witnessed what one might call a beautiful death—not something ugly or terrifying. Inge Sand was the first meaningful friendship I ever had when we were both students together. There was no one else."

Erik Bruhn made his formal debut as a dancer at the age of sixteen. It took place at the Pantomime Theatre of Copenhagen's world-renowned Tivoli Gardens. It was a debut memorable on several counts. Harald Lander, the director and ballet master of the Royal Danish Ballet, choreographed a short Russian dance for a boy and a girl. The work had been performed in previous years and Lander felt that it might serve as a suitable debut vehicle for Bruhn.

The debut was scheduled for May 4, 1945, which coincided with the war's end. Indeed, it was the day that the British entered Copenhagen by the thousands, overwhelming the surrendering Germans.

"It was a beautiful day," remembers Bruhn. "Naturally, I was very nervous backstage. I knew that a very large crowd had gathered at the Pantomime Theatre to witness my debut. Well, when the music started, my partner and I appeared and, just about two minutes before I was to go into my solo, the British entered the gates of the Tivoli Gardens. When that happened, the entire audience at the Pantomime Theatre turned on its heels and ran like mad to greet them. By the time I went on there wasn't one eye looking at me! And a good thing too, because I fell several times and when I had to tear off my hat at the end of the dance, I also took my black wig off with it. And *that* was my debut!"

The experience, funny or humiliating as it may have been, did not for a moment represent a setback in Erik Bruhn's continuing excellence as a ballet student. Still, it would take two more years of training before he would find himself accepted as a member of the Royal Danish Ballet. Prior to this singular honor, certain events brought Erik Bruhn into closer touch with himself as a person. Between the ages of sixteen and eighteen, he had abandoned his solitary ways. He made a strong and deliberate effort to develop relationships with his fellow students, and this made him far happier than he had ever been before. Of perhaps even greater importance, at around this time, he experienced his first sexual encounter with a girl.

⟦ CHAPTER 6 ⟧

WRITING on the nomenclature of dancers in the Royal Danish Ballet, the Danish dance critic Svend Kragh-Jacobsen explains how it differs from that in any other company: "When a student at sixteen graduates into the company from the school after examination, he or she is an *aspirant* for the first two years. After one final examination the aspirant, if taken permanently into the company, becomes a *ballet dancer*. There is only one other rank, that of *solo dancer*. A solo dancer at the top level is the equivalent of a ballerina or *premier danseur*."

Kragh-Jacobsen has been a Bruhn observer from the time that Erik was a pale, blond, and withdrawn boy of thirteen.

"The first time I saw Erik dance was when he was an apprentice in *Petrouchka*. Ever since then, I have seen everything Erik has ever danced in Copenhagen. I have also traveled to England, the United States, and Canada to see him perform. For me, he was the best *premier danseur noble* of my time. I was the first critic to understand that Erik Bruhn was a great talent. I have seen him grow and develop into even more than I had hoped for. In a way, I harbor fatherly feelings toward him. After all, I knew him as a young boy, and I also knew his mother.

"Of course, Erik's background is primarily Bournonville, but after he left Denmark he had the opportunity to expand his style and his technique. As a classical dancer he was unmatched by anyone. Possibly, Baryshnikov is the great new dancer in the tradition of Erik Bruhn.

"As I said, I have watched Erik grow into an unsurpassed artist. But Erik is a very private person. I think he is a distant person. He has many friends and countless admirers, but very few people can come near him. He is not exactly Greta Garbo, because he likes to live his life as fully as possible. But Erik never throws himself away to anyone. I think he is a man of great integrity, and he is a god of Danish dancers. A born Apollo of our century is Erik Bruhn, but ironically *Apollo*, that great work by George Balanchine, has never been danced by the greatest Apollo of them all!"

In 1946 Erik Bruhn made his unofficial debut on the stage of the Royal Opera House, dancing the role of Adonis in Harald Lander's ballet *Thorvaldsen*. This appearance was met with high praise from the company's administration and principal dancers. The management of the Royal Danish Ballet knew then that in Erik Bruhn they had found a young artist of exceptional gifts. They saw that the company would profit by his presence and relished the thought of retaining his services for many years to come.

In the company at that time was another highly talented young dancer, Poul Gnatt, who had befriended Erik Bruhn. Five years Bruhn's senior, Gnatt had been dancing in the Danish company with great success. A year or so earlier he had obtained a leave of absence for study and work in Paris, where he had joined Roland Petit's Les Ballets des Champs Elysées. Upon his return to Copenhagen Gnatt regaled Bruhn with stories of the glamour and excitement of life in Paris. Since his leave of absence was still in effect, Gnatt planned to travel next to London to join a new company called the Metropolitan Ballet and he invited Bruhn to visit him there. The eighteen-year-old Bruhn felt confined in Copenhagen and was ready to spread his wings. The Danish Ballet would be off for its annual vacation during the summer of 1947, and Bruhn was free to make his own vacation plans. So he resolved to join his friend Poul Gnatt in London, to observe the Metropolitan Ballet, take company class, and have some fun. Once the visit was over, Bruhn would return to Copenhagen and prepare for his official entry into the Royal Danish Ballet. As it turned out, the London experience was far more fulfilling than Bruhn had even imagined.

To begin with, there was the excitement of observing a brand-new ballet company in action. The Metropolitan Ballet, founded by Cecilia Blatch and Leon Hepner that year, included several international dancers and choreographers, such as Frank Staff and John Taras. The repertoire also included several works from the Diaghilev era. Its ballet master was

Victor Gsovsky, who would later be succeeded by Nicholas Beriosoff and Celia Franca, one of the company's dancers. Other dancers introduced to English audiences by the Metropolitan Ballet were Beriosoff's daughter, the fifteen-year-old Svetlana Beriosova, Colette Marchand, Serge Perrault, and David Adams. Also in its ranks was an extraordinary young Bulgarian ballerina named Sonia Arova. Although the Metropolitan Ballet survived for only two years, to 1949, it was among the best of the postwar British companies.

If the young Bruhn was enthralled by the Metropolitan Ballet, he was positively dazzled by other dance activities taking place in London at that time. "In London, I had my first glimpse of everything that would influence me in later life. I saw dancing that I had never seen before. I mean, I had left Denmark thinking that Bournonville was the only kind of dancing that existed. How wrong I was! I saw the Sadler's Wells Ballet perform and it was beautiful. There were the young Fonteyn, Moira Shearer, Beryl Grey—and they were a revelation! I had my very first glimpse of real Spanish dancing when I saw Carmen Amaya. Right then and there I fell in love with Spanish dancing. I thought, Why bother with classical dancing if I can't be a gypsy like Carmen Amaya! And I saw Katherine Dunham, and instantly I wanted to be a black dancer. I even remember sending her a fan letter. Seeing Dunham I thought, Nothing seems right about being white and doing classical ballet! There was Colonel de Basil's Original Ballet Russe. Well, that wasn't too impressive, but, oh, there was such glamour connected with it!

"But the biggest shock I got was watching Jean Babilée. I saw him dance Blue Bird and I immediately decided to stop dancing, because if I couldn't dance like Babilée, why dance?! Babilée was the very first dancer I felt I could really look up to. There certainly was no one at the Royal Danish Ballet whom I thought to be that exceptional. Yes, there was Børge Ralov, whom I really respected, but he was twenty years older than I was."

There was no question that Erik Bruhn felt immediately at home in London and in the international milieu of the Metropolitan Ballet. He had never seen any of Diaghilev's productions, nor was he acquainted with the fine dancers to whom he could now compare himself and with whom he could form friendships. He watched his friend Poul Gnatt give excellent performances in the classics and other works, and he marveled at the brilliance of the fifteen-year-old Beriosova. Above all, he was riveted by Sonia Arova, a twenty-year-old dancer with intense brown-black eyes and a particularly exotic manner. He considered her performances nothing short of electrifying. She had the spirit and élan of a bravura dancer, but projected a charm and femininity that altogether captivated Bruhn. Arova had also noticed Bruhn, who, while not performing with the company, had nevertheless taken daily classes with it.

If Bruhn was attracted to Arova's exoticism, Arova was equally drawn to Bruhn's Nordic good looks. "I was warming up for class on a stage in the north of England while we were on tour and out of the corner of my eye I saw a very blond, very fair, and very clean-looking young man in tights, pointing his foot. I thought, My God! What an incredible foot! Well, that was just a small part of it. I looked at his legs and I looked at his extension and I saw the incredible things he was doing and I couldn't believe it. I had no idea who this boy was. All I knew was that here was someone special. I quickly learned that this was Erik Bruhn from Denmark, a friend of Poul Gnatt's. After a performance I was presented to him and I must admit that I was quite smitten by his marvelous looks and beautiful smile."

Sonia Arova was born in Sofia, and began her training there at the age of six. By the age of eight she showed such potential that her teachers suggested she continue her ballet training in Paris. Letters of recommendation were sent to Olga Preobrajenska and Serge Lifar, each of whom accepted the child as their pupil. Sonia and her mother settled in a small apartment and were later joined by the rest of the family. The child progressed rapidly under the tutelage of her great Russian mentors, and it was everyone's hope that she might eventually join the Paris Opéra Ballet, then under the directorship of Serge Lifar. However, war was declared and the Germans advanced into France and eventually occupied Paris.

In terror of the approaching invasion, the family decided that twelve-year-old Sonia should leave the city and take shelter in Saint Malo—a suggestion made by the child's piano teacher, an Englishwoman who had taken a great interest in her. Upon their arrival in Saint Malo, however, the war situation became worse, for the Germans were fast approaching Brittany. The Englishwoman and her ward escaped to the Spanish border, where they hoped to find a means of getting to England. As Sonia had neither a passport nor official papers, the Englishwoman decided to smuggle Sonia out of Spain disguised as a boy. Traveling as mother and son, they found a fishing boat, secured passage, and sailed for England.

Sonia Arova eventually ended up in London, where she continued her training at the Cone-Ripman School. To her sorrow she later learned that her father had perished during the war, although in time she was reunited in London with her mother and sister. In 1942, at the age of fifteen, Sonia Arova made her debut with the International Ballet, where she danced for a number of years. In 1947 she entered the Metropolitan Ballet as one of its leading ballerinas, and it was at this point that she met Erik Bruhn, who would become the most important man in her young life.

In the short week that Erik Bruhn traveled with the Metropolitan Ballet, he not only developed a taste for independence but he too experienced the first strong stirrings of love. "When I had my first vision of Sonia Arova as a dancer, I thought she was fantastic. I had never seen a dancer move so beautifully. She was not exactly pretty, but the generosity and amplitude of her dancing made me fall in love with her instantly. I remember the company traveling by bus one day to some city or other and I was the last person to get on. There was no room for me to sit. For some reason I found myself sitting on Sonia Arova's lap and of course that was quite embarrassing, so I suggested that she sit on *my* lap, which she did for the next six hours! Well, on that day my love for her was sealed."

Much to Bruhn's regret, the time had come for him to return to Denmark. The Metropolitan Ballet was sorry to see him go, for the management had watched the boy taking classes and seen his outstanding capabilities, and so just before Bruhn's departure, they offered him a contract. When they told him he would be taken on as a principal dancer, Bruhn was immensely flattered. How marvelous to begin his career in leading roles and how splendid to be dancing them with Sonia Arova! Indeed, Sonia's presence was one of the chief attractions of the offer.

But could he in all good conscience leave the Royal Ballet when, in fact, he had yet to make his official debut with it as a full-fledged member of the company? The Danish Ballet School had trained him and educated him. It would not be fair to let them down. Besides, there would be a price to pay if he were to leave the company. Bruhn would lose his eventual pension were he to resign, and the thought gave him pause. He knew very well that to dance abroad, even with a well-known company, would mean taking a risk. Basically he would have to fend for himself in a profession notorious for its financial instability.

On the boat that took him back to Copenhagen, Bruhn pondered the question carefully. Finally he made a decision that would color the fabric of his professional and personal life henceforth. He resolved to resign from the Royal Danish Ballet. There was no point in asking for a leave of absence, for he knew it would not be granted. After all, he had not even begun working for the company, and a leave of absence was only granted to those dancers who had spent several years dancing there. But the die was cast. Bruhn was thirsty for adventure, he was eighteen years old, and for the first time in his life, he was deeply in love. Pensions seemed a long way off.

Upon his return to Copenhagen, Bruhn wrote a letter to Harald Lander, the director of the Royal Danish Ballet. In so many words he told Lander that he had received an offer to dance with the Metropolitan Ballet in London and that he would enter it as a principal dancer. Knowing that the Danish ballet would not grant him a leave of absence, the only course open to him was to resign. Amazed at his own boldness, yet slightly fearful of the consequences, he mailed the letter and waited.

Two days later he was summoned to Lander's office. "Lander had my letter in front of him, and he looked at me as though I were completely crazy. He thought it was madness for me to leave when I hadn't even begun my career with the company. He tried everything to persuade me to stay, but for the first time in my life I knew precisely what I wanted to do. I was certain that Lander would tell me to go ahead and resign and that they never wanted to see me again. Instead, and to my utter amazement, he granted me a six-month leave of absence, something unheard of for a dancer just entering the Royal Danish Ballet.

"Well, I couldn't believe it. I was in seventh heaven. I contacted the Metropolitan Ballet and gave them the news. I told them I would rejoin them immediately and, of course, I was dying to see Sonia again."

The six months with the Metropolitan Ballet proved to be an invaluable experience for Bruhn. Among other works, he danced in excerpts from *Aurora's Wedding*, the Blue Bird pas de deux, Fokine's *Les Sylphides* and *Spectre de la Rose*, as well as the second act of *Swan Lake*. While Sonia Arova was his principal partner, Bruhn also danced with the French ballerina Colette Marchand and with the young Russian, Svetlana Beriosova. During this period, John Taras came to choreograph for the company and he chose Bruhn and Beriosova for his ballet *Designs with Strings*. But the very first ballet specifically choreographed for Erik Bruhn was a work entitled *The Lovers' Gallery* by Frank Staff.

Erik Bruhn's appearances with this British company were met with high critical praise and the English public responded warmly to the handsome, blond Dane. Clive Barnes, the London-born critic, was then a young student attending Oxford University. Already deeply involved in watching dance, he had occasion to see Bruhn perform.

"I first saw Erik in a ghastly ballet by Victor Gsovsky called *Dances of Galatea,*" says Barnes. "In fact, there were two Danish boys in the ballet, Erik and Poul Gnatt. I also saw him do a ballet called *The Lovers' Gallery* by Frank Staff. Sonia Arova was brilliant in it and Erik had a very beautiful pas de deux with Celia Franca. Erik was incredibly handsome and he had a quite remarkable technique. I saw Erik dance with Svetlana Beriosova and they were absolutely stunning together. They were wonderful in *Le Spectre de la Rose.*

"What people tend to forget about Erik is that he had a most amazing elevation. People don't think of Erik as having a remarkable jump, but he did have it when he was younger. Later, it seemed that he almost consciously abandoned it so as not to mar his perfect classicism. But when he was young there was a much more open quality to his dancing. It was not nearly so polished and precise. He was not yet the great classicist that he would become."

Clive Barnes also recalled meeting the young Bruhn at a party given by the ballet critic and historian Richard Buckle. He found the dancer shy and, in many ways, aloof.

"Erik, I think, may have been a bit frightened by his remarkable good looks. It is very difficult for people like us to understand what it must be like to be either a man or a woman whom everyone looks at when they enter a room—not because they're famous but because they are so incredibly good-looking. Intellectual brilliance you can hide or you can flaunt. But that kind of physical beauty you simply can't hide. One is very exposed and I think it made Erik very nervous. Anyway, that was the first time I saw him at close range, but I don't remember having actually had any conversation with him. Of course, I followed Erik's career very closely throughout the years and we've become friends. But the point is, it was marvelous to have seen him dance at eighteen and most of the English ballet critics took note of him at that time."

There is no doubt that Erik Bruhn's professional dancing career was closely linked to that of his relationship with Sonia Arova.

In a way, Sonia acted as a catalyst to Bruhn's immense love for the
dance, for he was dancing with the girl he loved. "That early experience of
having my first truly physical involvement with another person was incredibly exciting. I mean, the dancing, the being in love, the traveling, was
fantastic. What was strange was that at the time England was in a terrible
state. There was rationing, there was no heat, and Sonia and I often lived
in terrible digs. We were freezing to death and we didn't have enough food
but it didn't matter because we were happy. I don't know *how* I could
have thought it was all so beautiful. But it was the experience of a young
person having something completely different enter his life.

"And everything was tied up with dancing. It was because of dancing
that we had met and it was because of dancing that we fell in love . . . and
it would be because of dancing that we would one day part. Still, we managed to be partners on and off until 1955, and also managed to maintain
some kind of a relationship as a couple."

Sonia Arova's feelings for Bruhn were equally deep. "I think I fell in
love with Erik the moment I saw him. I saw his talent and it was very exciting. I remember doing an *Aurora's Wedding* with him and neither of us
had ever done a fish dive before. But we did it as though we had done it all
our lives. How I didn't land on my nose and how he didn't drop me I'll
never know! I saw Erik dance *Spectre de la Rose*. To this day I consider his
the best Spectre I've ever seen. He would do these incredible things, like
double assemblés and double sauts de basque, and they just happened. I
would look at him and marvel at the ease with which he executed everything. He was just a natural dancer. And to be partnered by him was absolutely marvelous. We had a spontaneous rapport. We didn't need to tell
each other anything. What happened between us on stage was completely
natural—we had a total understanding.

"As for our relationship away from the dance, Erik awakened all my
young feelings. I was twenty, and we had an instinctive closeness. Of
course, Erik told me about his background—about having all those sisters
and about his mother and aunt. I could see even then that there was something diffident about him. Although our first encounter was very passion-
ate, I sensed a certain reserve. At times, he would become quiet, a little
moody. I had no idea that one day this reserve and moodiness would become an integral part of his personality."

Erik Bruhn's background could not help but confuse and restrict his relationships with other women. Reflecting on this, Bruhn admits that to be surrounded by so many women during his formative years was overwhelming. "As a youngster, I was exposed to a female force I couldn't cope with. I remember, as a boy, hating that female thing and wanting to get away from it. There was a period of time when I couldn't stand being with women."

And yet Erik Bruhn found something new with the exotic Sonia Arova. Certainly her personality was in total contrast to his own. He responded to her energy and joie de vivre, and if she was possessed of a strong personality, it was the kind of strength that he needed at that moment. Also, he doted on her admiration of him. Intelligent and perceptive, Sonia was well aware of his gifts and when talk between them turned to dance, a mutual understanding of the art nourished their personal passion for each other. Sonia boosted his ego and from the first was protective of his career. She cared deeply for Erik as a person, but was equally caring for his potential as an artist.

As the six months leave of absence from the Royal Danish Ballet drew to a close, Bruhn reluctantly prepared to return to Copenhagen. Although he would return to the Metropolitan Ballet the following summer, he was unhappy about being separated from Sonia. He knew, however, that the moment had come for him finally to establish a reputation with his parent company. For her part, Sonia was equally unhappy about his departure. She too would be leaving the Metropolitan Ballet in hopes of entering the Paris Opéra Ballet—a long-standing dream of hers.

The love between the two young dancers had culminated in a decision. Prior to Bruhn's return to Copenhagen, he presented Sonia with a beautiful engagement ring, its design shaping five rubies and four diamonds into a small cross. The ring sealed their love and although they would be temporarily separated, the two would be reunited and married—at least, that was the plan. Neither Sonia nor Erik believed it could be otherwise. At an emotional farewell the promise was made that Sonia would visit him in Copenhagen, so that she might meet his family and be with Erik in his home surroundings.

(ABOVE RIGHT) Erik Bruhn at the age of one and a half. (ABOVE) Erik, aged five, with his sister Benthe at the ballet school in Gentofte. (MIDDLE RIGHT) Erik surrounded by his family (*counterclockwise*): sisters Aase and Birthe, a cousin, his aunt Minna, stepsister, Else, father, Ernst, and sister, Benthe. (RIGHT) Erik standing in front of his mother with his sisters (*left to right*) Aase, Birthe, and Benthe.

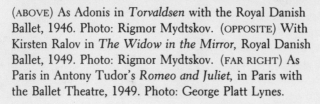

(ABOVE) As Adonis in *Torvaldsen* with the Royal Danish
Ballet, 1946. Photo: Rigmor Mydtskov. (OPPOSITE) With
Kirsten Ralov in *The Widow in the Mirror*, Royal Danish
Ballet, 1949. Photo: Rigmor Mydtskov. (FAR RIGHT) As
Paris in Antony Tudor's *Romeo and Juliet*, in Paris with
the Ballet Theatre, 1949. Photo: George Platt Lynes.

(LEFT) Bruhn's debut as Albrecht, with Alicia Markova, in *Giselle*, Ballet Theatre, 1955. Photo: Fred Fehl. (BELOW) With Carla Fracci in *Giselle*, American Ballet Theatre. Photo: Martha Swope. (OPPOSITE ABOVE) With Yvette Chauviré in *Giselle*, Berlin Opera Ballet, 1959. Photo: Serge Lido. (OPPOSITE BELOW) With Natalia Makarova in *Giselle*, American Ballet Theatre. Photo: Louis Péres.

(OPPOSITE) With Kirsten Simone in *Miss Julie*, Royal Danish Ballet, 1960. Photo: Rigmor Mydtskov. (RIGHT) With Cynthia Gregory in *Miss Julie*, American Ballet Theatre, 1967. (BELOW) As Jean in *Miss Julie* with Violette Verdy, American Ballet Theatre, 1958. Photo: Fred Fehl.

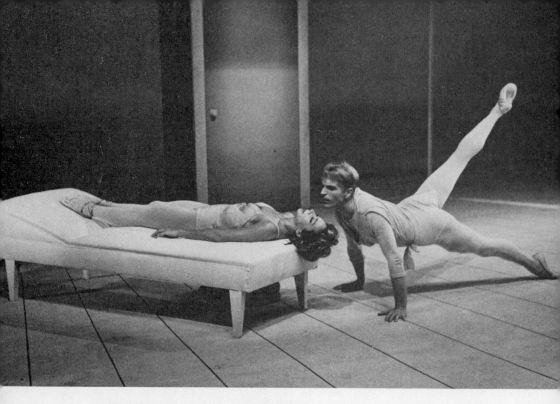

(ABOVE) With Nora Kaye in Herbert Ross's *Tristan*, American Ballet Theatre, 1958. Photo: Fred Fehl. (BELOW) With Serrano in *Helen of Troy*, Ballet Theatre, 1955. Photo: Fred Fehl.

〖 CHAPTER 7 〗

I N THE SPRING of 1948 the Royal Danish Ballet welcomed Erik Bruhn back into its ranks. Harald Lander and the rest of the management felt confident that Bruhn, having sown his balletic oats abroad, would now settle into the company and take up where he had left off. They noted a marked change in the young dancer's personality. He was far more outgoing, far more accessible, and in superb dancing form. The six months in England had obviously provided him with sufficiently varied roles to have given him a newfound sense of freedom. No longer the stony-faced technician, his stage persona blossomed into a far more theatrical presence.

Because he had performed leading roles with the Metropolitan Ballet, Bruhn seemed entirely ready for major parts in the Royal Danish Ballet's repertoire. As luck would have it, Léonide Massine, who had been Diaghilev's protégé after Nijinsky and had since gone on to establish himself as a major choreographer, was then in Copenhagen at the invitation of the Royal Danish Ballet. For the company he mounted his *Le Beau Danube* and *Symphonie Fantastique*. Although Bruhn had rejoined the Danish Ballet as a "ballet dancer" and was not yet a "solo dancer," Massine chose him for the pivotal role of the Hussar in *Le Beau Danube* and for the Pastorale section in *Symphonie Fantastique*. In these and other works, Bruhn continued to show his astonishing technical abilities, and dance critics in Denmark agreed that, technique aside, Bruhn displayed an altogether jaunty and endearing quality as the charming and romantic Hussar in *Le*

Beau Danube. They praised the open, fleet sweep of his dancing and were once more impressed by Bruhn's extraordinary beauty of line.

In June 1949 the Royal Danish Ballet gave a special performance in memory of Bournonville. For the occasion Harald Lander had put together a string of excerpts from the Bournonville repertoire and titled it *Bournonvilliana.* In it, Erik Bruhn performed two solos and a pas de deux with Margrethe Schanne from the second act of *La Sylphide.* Before the work's premiere, a general dress rehearsal was held, open to the public. In the Royal Theatre that evening Bournonville's reputed last pupil, the eighty-five-year-old Hans Beck, was seated in the first row of the orchestra. Sitting nearby, also in the first row, was a distinguished-looking gentleman by the name of Blevins Davis. Davis, a wealthy American theatrical impresario, was in Copenhagen with his production of Shakespeare's *Hamlet,* which was being performed at Elsinore Castle. But Blevins Davis was more than a theatrical impresario: he had just been appointed president of Ballet Theatre Foundation, the American company founded in 1940 by members of the Mordkin Ballet Company under the direction of Richard Pleasant and Lucia Chase. By 1949 Ballet Theatre—later to be known as American Ballet Theatre—had gone through a variety of financial crises, but somehow managed to survive, giving performances in New York and touring extensively throughout the United States. With the arrival of Blevins Davis, Ballet Theatre found itself a highly qualified "angel"—a wealthy Midwesterner. Not only did Davis have access to a considerable fortune but he moved in highly prestigious political circles. An intimate of President and Mrs. Harry S. Truman, Davis had befriended the Trumans in Independence, Missouri.

When the performance began at the Royal Theatre, both Hans Beck and Blevins Davis sat amazed at the sight of the handsome dancer interpreting the role of James in *La Sylphide.* The aged Beck had, of course, heard of the prodigal Erik Bruhn. What he hadn't fully realized was that this young dancer executed the Bournonville steps with the sort of élan and precision that Bournonville himself would have found exemplary. Then and there, Hans Beck resolved to meet Bruhn after the performance. For his part, Blevins Davis looked at the golden-haired dancer and, being partial to male beauty, found Bruhn not only magnificently gifted but also devastatingly handsome. Here was a talent that should be seen in America. As president of Ballet Theatre Foundation, he would go backstage and invite the dancer to come to New York, where he would be placed among the already distinguished international roster of male dancers with that company. Davis liked the idea of discovering new talent and Erik Bruhn was indeed a discovery. Once the performance was over, Hans Beck made his way backstage, found Bruhn's dressing room, and introduced himself to the dancer.

"Young man," he said, "as August Bournonville's last pupil, may I tell you what Bournonville said to *me* when he saw me dance. He said, 'You will go far!' Bournonville would have been proud of you. My congratulations."

Erik Bruhn's second visitor was Blevins Davis.

"Young man," he said, "I am the president of an American company called Ballet Theatre. You are an outstanding dancer, and you should be seen in America. Should you be interested in joining Ballet Theatre, I would be happy to make it possible for you."

Erik Bruhn was stunned by this dual encounter with Hans Beck and Blevins Davis. To be told that Bournonville himself would have been proud of him was a compliment to cherish; to be invited to dance in America was head-spinning. Bruhn recalls telling Davis that the idea of going to America was certainly exciting, but that he would have to think about it. Besides, he had to conclude his season with the Danes, and his summer plans would include a visit to Paris to be with his fiancée, Sonia Arova.

"When I told Blevins Davis that I planned to be in Paris during that summer, he told me that he too would be there at the same time. He said he would be staying at the Ritz, and I should look him up and tell him whether I was ready to sign with Ballet Theatre. Well, for me going to America was like going to the moon. Still, it was a tempting idea, and to dance with an American company would be a fantastic experience. Of course, in order for me to do this, it would mean having to ask for yet another leave of absence from the Royal Danish Ballet, and Harald Lander would again be furious."

With this exhilarating thought turning in his mind, Bruhn fulfilled his season of dancing with the Danes and prepared for that long-anticipated visit to Copenhagen by Sonia Arova. During the two years they had not seen each other, the couple corresponded almost daily. Sonia would be coming from Paris, where her great hope of entering the Paris Opéra Ballet had not been fulfilled. She had danced here and there with smaller companies, while continuing her training with various teachers. Arova had written to Bruhn telling him that she had arranged a summer engagement for them both with the Bordeaux Ballet. This would be their chance to dance together once more. In Copenhagen, Arova was delighted to be reunited with her handsome fiancé. "I loved Erik's family. I loved his home and got on very well with his mother. But I noticed that Erik was slightly fearful of her. I felt a certain tension between them. Anyway, I remember walking all over Copenhagen with Erik. We walked hand-in-hand and Erik showed me all the sights. I came to love the Danish people. They were very warm and friendly. Erik received permission for me to come and watch class. I recall watching Erik take the boys' class. Maybe it was because I was in love, but the only person who stood out was Erik. Again, I realized that Erik was going to go right to the top . . . that he would make it big very fast. One day I met Erik's father. He was a very handsome, very quiet, very gentle man. Erik was the image of his father. I saw no resemblance between him and his mother. Those few days in Copenhagen were wonderful. We were very much in love and we were very happy."

Upon Arova's return to Paris, Bruhn made up his mind to ask Harald Lander for one year's leave of absence from the Royal Danish Ballet. As expected, Lander turned down the request. Bruhn was becoming a valuable member of the company and Lander was not about to relinquish one of his prize dancers.

But, as in 1947, when Bruhn had asked for his initial leave, he was adamant. "This time I wasn't quite so scared about asking for a leave of absence. I felt I had to move around, dance elsewhere, see more of the world. Of course, I expected a scene. Lander said that they were just about to promote me to the rank of solo dancer, which is the equivalent of principal dancer. He said that if I left, I would not be promoted. The upshot was that not only did Lander finally agree to let me leave the company for one entire year but I was promoted as well. So, I had my leave of absence, and I was a principal dancer of the Royal Danish Ballet."

The summer of 1949 found Erik Bruhn planning to go to Paris, where he and Sonia Arova would share her small hotel room, and then travel to Bordeaux and dance with the Bordeaux Ballet. As it turned out, the plan had fallen through. Arova had gone to Bordeaux on her own in order to look at the company and deemed it of inferior quality. She did not feel that either she or Erik would be happy dancing there and she told him so when he arrived in Paris. She added that she had talked to Serge Lifar, the head of the Paris Opéra Ballet. Lifar had said that his company was short of boys and might take on Bruhn as one of its dancers. What Arova did not realize was that Lifar had no intention of admitting either Arova or Bruhn into the company. A man given to making extravagant promises, he knew perfectly well that the Opéra's administration did not, at that time, admit foreign-born dancers into its ranks. Lifar had filled Arova with false hopes, and in the end, both dancers found themselves at loose ends.

Bruhn now had one year to himself. He had not forgotten his meeting with Blevins Davis, nor Davis's promise of getting him into the New York-based Ballet Theatre. The question was: Would Davis keep his promise? And if so, what of Arova?

"Sonia and I ended up waiting in Paris for two months," remembers Bruhn. "Should we go to Bordeaux after all? Was Lifar serious about getting Sonia and me into the Paris Opéra or was he playing a game with us? We were running out of money and living in a flea-bitten hotel in Paris. I said, 'Sonia, what are we going to do?' She kept insisting that we'd both make it into the Paris Opéra Ballet. Finally, when it looked as though *nothing* was going to happen, I told Sonia that I simply couldn't go back to Denmark, that it would be too humiliating to do so after having gotten a year's leave of absence, and that some drastic decision would have to be made.

"Well, one day Sonia and I took a long walk and suddenly found ourselves in front of the Hotel Ritz on the Place Vendôme. I stopped and said to Sonia, 'You know, Blevins Davis told me I should contact him at the Ritz and here it is.' She said, 'Don't believe it!' But I went into the hotel anyway and to my complete amazement found a message for me from Davis. It said that he was out of the city for two days but that he had a contract for me with Ballet Theatre and that he had booked passage for me to go to America with him. I was to wait for him and call him in two days' time. I couldn't believe it, and Sonia's face just dropped."

Arova's memory of this course of events differs from that of Bruhn's recollection. "It wasn't *par hasard* that we were walking past the Ritz. Erik had a definite date with Blevins Davis and Erik already knew about Ballet Theatre, the contract, and the boat trip. Everything had already been prearranged and I knew about it. I was terribly upset that Erik would be leaving for the States. Because, you see, we could have gotten married in Paris. We could have had a child. Still, I knew in my heart of hearts that it would have been wrong to hold him back. Obviously, things were beginning to open up for him and I felt that I would have been in his way if I had pressured him to stay. But Erik was talking about the States and Blevins Davis. It was a difficult moment for me—to say the least. In fact—and to this day Erik doesn't know this—I wrote a letter to George Balanchine asking him if I could come to the States and study at the School of American Ballet. I remember writing the letter twenty-five times before mailing it. I told Balanchine that I had no money for the trip, but that I wanted desperately to work with him. I never got an answer. The whole point, of course, was that I wanted to be near Erik. I didn't want to lose him."

When Erik Bruhn and Blevins Davis met in Paris, the dancer noted Davis's very particular delight when he agreed to accompany him to America. "Blevins Davis couldn't have been nicer to me," recalls Bruhn. "He arranged for my visa to the States and even advanced me some money. He handed me five hundred dollars, and I felt like a millionaire. I did feel badly about leaving Sonia, but *somebody* had to work. Of course, it didn't improve our relationship, but what were we going to do? I mean, even if she did get into the Paris Opéra Ballet—which she didn't—what would I be doing? I certainly didn't get an offer to join the Paris company. The only sane thing to do would be to try my luck in New York. So, Blevins Davis and I boarded the S.S. *America*, and it was like a dream. We traveled first-class, and the whole thing was terribly chic. The only problem was Blevins Davis. During the trip I realized that he had certain inclinations. He paid attention to me in certain ways. I was quite innocent about all that and I was still happily engaged to Sonia Arova. Anyway, I had an absolutely marvelous time on the boat, although I only had one suit and one tie. I couldn't compete with all that elegance. But nothing mattered. I was going to the United States and I was going to dance with an important American ballet company. When we landed, it seemed that a whole new world was awaiting me."

[CHAPTER 8]

WHEN Erik Bruhn joined Ballet Theatre in 1949 at the age of twenty-one, he was totally unknown in America. In Denmark, on the other hand, Bruhn had already become a celebrity. The Danish press had taken the young dancer to its heart and lavished praise upon him as an artist clearly destined for greatness. When news reached the Danish papers that Bruhn would be joining an American company, major articles appeared citing Bruhn's background and his swift rise within the ranks of the Royal Danish Ballet. Their native son was about to conquer a new continent and spread the glories of Danish ballet training abroad.

Soon after his arrival in New York, Bruhn was introduced to Lucia Chase, whose private fortune had partially subsidized the financially shaky Ballet Theatre since its inception. She had never previously heard of Erik Bruhn, but she took Blevins Davis's word that Bruhn would be an exceptional addition to her fine roster of male dancers, which, as of 1949 and 1950, included Igor Youskevitch, John Kriza, Hugh Laing, Scott Douglas, James Mitchell, Eric Braun, Kelly Brown, Enrique Martinez, Fernand Nault, Michael Lland, and Michael Maule.

"Of course, at the time, Blevins Davis was the president of our foundation," remembers Lucia Chase. "And when Blevins wrote to me about this wonderful young Danish dancer I was delighted. Later, when I saw Erik dance, it was a perfect revelation. I just adored him. I am so proud that we were able to present Erik Bruhn for the first time in America. Of course, our association has lasted for many years and we have become very close friends. But from the very beginning, Erik was a total joy. I like to think that we had some share in Erik's development as one of this century's greatest artists."

The only cloud marring Bruhn's entry into the company was the fact that, as Bruhn puts it, Lucia Chase and everyone else were under the impression that he was Blevins Davis's special friend. Indeed, Bruhn was unaware that Davis himself had guaranteed his salary for the year he would be working with Ballet Theatre. It was obvious that Davis had taken Bruhn totally under his wing—a wing that Bruhn could surely have done without. A further disappointment was that Ballet Theatre would not be performing for at least six weeks and that Bruhn was expected to spend a great deal of time in Davis's company.

"What was very annoying was that Blevins wanted me to go and live with him at his estate in Independence, Missouri. He said that he knew a wonderful teacher in Kansas City and that I would be driven there every day to take class. I told him that I didn't want to go to Independence and that I could take class in New York. Finally Lucia Chase entered the picture and she too told me that it would be a wonderful idea for me to go to Missouri with Blevins Davis. I think she wanted Blevins to be happy, since he was Mr. Moneybags. Well, what with one thing and another, I reluctantly ended up going to Independence with Blevins and there was this big house with several servants. I must say, Blevins turned out to be very nice and he put his car at my disposal and I *did* go to Kansas City to take class. Only occasionally would things get sticky, like his asking me whether I needed a massage, which he volunteered to give me. Naturally I refused and he didn't persist. I remember turning twenty-one when I stayed with Blevins and he gave me a birthday party. One of the guests was Bess Truman, the president's wife. The Trumans had been Davis's neighbors in Independence and were very good friends.

"Anyway, the weeks with Blevins were somewhat difficult to cope with. I was very angry with Lucia Chase for putting me through this. But she thought that I was Blevins' boyfriend. Still, I couldn't forgive Lucia for several years. Much later Blevins Davis and I became good friends, especially as we saw each other less and less. When I became a principal dancer with Ballet Theatre in 1955, I recall receiving a letter from him telling me how proud he was about having discovered me, and how Lucia had never really realized that I was a talent during those first years with the company. Only *he* realized it. Well, Blevins Davis finally lost all his money and, of course, he was out of Ballet Theatre. Then, years later, he died. But despite my problems with him, it's true that he gave me my first opportunity in America."

When Bruhn returned from Independence to take up his career with Ballet Theatre, the company gave a season at the Center Theater in New York. Bruhn was finally able to dance in a company that boasted such ballerinas as Nora Kaye, Nana Gollner, and eventually, Mary Ellen Moylan, Lupe Serrano, Diana Adams, and Alicia Alonso. He danced in John Taras's *Designs with Strings*, the *Nutcracker* pas de deux (alternately with Gollner and Moylan), and appeared in various other works. He had occasion to watch Nora Kaye in Antony Tudor's *Pillar of Fire*—the work that catapulted Kaye to fame—and he was struck by the ballerina's superb dramatic gifts and exotic appearance.

"Nora and I became very close friends," recalls Bruhn. "At one time we came close to having a love affair. Nora, like Sonia, had those dark, smoldering looks, and I was very attracted to that kind of exotic woman. But, again, everyone in the company thought I was Blevins Davis's boyfriend. I had to do something about that. I was determined that were I ever to return to Ballet Theatre, it would be because of my value as a dancer, not because of Blevins Davis.

"Actually, I danced very little during that first Ballet Theatre season, but I went on tour with them and I laughed a lot, drank a lot, and had lots and lots of fun."

Being in America and part of a whole new dancing environment, Erik Bruhn could not be expected to brood too heavily about his absence from his fiancée, Sonia Arova. Certainly he thought of her and there were times when he genuinely missed her, but on the whole he was far too busy accustoming himself to the rigors of touring and to learning and performing new roles. Besides, he would soon be returning to Denmark and would no doubt be reunited with Sonia, whom he still had every intention of marrying.

Sonia Arova found herself veritably stranded, not quite knowing where to turn next. "I knew that people would recognize Erik's great talent," Arova says. "And I also knew that no one could hold him back, least of all me. I felt that our relationship was still there, but Erik was changing all the time. I felt that I simply had to wait it out. I realized that it would be wrong for us to get married.

"Naturally, I didn't give up on Erik—at least in my heart and in my mind. I thought that if we could just see each other we would know exactly where matters stood between us. So that was my dream—to find a way of being together with Erik."

When the year with Ballet Theatre drew to a close, Erik Bruhn returned to Copenhagen and, once more, the Royal Danish Ballet greeted him warmly. As it turned out, however, the Danes were just then in the midst of an artistic and political upheaval. Harald Lander, the company's ballet master and director since the early thirties, had begun to meet with a number of complaints from members of the company regarding his artistic policies.

Bruhn recalled the complexity of the situation. "The fact is that Lander favored me. He was not an easy man, but I could never say that he ever treated me badly. He encouraged me to dance with his wife, Toni, and would also invite me to their home, which was a great privilege. But somehow there was general dissatisfaction with him among certain factions of the company. It had to do with the general running of the company. And I must say I agreed that the company was being mismanaged. Anyway, three dancers in the company organized an anti-Lander group and they came to me and persuaded me to write my own artistic complaints. I should add that these complaints had nothing to do with the way I was personally being treated, but were simply my views of how matters could be improved within the company. So I wrote a general statement and it was published in the press. Of course, Lander saw it and was very upset.

"Now, you must understand that nobody can be dismissed from the Royal Danish Ballet unless they commit some sort of crime. So my writing that statement would not have contributed to Lander's fall. What *did* contribute to his dismissal was the accusation by some teenage girls in the ballet school that Lander had made sexual advances. *That* was considered a crime and it caused a big scandal and made all the Danish papers. It was a horrible thing, and Lander was suspended immediately. Of course, there were several important critics and writers who defended Lander in the press, including Svend Kragh-Jacobsen. He liked Lander and went all-out for him. What finally happened was that Harald Lander left the Royal Danish Ballet and Toni Lander, his wife, left with him. They went to Paris and Lander staged various works, including his own, for the Paris Opéra Ballet."

After Lander's dismissal, Niels Bjørn Larsen, one of the senior dancers of the company, assumed the company's directorship. Larsen had been among the anti-Lander faction and those who favored Lander made life difficult for the new director. Life was also made difficult for Erik Bruhn, who was ridiculed for having published his statement in the press. But, by this time, the young dancer had had his fill of political intrigue and bickerings and wrote a letter to Lucia Chase saying that he wanted to return to Ballet Theatre as quickly as possible. He wanted to be free, and he once again resolved to ask for a leave of absence—his third within the span of four years. He knew that dancers with the Royal Danish Ballet were allowed only three such absences throughout their tenure with the company. Still, what mattered most to him at this point was to return to America.

In due time Lucia Chase answered his letter and invited Bruhn to rejoin Ballet Theatre for its 1951–52 season. She added that he would henceforth be dancing as a second soloist. Overjoyed, Bruhn prepared to leave for New York.

"It was a triumph for me that Lucia Chase wanted me back. It was Lucia and not Blevins Davis who wrote to me. I would be returning to Ballet Theatre under very different circumstances and I couldn't have been more pleased."

Bruhn's return to Ballet Theatre found him dancing more and more roles. Still a relatively unknown figure in American dance, he made his presence felt by virtue of his impeccable technique and superb interpretation of the various roles he assumed.

"The American press began to notice me more and more," says Bruhn. "But I was still fairly overshadowed by other male dancers in the company. I remember the groans that would go up when it was announced that I would be replacing Igor Youskevitch. Well, I suffered those groans, but I survived them. By the end of the season, things improved considerably, and I even heard some cheers from the audience."

Bruhn's dancing and personality were beginning to take hold in America. His one regret at this time was the fact that he had committed himself to return to Denmark for a period of two years, and so, after concluding his season with Ballet Theatre he regretfully traveled back to Copenhagen, resuming his duties as a principal dancer with the Danish company.

This time his reception was far from pleasant. "When I got back in 1952, my role in the Lander affair had obviously harmed my reputation and people were out to get me. For one whole year the press treated me abominably. They wrote that I was the most horrible and inartistic dancer. They wrote I was star-conscious. They said, 'Who does this twenty-three-year-old dancer think he is?' And they pointed out the name of younger dancers, saying that I had better watch out or I would be out of the ballet business quicker than I thought.

"If I had taken all that abuse seriously I would be dead by now. Of course, the whole thing was a political maneuver, but it was very painful. It was especially upsetting because my family and friends suffered when they read all that in the papers. My family seemed ashamed of me and that was hard to live with, too. I should also say here that Svend Kragh-Jacobsen, who was supposed to be my great champion, also threw dirt at me. Svend has forgotten that. Well, he may have forgotten it, but I haven't. Still, I didn't go around whimpering, and little by little I won the audience back. It took a long time but I managed to survive."

Even as Bruhn suffered the calumnies of the critics during his return to his parent company, his performances matured to an extraordinary degree. The personal anguish he felt was transformed into high art during performances of such classics as *Swan Lake, Sleeping Beauty, The Nutcracker, Les Sylphides*, and, above all, Bournonville's *La Sylphide*.

James had been Bruhn's first major role when he was still a student at the Royal Danish Ballet School, though at the age of seventeen he had barely begun to understand just how the role should be interpreted.

Bruhn recalls working with the former dancer Valborg Borchsenius, who was also known for her extraordinary talent as a mime. "This woman was teaching us very traditional mime movements. She did the gestures and we would imitate them. Most of the boys and girls in the class had the ability to imitate perfectly. I, on the other hand, stood there as though paralyzed. I was like a stick and the reason was that no one was telling me *why* I was supposed to be doing these things. Already at that age I rejected that which I couldn't psychologically relate to. The point is, Valborg Borchsenius simply demonstrated the gestures without explanation. Well, when I couldn't do these things, she just gave me up as hopeless. I mean, when it came to dancing, everyone admired my technique, the body, the facility, but when it came to miming, I just froze. I had no expression, no smile, nothing.

"When I made my debut at twenty-two in the full-length *La Sylphide*, I was terrified. And because I was terrified, it turned out to be the biggest flop. Now remember, I was still very young at the time, but I felt that I was marked for life. It seemed I could dance but I couldn't act. I had no feeling for drama or for interpretative expression. Then, all at once, I began to get stubborn. I decided to think carefully about James—about who this man was. In subsequent performances I would try to motivate myself more fully. I was beginning to build the portrait of James that I would paint many years later. This process of understanding a role wasn't just a question of miming, of aping certain traditional gestures. It was more a question of getting to the psychological root of the character, of making this person become a living human being, rather than some dusty relic of the past.

"As the years progressed, I felt I understood the character of James better and better and I found it all by myself. So, when the Royal Danish Ballet performed in London in 1953, I portrayed a James that was acclaimed on all levels. What is so amusing is that the management didn't realize what was happening. They had to read it in the newspapers. They looked at those reviews in London and then they believed it. They read that my interpretation of James came out of a true understanding of the character and that the expressiveness, wedded to technique, was psychologically motivated rather than being employed for effect. Also it was a matter of sustaining the characterization."

Bruhn went on to become the greatest James of his generation, and his interpretation of this major Bournonville role was considered to be definitive. Summarizing his feelings about the role in *Dance Perspectives 36*, published in the winter of 1968, he states:

> For me, James is the youngest in the gallery of Romantic ballet heroes. He is an idealist, a poet. In the end, when he tries to grasp his ideal and tries to make her a real woman, he dies. Without this dream, this illusion, he can no longer exist. He is a true escapist. Nobody can actually get hold of James. His mother, his fiancée—none of the real people understand him. But when he is alone with his dream he is quite himself; he is a total being. When the dream is gone, he must die with it.

Bruhn's appearance with the Danish ballet in London was a major step forward. While his technical prowess was considered to be a marvel, Erik Bruhn now brought his intelligence to bear upon matters of interpretation. Bruhn began to question every last detail of every role he undertook. He believed that the classics, handed down from generation to generation, had to be looked at in the light of contemporary attitudes and feelings. Although the stories of such classics as *La Sylphide, Giselle, Swan Lake, Sleeping Beauty, Nutcracker,* and *Coppélia* were essentially cast in the mold of naïve fairy tales and simplistic plot construction, they each contained a moral applicable to any age. The leading characters in these famous story-ballets can be interpreted in myriad ways, and artists who go to the trouble to intuit their deeper meaning invariably emerge with interpretations that give these characters size, depth, and dimension. In the years to come, Erik Bruhn would bring truth and meaning to roles that in other dancers' hands had been mere ciphers.

〚 CHAPTER 9 〛

A S FAR AS technique is concerned, Erik Bruhn has never been one to rest on his laurels. What is more, he has always sought the best help available by going to teachers who would strengthen and deepen his technical range. It was fortunate that in 1951 an extraordinary Russian teacher made her appearance at the Royal Danish Ballet School. Her name was Vera Volkova.

Volkova was born in St. Petersburg in 1904 and studied at the School of Russian Ballet as well as with Agrippina Vaganova, one of the foremost Soviet teachers of her time. Volkova's career as a dancer found her touring Japan and China in 1929 with a Soviet group. For several years she lived in Shanghai, where she danced with the George Goncharov Company and also taught in its school (the young Margot Fonteyn received her early training there with Volkova). In 1936, she married the English painter and architect Hugh Williams and the couple moved to London, where Volkova opened her own school and taught at the Sadler's Wells Ballet.

Between 1943 and 1950, Vera Volkova became the most respected Western authority on the Vaganova system and an extremely influential teacher to a whole generation of British dancers in the postwar years. In 1950, Volkova taught at La Scala in Milan, and in 1951 she became artistic adviser to the Royal Danish Ballet. She remained in Denmark for twenty-four years and died there in 1975. Bruhn, as well as every other dancer of the Danish ballet, benefited enormously from her training.

"Just before Harald Lander left Denmark," Bruhn recalls, "he did the Danish ballet a great service by bringing Volkova to the school. At the time, I had been asked by the direction to teach class to the younger boys in the school. I didn't know what to do with them at first. I would demonstrate things very clearly and cleanly and they would distort what I was showing them to such a degree that I thought they were making fun of me. Volkova taught me that, in order to teach, one should demonstrate as little as possible. She said that I should make them do the movements themselves, and then refine things from there. That was one of the first lessons I learned from Volkova. When I myself took classes with her I was her prime target for demonstrations. She helped me enormously—especially with my neck and my chest. The fact is, my chest was sunken—I was simply built that way. She corrected that within a year.

"The happiest memories I have of Volkova were our many talks. We talked every day when I was not performing. And we would talk about every limb, ligament, and muscle. She was fantastic for the Danish dancers, all of whom had been trained in the Bournonville style. You see, the Bournonville technique is very good for the male dancer, but it had certain limitations which Volkova, with her Russian background, improved upon. She didn't change the Bournonville technique but added to it. The Russian male dancers generally have a sturdier physique and they are required to do more physically strenuous things than is demanded by the Bournonville school. The Danish 'line' is very long. If you make one slight mistake it looks as though you've lost all your technique. Well, any wrong move that would show up in a Danish dancer would *not* show up in a Russian dancer. His muscles would cover it up. I was always jealous of Russian dancers, because they could just stand there and look so strong and attractive. I always had to work very hard to make my muscles look that way. Often, I would have to force and strain my muscles to achieve that particular look.

"Anyway, Volkova improved what was already there and she really made me think. In class she was very specific. For example, when she didn't want you to move your shoulders she would put a matchbox on one of them. If the matchbox fell off, you were doing something wrong. If she wanted you to contract your buttocks, she would place a handkerchief between the cheeks. If you lost it, it meant you were relaxing your ass. She had little tricks like that. They were simple things, nothing you couldn't understand. Except that you realized that you never thought—how simple it *could* be. And, of course, that's what made it so difficult. She had all these little symbols to make you understand what she was saying. She would make me visualize a button at the center of my chest and she would want me to raise that button, and the only way I could do that was to inhale very deeply. When I achieved this chest expansion, I had to learn how to breathe properly so as not to lose it. She helped to correct the position of my neck. She made it sit in the right position. She was absolutely marvelous!"

Bruhn's relationship with Vera Volkova was as instructive as it was intense. And yet, as helpful as she was and as concentrated as her teaching methods were, Bruhn would often lose patience. This was not a personal thing but was entirely connected with Volkova's working methods. Because she had taken such enormous interest in her brilliant young pupil, she imbued him with almost more information that he could assimilate.

Indeed, there were times when the lessons of Volkova became an impediment to Bruhn's performances. "Suddenly, I began to have stage fright. Of course, there is always some fear connected with any performance, but this was something else. I remember dancing in Balanchine's *Symphony in C*, a work that I had danced several times before, when I suddenly began to get scared. I found it difficult to execute steps that I had executed with the greatest of ease and confidence in the past. It finally dawned on me that I was *thinking* too much. Through Volkova, I had trained myself to think and think and think! I was overanalyzing everything and it got to a point where I couldn't move. I remember deciding not to dance certain performances and Volkova would get absolutely furious. Things got progressively worse between us. We would quarrel. We would even throw things at each other. There came a moment when I couldn't stand to look at her. Once, I got so mad at her that I called her a bitch, at which point she threw her purse at me. It was wild and it all lasted for about two weeks.

"I was getting ready then to leave Denmark to return to Ballet Theatre. Volkova and I parted on rather cool terms, but when I began dancing with Ballet Theatre, I realized what a bank account she had given me. Everything she taught me began to be released and during those years with Ballet Theatre I began to climb to the top. She gave me a freedom and a richness that was absolutely unique. No one did more for me than Vera

Volkova and, of course, when I returned to Denmark in later years we became very close friends. I told her how grateful I felt and we would laugh and talk and have a marvelous time together. However, I needed that break from her, because it was when I was away from her that everything she taught me seemed to fall into place. The fact is, Volkova was my primary influence—the biggest and the best!"

The years 1952 to 1954 spent in Denmark were enormously productive for Erik Bruhn. His repertoire was increased to include such roles as Ove in Bournonville's *A Legend*, the title role in Frank Schaufuss's *Idolon*, and the student in Birger Bartholin's *Parisiana*. Although he was berated by the press over his participation in the Lander affair, he had ultimately managed to overcome the resentment shown to him through the sheer strength and beauty of his dancing. Bruhn was determined to prove himself an artist first.

He worked hard to perfect his technique and to broaden the scope of his interpretative gifts. As it turned out, Bruhn's career was blossoming in all directions. In 1952 he had been summoned to Hollywood by Samuel Goldwyn, who had asked him to participate in the filming of *Hans Christian Andersen*, starring Danny Kaye and Renée Jeanmaire. The dance sequences were choreographed by Roland Petit. This was Bruhn's first venture in feature–filmmaking, although his was purely a dancing role. In 1953 he was acclaimed for his James in *La Sylphide* in London and he created his first choreographic work—*Concertette*—set to music of Morton Gould's *Interplay*. This was performed by the younger members of the Royal Danish Ballet and was deemed to be a straightforward and promising ballet—a carefree entertainment devoid of psychological probings. In addition, it was during these two years that Bruhn made his first serious foray into teaching. His work with the young Danish students would prove seminal to his teaching ventures in later years.

⟦ CHAPTER 10 ⟧

THE EARLY RISE of Erik Bruhn was intermittently publicized in various dance publications and newspapers, and his progress was keenly followed by Sonia Arova, who still harbored the hope of resuming her relationship with him. Since 1949, when Bruhn had left her for New York, she had made strides in her career, although she did not have the good fortune to be associated with a parent company—she had no Royal Danish Ballet to return to—and was, in every sense of the word, a dancer in search of a home. She had, nevertheless, danced with the Metropolitan Ballet, the London Festival Ballet, The Komaki Ballet in Japan, and had fulfilled various guest engagements with companies throughout Europe.

In 1954, at the time when Erik Bruhn was dancing with Ballet Theatre in New York, she found herself in Paris performing with the Marquis de Cuevas company. She and the marquis had become good friends, and the director would often invite her to soirées held in his sumptuous Paris apartment on the Quai d'Orsay. On one such occasion, the guests included none other than Blevins Davis. Davis had, of course, heard of Sonia Arova from Erik Bruhn. The ballerina was full of questions about Ballet Theatre and told him of her various dancing engagements. The conversation soon turned to the possibility of her coming to America and joining Ballet Theatre. Davis was fully aware of Arova's feelings for Bruhn and of the fact that she was a first-rate ballerina. She might indeed prove a splendid addition to Ballet Theatre's roster of dancers. It was decided that

Davis would make inquiries in New York regarding Arova and that she
would hear from him one way or the other. Within two weeks she received
a cable from Davis advising her that she had been accepted into Ballet
Theatre and was to take the next boat to New York.

"I was overjoyed!" recalls Arova. "But I was also a little apprehensive
about seeing Erik again. It had now been five years since we last saw each
other and, of course, I knew that Erik had already become *Erik Bruhn*. At
any rate, I arrived in New York and entered the company. When I saw
Erik for the first time, he seemed much happier than when I had left him,
but I instantly sensed a tremendous change in him. I felt that our relationship was still there and, yet, it was a different Erik I was looking at. When I
first entered the company, everyone seemed to know that I was Erik's
fiancée. I was still wearing his engagement ring. All too soon, however, I
noticed that there were many people around Erik—people whom he enjoyed having around. I began to feel somewhat superfluous. Rather than
becoming a burden to him I decided to pull back. Of course, Erik was terribly nice to me, but I felt that I had to be careful. I didn't want to be a
millstone around his neck. I didn't want to say to him, 'Erik, I still feel the
same way about you. We have been engaged for five years. Perhaps it's
time we married.' That would not have been right. I believe he would have
married me if I had asked him to. But I didn't. Somewhere I felt that Erik
really didn't need me.

"You see, everything had been so easy for Erik. He was the Golden Boy.
People wanted to do things for Erik. They adored him. And, as I say, there
was a very definite change in him. He had made close friendships in the
company. He was close to dancers like Scott Douglas and Ray Barra. I was
aware of this, and I had two choices: either fight the problem and make
him unhappy or just let things drift. My feelings were that I was going to
be in his way. I felt it was best that we end our relationship. It's very sad
but that's what *had* to happen. Neither of us ever said, 'Let's break this
off.' But we both understood that whatever there was between us was now
over. Erik wrote me a beautiful letter in which he really tried to put his
thoughts into words. We also had a very long talk. I told him I understood
him and that I hoped we would always have a friendship. I told him not to
feel guilty and we both promised to keep our beautiful memories alive."

Sonia Arova's career with Ballet Theatre lasted for about three years.
She was not frequently called upon to dance with Bruhn, although they

both appeared in two important works—Massine's *Mam'zelle Angot* and John Taras's *Designs with Strings*. For the most part, she was partnered by Igor Youskevitch and John Kriza, with whom she danced *Swan Lake*, Lichine's *Helen of Troy*, and various other works. A highlight of her tenure with Ballet Theatre was her performance in Robert Joffrey's *Pas des Déesses*, in which she danced a leading role with Bruhn, Lupe Serrano, and Ruth Ann Koesun.

Lucia Chase, the company's director, was very mindful about matters of seniority. From the first, she liked the idea of her dancers rising from within the ranks and meriting their promotions. Bruhn was basically a newcomer and, while Chase was well aware of his rank as principal dancer with the Royal Danish Ballet, she hesitated to push him ahead of dancers who had been with her for many years.

But Bruhn was garnering superb reviews from performances on tour and felt that it was now time to be promoted from the rank of second soloist to that of first soloist. He was not asking for a place as principal dancer, merely a slight upgrading of his position with the company. Chase said she would think about it. A less nettling matter was the fact that in the company were two dancers named Eric Braun and Kelly Brown, respectively. Bruhn felt that three soloists with such similar names would confuse the public. He mentioned this to Lucia Chase. She agreed that the three dancers were continually being confused by the critics and suggested that he change his name. Upon reflection, Bruhn thought that he might take on his mother's maiden name and become known as Erik Evers. Chase was quick to approve, but Charles Payne, an administrative assistant with the company, felt it would be a mistake. He urged Bruhn to hold on to his name—and Bruhn did.

During the 1954 tour, Bruhn danced the Black Swan pas de deux with Nora Kaye, which met with enormous success, as did his *Don Quixote* pas de deux with Lupe Serrano. Indeed, Bruhn and Serrano were frequent partners in a number of the company's works, and Bruhn remembers the ballerina with special affection.

"I had a wonderful, energetic time with Lupe, and we had tremendous fun on stage. She was so physical and she loved a challenge. We could have gone on to have a great partnership, but it wasn't to be. In later years, I was advanced in the ranks before her and she continued her career dancing mainly with Royes Fernandez."

Bruhn also remembers other partnerships during his first years with Ballet Theatre. He recalls how, as early as 1951, he first partnered the fiery Alicia Alonso. "Of course, I had seen Alicia dance with the company and she was an incredible technician. She had a vibrant personality that could be scary at times. She was a strong lady who knew exactly what she wanted. There was never any doubt in Alicia's mind as to why she was doing *anything.* Well, back in 1951, we did a *Don Quixote* pas de deux. When we rehearsed it, I noticed that the tempos were unbelievably slow. That's what Alicia liked. When we came to do the performance, I couldn't bear the thought of dancing to such slow tempos. So, because I was very young and a little brash, I went to the conductor and told him to speed up the tempos. Naturally I didn't tell Alonso. The conductor asked me if I had told Alicia and, lying, I said yes. Well, from the first bar of music, Alicia knew that something was wrong, and, being Alicia, she paid no attention to the music and did her variations in her own tempo, disregarding the music completely. And so it went throughout the entire pas de deux. Of course, she was quick to realize who had requested the changes, and during the performance she whispered in her lovely, Latin way, 'I am going to *k e e l* you!' I got through the pas de deux shaking in my pants. Alicia didn't kill me but the tempos were restored to the way she liked them.

"I didn't dance with Alonso very often, but our performances were so memorable for me that it seemed as though we had danced a great deal together. In a way, I remember dancing with Alicia far more than I do dancing with Nora Kaye, who was a frequent partner."

There were other happy partnerships for Bruhn: Nana Gollner, whom Bruhn considered to have been one of the most beautiful and gifted of the American classical ballerinas, and Mary Ellen Moylan, with whom he developed a special artistic rapport.

"Mary Ellen Moylan was one of the few dancers who made me realize that I was partnering a real person—not just another dancer. Dancing with Mary Ellen was not just dancing for the public. It was dancing *with* someone and *for* someone. It was with Mary Ellen Moylan that I achieved my first early success in America. We did not dance too often—only one season—but I remember doing a *Nutcracker* pas de deux with her as well as a ballet called *Constantia* by William Dollar."

Another of Bruhn's favorite partners at Ballet Theatre was the ballerina

Rosella Hightower. In 1948 Bruhn had seen Hightower dance with André Eglevsky in London with the Marquis de Cuevas Ballet, and remembers her as an artist of unusual depth and éclat. Hightower, who guested periodically with Ballet Theatre during the fifties, was de Cuevas's prima ballerina and her experience gave her appearances with Ballet Theatre a very special glow.

"Rosella was the kind of dancer who loved to work. She would work for hours to refine her movements—she was indefatigable. She was something of a shy person, but she also loved a good laugh and a good glass of scotch. I shared the same roles with her and Nora Kaye, but, again, I remember Rosella better than I do Nora. She left more of an impression on me. I remember dancing a Black Swan pas de deux with her in Chicago, and Claudia Cassidy, who was a powerful columnist—the kind who could make you or break you—wrote: 'This couple will shake the world!' So, there was something great going on between us and most of it was simply a lot of sweat and a lot of work."

Bruhn's relationship with Nora Kaye had begun when he first danced with Ballet Theatre in 1949. Kaye had achieved stardom with her portrayal of the role of Hagar in Antony Tudor's 1942 masterpiece, *Pillar of Fire*, and went on to become celebrated in other dramatic works such as Agnes de Mille's *Fall River Legend* and Tudor's *Jardin aux Lilas*. Although Nora Kaye danced the classics, notably *Swan Lake* and *Giselle*, her fame rested mainly on the contemporary repertoire. Erik Bruhn's pure classicism seemed oddly mismatched when contrasted with Kaye's somewhat more earthy approach to the classics.

"I danced with Nora Kaye a great deal throughout my years with Ballet Theatre. When I was a principal dancer, it was Nora and me. I had already danced the classics with the company and I was now dancing them with Nora. It was something of a trial, because Nora thought that it was enough to know the steps, to know the music, and then you just go out and do it. When we did *Giselle* together she kept saying she knew the role and that *I* knew the role too. I would tell her that we *both* would have to know our roles *together* so that they would work well between us. Some people, like Balanchine, would say, 'Ballet is not something you talk about, you do it.' But I don't agree with that. If you do a ballet your mind has to be at work, because if you don't really understand what you are doing, how will anybody else understand it? The point is, what was enough for Nora was not

enough for me. I tried to get her to do more and to work more. Well, ultimately, things did begin to work for us and we began to relate to each
other on stage. In fact, John Martin, who in those years was the dance
critic of *The New York Times*, extolled our partnership and said that we
had reached a peak together.

"I would say that my partnership with Nora Kaye was an important
one, and she was a magnificent dancer. My regret is that something more
vital didn't happen between us. It was just one of those things."

Oddly enough, the turning point in Erik Bruhn's American career did
not happen with any of his regular partners at Ballet Theatre. Instead, it
took place in May 1955 when the great English ballerina Alicia Markova
came to dance as a guest artist with the company. She had formed a legendary partnership in the thirties with Anton Dolin, and in time the two
became known as their period's greatest interpreters of *Giselle*. Markova
had made the role of Giselle her own and Dolin was considered the definitive Albrecht. By the time of her engagement with Ballet Theatre in 1955,
the Markova-Dolin partnership had dissolved and during that season the
ballerina was offered her choice of partners out of Ballet Theatre's roster of
male dancers. As a guest with the company, she would be performing in
Fokine's *Les Sylphides* and in *Giselle*. It may have been Lucia Chase who
pointed to the young Erik Bruhn, suggesting that his impeccable purity of
line, superb classicism, and innate musicality would complement Markova's own rare artistry.

The ballerina agreed that Bruhn might indeed be a suitable partner, but
before committing herself to dancing with him in *Giselle*, she elected to
test the partnership in *Les Sylphides*.

Bruhn recalls that first encounter: "I realized that if *Les Sylphides*
would work out between us I might also get to do *Giselle*. The rehearsals
were entirely amiable and Markova, who was nearly twenty years older
than I was, explained how certain things should be done. I remember that
while we rehearsed our pas de deux she wanted me to grab her in such a
way that it would appear as though I were catching her in mid-air and
pulling her back. Of course, that was a beautiful idea . . . the Poet trying to
catch his dream in the air and bringing her back to earth. So, we tried to
materialize this thought. We began the pas de deux and at a certain moment she said to me, 'Now lift.' Well, I started to lift her but she was still

on the ground. You see, she had a certain preparation that I wasn't used to, and perhaps she didn't push her body up when it was time for me to lift her. It was very embarrassing. She stopped and said that she was used to stronger partners.

"Naturally, I felt this was the end. If I couldn't get her off the ground in *Les Sylphides*, what would happen in *Giselle*? However, the next time we tried the lift it worked. She must have changed her preparation, or done something to make it easier, because we were creating the effect that she wanted. I must say, Markova was extremely generous. During subsequent rehearsals she asked to see my own variation and showed great interest in me as a dancer. Generally, other ballerinas cared very little about how *I* looked, as long as *they* were being displayed to best advantage. But Markova showed me how Fokine himself had done the steps for the male variation in *Les Sylphides*. I learned the quality that was needed to make the variation just right and it was Markova who helped me on that. When we gave the performance, it turned out to be a success. Markova must have been pleased, because she said yes to *Giselle*. It was a chance of a lifetime, because I was going to do my very first Albrecht with the great Alicia Markova."

With the prospect of this unique opportunity and with the excellent reviews Bruhn had been gathering during his Ballet Theatre tour, he was more anxious than ever to have some tangible reward from the management. He was still only a second soloist. With *Giselle* in the offing, he felt it was decidedly time to be promoted to the rank of first soloist. He again approached Lucia Chase, who firmly turned down his request. It was a matter of seniority, she told him. Bruhn was crestfallen. He had already begun rehearsing with Markova on *Giselle* and he was prepared to fight on this issue.

As it turned out, Chase was just then in the process of negotiating contracts with her dancers. She wanted Bruhn to sign his second soloist contract for the upcoming season.

This he refused to do. "Lucia was willing to give me more money, but she wouldn't promote me. It wasn't money I wanted, only some credit for what I had been accomplishing on the stage. Ballet Theatre would be off for several months, and I would be returning to Denmark, but Lucia wanted me to sign the contract beforehand, so that she would be sure I would come back to her. I told her plainly that I wasn't going to sign, and that I would not come back from Denmark unless I was made a first soloist. I was becoming stubborn and she knew it. Well, she said she would think about it. Then, two days before my debut in *Giselle*, she called me into her office and told me that unless I signed the original contract I would not be dancing Albrecht! I told her that it was perfectly all right with me, because I had no intention of signing this contract. Lucia kept on threatening me, until practically the last moment, and it was extremely demoralizing, particularly since I was rehearsing like crazy with Markova.

"I needed some encouragement because Lucia was putting me through hell. I told Markova what was going on and Alicia said, 'Pay no attention to Lucia, because I am signed and I have to be paid, and without you I would have no partner. Rest assured that I will be on that stage and my partner can only be you!' Markova was marvelous and the upshot was that I did *not* sign the contract and I *did* dance *Giselle*."

During rehearsals, the dancers worked with Dmitri Romanoff, the company's regisseur, and with conductor Joseph Levine. The tempos were set according to Markova's and Dolin's own version of the ballet. Sonia Arova was cast in the pivotal role of Myrtha, Queen of the Wilis. But this important performance received relatively little rehearsal time—less than a week—and tensions were mounting. Matters were not helped by the presence one day of Anton Dolin in the rehearsal room.

"Actually, Dolin only came to one rehearsal," remembers Bruhn, "and he spent the entire time insulting Alicia. We were working on the second act and I had already managed to be able to lift her without having to worry about it. But Dolin kept saying, 'In order to get her off the ground you have to be as strong as an ox. Are you strong enough? You *do* realize how heavy she is, don't you?' He went on like that and Alicia never said a word. Her face was like a stone. I felt quite embarrassed. Finally Alicia gave orders that no one was to be present during future rehearsals. Of course, Dolin was wrong. Alicia was physically quite light and she knew how to create an illusion which needed just a little extra help from her partner. Anyway, I had nothing but the greatest admiration for Alicia Markova and she helped me enormously to understand my role and to give me the confidence to dance it with security and ease."

The matinee performance of *Giselle*, held on May 1, 1955, at the old Metropolitan Opera House in New York, proved to be a milestone in the history of ballet. Markova and Erik Bruhn gave a performance that brought endless cheers from the audience and unparalleled reviews from the critics. Writing in *The New York Times,* John Martin opened his review by stating:

> One of the most notable events of the Ballet Theatre's season at the Metropolitan Opera House was reserved for the last day. Yesterday afternoon, Alicia Markova made her appearance in *Giselle* and Erik Bruhn appeared opposite her in his very first Albrecht. It may well be a date to write down in the history books, for it was as if the greatest Giselle of today were handing over a sacred trust to what is probably the greatest Albrecht of tomorrow. . . . In the second act, Mr. Bruhn really came into his own. His dancing was like velvet, and his support of Miss Markova was easy, gracious, and totally in accord with her, in both mood and technique. Through his sense of her as a disembodied spirit, he made her seem even more ethereal than she is. Never for an instant did he lose the dramatic line. Here was a young lover, truly possessed. The final parting, when at dawn Giselle must return to the grave, was as deeply moving a scene as one has ever encountered in the ballet.

In an article entitled "The Matinee That Made History," written by P. W. Manchester and published in *Dance News* in June 1955, Manchester reports her version of the event in even greater detail:

> Technically exacting as it is, the role of Albrecht is not beyond the capabilities of any competent *premier danseur*, and Erik Bruhn is infinitely more than that; he is probably the most completely equipped male dancer of the day, with the flawlessly clean technique that comes only through a combination of enormous talent allied to the correct day-by-day training from childhood. . . . If his dancing was magnificent, and it was, his partnering of and playing to Markova was no less so. The result was one of those electrifying performances when everyone both in the audience and on the stage is aware that something extraordinary is happening.

In the relatively closed world of the ballet in those years, news spread like wildfire about Erik Bruhn's phenomenal success in *Giselle*. The reviews and articles traveled abroad and all of Europe became aware of Bruhn's newfound stardom in America. Bruhn himself was stunned by his reception in *Giselle*. As he told John Martin in a *Dance Magazine* interview shortly after the performance: "When I came offstage for the last time and walked in a daze to my dressing room, I suddenly began to get frightened. I had been so involved during the performance that when I tried to remember what I had done, I found I could remember nothing, and I was mortified that I might have done dreadful things and been all wrong."

Lucia Chase was, of course, thrilled by the critical reception allotted her young second soloist; but she was decidedly dazed over another piece of news she had received on the morning prior to the memorable *Giselle*: Igor Youskevitch and Alicia Alonso, two of her leading dancers, had come to her and announced that they would be leaving Ballet Theatre to join its strongest competition, the Ballet Russe de Monte Carlo. Chase was losing vital members of her company and she was particularly distressed over the loss of Youskevitch, who had been Ballet Theatre's premier danseur. The advent of Erik Bruhn's enormous acclaim—something she had undoubtedly anticipated—couldn't have been better timed. Bruhn might become an extraordinary drawing card and, with Youskevitch gone, might easily fill his place. She would most definitely have to reconsider his request for a promotion.

Bruhn recalls Lucia Chase's new mood. "Suddenly, she came around to me and said, 'Erik, dear, I am going to make you one of my stars! You will make a lot of money.' It seemed that now she needed me. I told her how badly she had behaved, putting me through the wringer just at a time when I needed to concentrate on what I was doing. I told her that instead of giving me her support, all she did was fight with me. Well, she soothed me and was sweet as all get-out, and finally offered me a contract as a principal dancer with the company. From that moment on my relationship with Lucia changed for the better."

Ballet Theatre's historic *Giselle* ended the company's 1955 spring season at the old Met. The company would travel to Boston for a brief tour and then go off on vacation. For Erik Bruhn, the tide had turned. While not totally aware of it at the time, he had emerged as one of the world's greatest exponents of male classical dancing. Indeed, his Albrecht had placed him on the international-ballet map, and henceforth his name would become synonymous with all that was pure and technically perfect in an art form that had for centuries regarded itself as among the noblest of all creative expressions. In short, the ballet world had found in Erik Bruhn a new god of the dance.

〖 CHAPTER 11 〗

I N JULY 1955 Ted Shawn, one of America's prime figures in the American modern dance movement, and the long-time director of the Jacob's Pillow Dance Festival in Lee, Massachusetts, invited ten members of the Royal Danish Ballet to come from Copenhagen and demonstrate the art of Bournonville to the American public. This invitation would give the United States its very first glimpse of the two-hundred-year-old Danish ballet through several of its stars. To that end, Shawn invited Mona Vangsaa, Kirsten Ralov, Inge Sand, Svend Erik Jensen, Frank Schaufuss, Stanley Williams, Fredbjørn Bjørnsson, and the young dancers Mette Mollerup, Viveka Segerskov, and Flemming Flindt.

To round out his program for the summer Ted Shawn also invited Erik Bruhn to the Pillow. The two had become good friends some years earlier and, after Bruhn's spectacular debut in *Giselle*, Shawn was particularly delighted when the dancer agreed to participate. He would appear with Mary Ellen Moylan in the *Don Quixote* and *Nutcracker* pas de deux and with Alicia Alonso in the Black Swan pas de deux and in excerpts from *Giselle*. Learning that Shawn had plans to bring members of the Royal Danish Ballet to America, Bruhn made every effort to help him complete negotiations with the Danes. News had by then reached Denmark of Bruhn's great success as Albrecht and, when the Danish dancers made their appearance at Jacob's Pillow, they were thrilled to be reunited with their now-famous countryman.

The performances held under the aegis of Ted Shawn were a huge success and Bruhn was outstanding in his share of the program. When Shawn turned eighty in 1971, a year before his death, the dance world paid him homage. He and Ruth St. Denis had pioneered the modern dance movement in America and the accolades that came to Shawn were as merited as they were poignant. Bruhn wrote Shawn a warm and heartfelt birthday greeting, which Shawn answered from his home in Florida. His letter, dated November 23, 1971, offers a glimpse of the friendship between the two men:

Dearly beloved Erik:

It has taken me over a month to thank you for the beautiful letter which you sent for my 80th birthday and which Genevieve Oswald [curator of the Dance Collection of the Lincoln Center Library for the Performing Arts] read aloud to the nearly 400 guests at the party. It was so beautiful it brought tears to my eyes and a lump in my throat! As our American Thanksgiving Day approaches, and we think of the things we have to be thankful for, one of the things on the top of my list is that I live in the same age so that I could see you dance—see the absolute perfection of my every ideal of what a man dancer should be—and to call you a friend, and to be called friend by you!

So many tender and precious memories come out as I write—that fabulous matinee on May 1, 1955, when you did your first Albrecht with Alicia, and I cooked for you and fed you after that matinee; the next morning when sleepy-eyed you and Ray came in with leftover eggs and butter, etc. . . . And your visit here [to Florida]—I have the Kodak pictures—your serious expression as you contemplated the first orange you ever picked from a tree and then cutting into it and eating it. And the many memories of you at Jacob's Pillow and the thrills of your performances there that never were and never can be matched by anyone else. . . . Well, I could go on and on! . . . You have been in my mind and heart all the time. . . . I hope there will be a chance to see you at least once again, and embrace you and say in gesture what cannot be said in words!

Your ever devoted friend

"Papa" Shawn.

Following his engagement at Jacob's Pillow in July 1955 Erik Bruhn returned to Copenhagen, where he was invited by the Royal Danish Ballet to repeat his triumph in *Giselle* with Alicia Markova. The two danced two performances at the Royal Opera House and also did excerpts of the ballet for Danish television in honor of the British Trade Fair being held in Copenhagen that year.

While Bruhn was in Copenhagen, he had occasion to learn the role of Romeo in Frederick Ashton's *Romeo and Juliet,* which the British choreographer had come to set on the Danes that summer. The work had been given its premiere in May 1955 and had made a star of Henning Kronstam, who created the role of Romeo. Bruhn was asked to perform in it when the company appeared at the Edinburgh Festival that August. Ashton's three-act *Romeo* was one of the Royal Danish Ballet's most ambitious presentations and, to this day, many ballet cognoscenti consider it the best of the various productions on the Shakespeare play. As it turned out, however, Ashton's *Romeo and Juliet* did not prove popular with the Danish public and has not survived in the Royal Danish Ballet repertoire. The production was dropped and the work, a treasure among Ashton's large oeuvre, has been tragically lost.

Bruhn's memories of his appearance in this *Romeo* are vivid. "Henning Kronstam did the premiere, and he was marvelous as Romeo. It made his career. But then, all the people in the cast were wonderful—Mona Vangsaa as Juliet, Frank Schaufuss as Mercutio, and Niels Bjørn Larsen as Tybalt. Anyway, I danced Romeo in Edinburgh and my interpretation was very different from that of Henning's. It is a beautiful ballet, perhaps a little weak in the mass dancing but unequaled in the pas de deux. This was the first full-length ballet Ashton had ever created for an outside company and we Danes should all feel like criminals for having let it go."

Bruhn continued dancing with the Danes until the conclusion of their season and then found time to spend some weeks with his family in Gentofte. His mother, aunt, and sisters had, of course, kept up with his great success in America and were delighted to have Erik back in their midst. Ellen Bruhn's hairdressing salon was all abuzz with talk of Erik's fame and even his half sister, Else, seemed happy to see him, while Birthe and Aase looked upon him with awe and pride. (Bruhn's youngest sister, Benthe, was living in Canada.)

All too soon, it was time for Bruhn to return to New York, where he would rejoin Ballet Theatre as one of its star dancers. Bidding his family and friends farewell, he looked forward to the flight that would bring him to the country in which he would achieve even greater renown. He had signed an exclusive contract with Ballet Theatre (which had now changed its name to American Ballet Theatre), one that would run until June 1957, with an option for an additional year. Bruhn realized that under this exclusive contract he would be unable to appear with the Royal Danish Ballet, which would be performing in New York for the first time during the fall of 1956. But Bruhn was content to dance with the American company, now operating under the management of Sol Hurok.

Bruhn looks back on this particular period of his career with a certain ambiguity. "Being a so-called star was not particularly easy for me. The first problem was Lucia's pushing me to dance much too often. Also, I was dancing the same roles over and over again and we fought about that. There was a time when I refused to speak to Lucia. She couldn't get one word out of me. The work load was just getting to be too much. It was a question of tremendous responsibility that brought a lot of tension. I mean, I was expected to deliver practically every night. It was getting to a point where I was hurting myself and being off, and that, of course, was a way out. The fact is, I was not being properly directed, and when I became the director of a ballet company myself later on, I never forgot how important it was to use one's dancers well and not burn them out."

Despite his sense of being overworked, Bruhn *did* deliver—and magnificently. He appeared in such New York premieres as Joffrey's *Pas des Déesses*, Alexandra Fedorova's version of *Paquita*, Anton Dolin's *Variations for Four*, Enrique Martinez's *La Muerte Enamorada*, Kenneth MacMillan's *Journey*, Alfred Rodrigues's *Blood Wedding*, Job Sanders' *The Careless Burghers*, Herbert Ross's *Concerto* and *Tristan*. In May 1957 Bruhn created his second original ballet, *Festa* (in which he did not appear), set to music of Rossini, and it proved a popular success.

Of the dancers in the company at that time, Nora Kaye was Bruhn's most frequent partner. They performed in the classics—the second act of *Swan Lake* and *Giselle*, among others—and were paired in various contemporary works. He also danced frequently with Lupe Serrano and Ruth Ann Koesun. He had danced only occasionally with Sonia Arova, who by 1956 had decided to leave the company.

Says Arova: "I realized that Lucia Chase was never really going to accept me, because she liked to discover people herself, and she hadn't really discovered me. With Erik it was another matter. Although Blevins Davis had brought both of us into Ballet Theatre, Lucia basically liked her other ballerinas more. I found myself in a stagnant situation. I thought, Well, there's no more Erik for me. Was there any real reason for me to remain in the company? I discussed my status with Lucia and she said that she had her established ballerinas and for me to dance more would mean having to wait. Well, I was not prepared to wait.

"Also, in 1956, I began a relationship with Job Sanders, one of the company's dancers and choreographers. When it became clear to me that my career was not moving forward with Ballet Theatre, Job and I decided to go to Europe and to get married. We joined a company called American Festival Ballet, an American-based company that performed mainly in Europe. For this company Job choreographed new works and I danced in them. Job Sanders and I stayed together until 1959, but it was not a happy marriage and later that year we were divorced."

If Arova did not marry Erik Bruhn, it did not mean the end of their relationship. Indeed, Erik Bruhn would be part of her private and professional life for many years to come. Erik Bruhn confesses to some regret in not having made Sonia Arova his wife. Still, he claims that Arova herself was partially to blame for this. "Sonia was my first love. We got engaged. I was nineteen. She was twenty. We could have had a child. The fact is, I wanted to marry her at that time, but she told me that I was too young. Also, she was thinking more about her career than about marriage and that was understandable. I too thought about my career, but I still wanted to marry her. It's hard to say what kind of a career I would have had if I had done that. Sonia might not have had a career at all, especially if we started having children. Anyway, it obviously wasn't meant to be, and I have no regrets about never having married."

The year 1958 was an important one in Bruhn's artistic development. Bruhn had proven himself a major asset to American Ballet Theatre and was now in a position to demand particular roles that he wanted to perform. In Copenhagen in 1957, he had chanced to see a work by the Swedish choreographer Birgit Cullberg. It was called *Miss Julie* and was based on the play by August Strindberg. Bruhn asked Lucia Chase to ask Cullberg for the ballet, which had originally been created in 1950. He wanted to portray the role of Jean, a valet, who seduces the daughter of the house, a young noblewoman who has been brought up to loathe the idea of love between a man and a woman. Miss Julie taunts the valet, berates him, and physically abuses him until he retaliates with a venomous sexual attack on her. It would be a dramatic role in total contrast to anything Bruhn had danced in the past and he would be called upon to make use of his acting ability. While the dancing was fairly complex, it made little use of the classicism with which Bruhn had been associated. He would have to abandon matters of conventional pyrotechnics, lose his image of the danseur noble, and give himself over to a characterization demanding the utmost dramatic intensity. Furthermore, it would not be a sympathetic role, but one in which Bruhn would have to portray a boorish and hateful villain, whose progressive sadism culminates in the heroine's demise. Equally demanding would be the role of Miss Julie. Whoever would portray her would have to match Bruhn's dramatic power and be possessed of a strong sense of theatricality. Bruhn thought the role of Miss Julie would be an ideal vehicle for Nora Kaye, who had proven herself a great actress on the ballet stage and would no doubt lend the role the required intensity.

As it turned out, what Bruhn had seen in Copenhagen was not the full-length ballet, but only the so-called "kitchen scene." Bruhn had no idea that there was far more to the work than this single scene, and when Lucia Chase contacted Cullberg and talked to her about wanting it for ABT, she learned that *Miss Julie* was a ballet of thirty-five minutes' duration, employing a number of dancers besides the leading roles. When Chase told Cullberg that she wanted *Miss Julie* specifically for Erik Bruhn, the Swedish choreographer considered Bruhn entirely wrong for the part. She felt that he was a classical dancer, not a character dancer, and that as Jean he would be decidedly miscast. On the other hand, Cullberg had never had a ballet of hers performed in America and she was anxious to be presented by so important a company as ABT. Despite her misgivings about Bruhn, she accepted Lucia Chase's invitation and agreed to join the company to stage the ballet herself.

"Birgit Cullberg came to set *Miss Julie*, and I had no idea that she didn't really think I was right for the role of Jean," says Bruhn. "Lucia never told me that. At any rate, Nora and I began to rehearse and as the rehearsals progressed, Nora began to complain that she didn't like her role. She said, 'I can't stand these steps.' Well, we had to find another dancer, because we were planning to present *Miss Julie* at the Metropolitan Opera House in New York in 1958. The girl I thought would be just right was Violette Verdy, who came in very late in the rehearsal period. The fact is that Nora kept hedging about actually backing out of the role. She kept being very much around, making Violette extremely nervous."

A French-born ballerina, Violette Verdy had joined American Ballet Theatre in 1957. As a child prodigy, she trained with her mother and Vic-

tor Gsovsky and danced with Les Ballets des Champs Elysées until 1949.
From 1950 until 1956 she danced with the Ballets de Paris de Roland
Petit, where she created her best-known roles, notably the Bride in Petit's
Le Loup. Verdy then danced several seasons with London's Festival Ballet
and was a guest artist at the Teatro alla Scala and Ballet Rambert. It was
during her brief tenure with Ballet Rambert that she danced her first full-
length *Giselle* and *Coppélia*, scoring a great success in both productions.

Verdy was discovered by American Ballet Theatre through a film performance, photographed by Ann Barzel, of the *Nutcracker* pas de deux, in
which she was partnered by the English dancer John Gilpin. The film was
screened at a party attended by Nora Kaye, who was impressed enough
with Verdy's performance to mention the film to Lucia Chase, who then
saw the film herself and hired Verdy as a ballerina. At ABT, the vivacious
and gifted Miss Verdy had danced with Erik Bruhn on several occasions,
notably in *Les Sylphides, Theme and Variations*, and the *Nutcracker* pas
de deux, and the two had become good friends.

When she was offered the role of Miss Julie, Verdy was delighted. "The
minute I grabbed the riding whip and did the first entrance with the jeté, I
said, 'This is something for me to chew on!' I felt like a dog who had
found the right bone. Erik seemed pleased with me and felt I was right for
the part. Finally, when the company returned to New York, Erik and I
really launched ourselves into rehearsals. Erik was incredibly brilliant. We
exchanged thoughts about our roles and the kind of communication we
had was exceptional. The point is that Erik was being a perfectionist and
was alert to every last nuance of his character and of mine. Cullberg had
taught us the steps, but Erik infused the ballet with an extra dimension.
Our rapport was total, and working with Erik on *Miss Julie* was one of the
greatest dancing experiences of my life."

Miss Julie was part of a mixed bill presented at the Metropolitan Opera
House on September 18, 1958. John Martin in *The New York Times*
praised the ballet unstintingly. After extolling Birgit Cullberg's conception
and staging, he went on to say: "The central figures are excellently danced
(and acted, make no mistake) by Violette Verdy and Erik Bruhn. One
would have liked, perhaps, more easy breeding and aristocracy behind
Miss Verdy's vicious Julie, but that is something of a quibble. Mr. Bruhn
as the valet proves himself once again to be a superb actor-dancer and an
artist of the first rank."

Miss Julie became a resounding success and since its premiere at ABT has remained a staple of the repertoire. Bruhn appeared in it many times, making clear his dramatic gifts, while concurrently performing in the classics where as a danseur noble he continued to reign supreme. Eventually, Bruhn would dance *Miss Julie* at the Royal Danish Ballet, where he again triumphed in the role of Jean, and would succeed in transforming the classically trained Kirsten Simone into a dramatic actress.

Reflecting on his role of Jean, Bruhn says: "The reason I wanted to do *Miss Julie* in the first place was to prove to the public that I could portray a dreadful and awful character. Actually, portraying such a role comes very easily to me, whereas being the noble prince did not come as naturally as people might suppose."

The 1957–58 season of American Ballet Theatre had found the company undergoing a severe financial crisis. Despite a long tour and a successful New York engagement, prospects for further bookings into 1959 were extremely dim. Lucia Chase and her co-director, Oliver Smith, found no way to ameliorate the situation and with the greatest reluctance felt obliged to suspend operations temporarily. The company, they hoped, would resume its activities when greater financial backing could be secured and when sufficient engagements would make resumption feasible.

It would not be until the spring of 1960 that American Ballet Theatre would get back on its feet, and in the meantime, its dancers had to seek employment elsewhere. In 1959 Erik Bruhn was invited to return to Copenhagen and resume his place as principal dancer with the Royal Danish Ballet, now headed by a new ballet master, Frank Schaufuss. Schaufuss offered Bruhn a three-year contract and Bruhn accepted it on the condition that he would have control of his repertoire. When he arrived in Copenhagen, he found the Danish company in an uproar—one that would precipitate any number of conflicts between Bruhn and the management.

〖 CHAPTER 12 〗

T HE ROYAL DANISH BALLET had become one of the most important
companies in the world under the guidance of Harald Lander, its
ballet master, who saw to it that the Bournonville tradition would
be carefully preserved. It was also during Lander's regime that Erik Bruhn
first came to the attention of the public. Clearly, Lander was a man of
great artistic and administrative acumen, and his abrupt dismissal in 1951
was beginning to be regretted by the hierarchy at the Royal Opera House.

Although the intervening ballet masters of the company—Niels Bjørn
Larsen and Frank Schaufuss—had guided the company with relative care,
some of its glitter was fading. At the time of Erik Bruhn's return to Copenhagen in 1959, a strong movement was afoot to bring Lander back as a
guest choreographer. Lander had made a distinguished career for himself
as ballet master and teacher with the Paris Opéra Ballet and had been
highly productive as a choreographer. Perhaps it was time now to let bygones be bygones and bring Lander back. As things turned out, a large
number of the Danish dancers protested such a move; they were unwilling
to have Lander back and petitions were drawn up against his return. The
dancers were perfectly satisfied to continue under Schaufuss, whose wife,
Mona Vangsaa, was one of the company's leading ballerinas.

"It was Schaufuss who offered me my three-year contract," explains
Bruhn, "but when I got to Copenhagen things were in a tremendous turmoil there. I found myself in the middle of a political struggle that I really

wanted no part of. I mean, even the king was brought into it! The management and a lot of Danish politicians wanted Lander back, but fifty percent of the dancers wanted Schaufuss to remain in power. At one point, the entire ballet company was threatened with being fired if they continued to refuse Lander's return. When they heard that, they got scared, because it meant they would lose their pensions, so, practically en masse, they turned around and said 'Fine, we'll accept Lander!' Of course, I'm simplifying, but it was a holy mess.

"I had a three-year contract, but within a month's time, my contract was canceled, because of the political turmoil. Frank Schaufuss was dismissed as ballet master, so, again, that was a mess. The upshot of it all was that I engaged my Danish lawyer, Esther Tonsgaard, to look into the situation. To make matters even more confusing, Harald Lander heard that none of the dancers of the Royal Danish Ballet wanted him back and so, naturally, he had no intention of returning to Denmark. In fact, he did *not* return to Denmark until several years later, and then only to stage some of his works. As matters stood, Lander didn't come, Schaufuss was fired, and I had no contract. I got thoroughly disgusted and told my lawyer that I would leave immediately. When word got out that I was leaving the company, having just arrived, everyone got panicky. It wouldn't look good for the company. Hours after I made my announcement, my lawyer received a telephone call from Denmark's prime minister, H. C. Hansen. He begged her to tell me not to leave and told her that my presence there might bring some peace into the company. But I was fed up. I took off for Germany and communicated with my lawyer by phone. Finally, at Esther Tonsgaard's suggestion, I made a whole other arrangement with the Royal Danish Ballet. We drew up a contract stating that I would dance three months out of each subsequent three years, and that the choice of those months would be mine. In other words, I would be a guest artist for certain specified periods over the next three years. This was a very agreeable arrangement for me, because it gave me the freedom to travel and not be tied down. I should add that during those three years the ballet master of the Royal Danish Ballet was Niels Bjørn Larsen."

With his new contract firmly negotiated, Bruhn returned to the fold and staged a new version of *Giselle* for the Royal Danish Ballet. The company felt that their production had become somewhat antiquated and wanted Bruhn to revamp it, remembering how he and Markova had triumphed in the Markova-Dolin version staged for American Ballet Theatre. This Bruhn did and, as was his custom when staging his own works, he did not place himself in the leading role. For the 1959 season, the Royal Danish Ballet presented Bruhn's *Giselle* with Kirsten Simone in the title role and Henning Kronstam as Albrecht. The two dancers, as well as the production, received unqualified praise in the press.

Bruhn had always felt a special fondness for the unusually gifted Kirsten Simone, who became one of the Royal Danish Ballet's most prominent ballerinas. Although she had formed an important partnership with Henning Kronstam, Bruhn invariably chose her as a partner whenever he danced in Denmark.

"When Kirsten made her debut at the age of seventeen with the Royal Danish Ballet, it was I who partnered her in the *Nutcracker* pas de deux," says Bruhn. "Vera Volkova had been her principal teacher and she developed into an excellent technician. I liked Kirsten. When she was younger, she had a wonderful sense of humor and it was fun to be with her. I remember one night early in her career taking her out on the town and getting her drunk. I don't think she's ever forgiven me for that, and she has stayed sober for years! Anyway, she was a good sport. As time went on, we became very good friends and she would often visit me in my house in Gentofte. I must say, she was very domestic and I recall my housekeeper, Ella Schram, being rather put out over Kirsten's zealousness around the house.

"Of all the ballerinas in the Danish company, Kirsten was the only partner I felt comfortable dancing with. We did *La Sylphide, Miss Julie,* and *Carmen* together. Eventually, however, I felt that her interpretations were beginning to get somewhat routine. She would get rigid in a part. When that happened, I would terrify her by telling her that on a particular night I would not be doing a certain lift. That would perk her up no end, because she didn't know what was going to happen onstage. She would live in terror about my not catching her during a pas de deux—and she actually claims that I once let her fall on her ass, because I wasn't there to catch her. Well, when she did fall on her ass she got herself up and danced even better than before. The point is that Kirsten had a way of getting in a rut with her roles, and she needed to be shaken up.

"Many years later, when I returned to Denmark, I again chose Kirsten as my partner for *La Sylphide,* but on this occasion we had a very serious argument, because throughout the years that she had been dancing the role, she had not felt that she needed to rethink it. Well, I had been reading some of her reviews and told her that she didn't, in fact, know the ballet in the first place. She said she knew the role perfectly. I said to her: 'You should not say that about any role in any ballet. I have heard that people are bored looking at you and that's because you think you know *La Sylphide* inside and out and could do it in your sleep. Well, that's what it's been looking like!' Poor Kirsten was so upset. But *somebody* had to tell her she was getting stale and that she would have to pull herself together. Still, she gave me a big argument and I suddenly lost interest.

"What happened next was that I talked to my friend the dancer Inge Sand and asked her who among the new girls would make a good Sylphide. Inge said that Anna Laerkesen had been dancing the role very well in the past, and so I chose her as my partner. People were shocked and everybody was saying, 'Who is going to tell Kirsten?' I decided that I would write Kirsten a letter telling her that I would dance *La Sylphide* with Anna Laerkesen and I also told her exactly why. Two or three days later the casting was posted, and Kirsten was furious. But I would not give in. I danced with Anna, and Kirsten Simone and I were very cool to each other for a very long time.

"Actually Kirsten knew that things were not going well for her in the company. Just a few years ago I invited her to come to Spain with me. We stayed there for a week and we talked endlessly. She had problems about her career. She was still an excellent dancer, but she was not fulfilling her promise and very soon she would be on the list of those dancers waiting to get their pension. I tried to tell her that she had not permitted herself to blossom fully as a dancer. I kept telling her not to sit back, not to wait and depend on others. I burned myself out talking to her and finally suggested that she simply take charge of her life and of her career before it was too late. These days, Kirsten is still very involved in the theater and devotes herself to it completely. She still dances occasionally and I'm sure that when she stops she will be a valuable asset in some other capacity. We are now back on good terms and since Henning Kronstam is the current director of the Danish ballet, as well as being one of her closest friends, he will almost certainly want to put her in a position that would be of benefit to her and the Royal Danish Ballet."

Kirsten Simone recalls seeing Erik Bruhn in 1952 as a young dancer destined for greatness. "We all called him 'King of Dance.' I was in the Royal Ballet School and of course was immensely flattered when Erik partnered me in my debut when I was seventeen. Later we danced a great deal together, and we had a lot of fun. Often, we would talk through whole performances! With Erik I could laugh a lot and we felt very comfortable in each other's company. When he danced, he never abandoned his great purity of style. I mean, he was the greatest! I have never seen anything like it. We danced together in many works—*La Sylphide, Les Sylphides, Giselle, Nutcracker, Night Shadow, Don Quixote,* and, of course, all the Bournonville works in our repertoire. The most thrilling things for me were *Miss Julie* and *Carmen,* because Erik was able to bring out my qualities as an actress. He would discuss these roles so intelligently!

"Like every artist, Erik is complicated. He has his moods. But, for the most part, he is sweet and very helpful. I remember that whenever I was unsure of myself, he would give me very good advice and I would usually take it. I trust Erik completely. By now we are very old friends. We have traveled together and I have been with him during our summer holidays. Always we laughed and joked. I suppose it is our sense of humor that has kept our friendship going."

Bruhn's contractual arrangement with the Royal Danish Ballet was entirely satisfactory to him. He would be dancing with the company three months a year for three years, and by September 1959 he had completed the first of these three months, dancing in various roles and also teaching some classes at the Royal Ballet School. The youngsters looked to Bruhn as an inspiration. He was, after all, the greatest dancer Denmark produced during their lifetime and his classes were eagerly anticipated, particularly by the young male students whose dream it was to emulate the refinements of their celebrated teacher.

Now thirty-one, Erik Bruhn had accomplished much. He could look back on a career that was nothing if not phenomenal and know that his fame had not been earned through talent or genius alone. The daily classes, the endless rehearsals, the repeated performances, and the rigorous and exhausting travel had all contributed to his development as a complete artist. A perfectionist, Bruhn would give of himself unstintingly, often at the sacrifice of a rich or fulfilling personal life. It was not that he avoided personal relationships or that he did not enjoy close or casual friendships, but the demands of his career left him relatively little time to engage in involvements commensurate with the depth of his art.

His years with American Ballet Theatre, and particularly the long months of one-night stands on tour, brought home to him the knowledge that the life of a dancer was indeed a lonely one. Solitary by nature, Bruhn would often retreat into himself or even disappear for months at a time. When dancing, personal involvements, and the constant presence of other people became too much for him, Bruhn would occasionally take leaves of absence, letting no one know his whereabouts.

"There were times during my twenties when I wanted to stop dancing altogether," claims Bruhn. "I remember, after having done four years of one-night stands with Ballet Theatre, that I simply could not go on. Of course, it was hard on everybody, but there were moments when it got to be unbearable. Those one-night stands were simply not for me. But in those years that was the only way a company could survive. And when you do one-night stands, you also have them as a person—sexually. Believe me I tried them, but they were so unfulfilling that in the end I stopped. I wanted full relationships, not in terms of years but in terms of intensity. Some relationships last a long time and some don't, but within a span of time it is possible to be passionately involved. For me, everything depended on the degree of intensity that I experienced with another person. I applied that principle to my dancing as well. When the intensity diminished I felt burned out, and the only way I could get my strength back was to leave—to return to nature—not the woods or the fields but back into another stream of life where I would meet entirely different people. Through new people I would discover new ideas and be inspired and could replenish myself as a thinking and feeling human being, rather than a machine that dances. I have always needed to do that. Of course, people were not the only source of this replenishment. Just being by myself would often be enough. I remember, looking back on it, that my agents would be appalled at my taking off just like that. They would say, 'People will forget you!' But you see, I needed to make that space for myself. I felt that if I didn't have that space it would be very destructive to me. I needed to get life back into me—to renew myself. Besides, I would always make sure that the public would not forget me, because the minute I felt the physical energy coming back, I would immediately be back on stage and dance like a new person."

Pas de Dix with Maria Tallchief, New York City Ballet, 1959. Photo: Rigmor Mydtskov.

(ABOVE) With Sonia Arova in *Swan Lake*, American Ballet Theatre on Russian tour, 1959. Photo: David Mist. (OPPOSITE LEFT) With Arova on tour in Australia, 1962. (OPPOSITE RIGHT) With Lupe Serrano in *Lady from the Sea*, American Ballet Theatre, 1960. Photo: Fred Fehl. (OPPOSITE BELOW) With Patricia Wilde in *Panamerica*, New York City Ballet, 1960. Photo: Fred Fehl.

(RIGHT) With Sonia Arova in *Don Quixote*, American Ballet Theatre. (BELOW) As Don José in *Carmen* with Kirsten Simone, Royal Danish Ballet, 1960. Photo: Rigmor Mydtskov. (OPPOSITE) In *Don Quixote*, American Ballet Theatre. Photo: Martha Swope.

(OPPOSITE LEFT) As James in *La Sylphide* with Margarette Schanne, Royal Danish Ballet, 1952. (LEFT) *La Sylphide* with Kirsten Simone, Royal Danish Ballet, 1965. Photo: Fred Fehl. (OPPOSITE BELOW) As James, American Ballet Theatre, 1967. Photo: Fred Fehl. (BELOW) *La Sylphide* with Carla Fracci, American Ballet Theatre, 1967. Photo: Fred Fehl.

(ABOVE) Rudolf Nureyev and Bruhn at Maxim's in Paris, 1963. (OPPOSITE ABOVE) Bruhn giving a class to Nureyev, 1965. Photo: Jack Mitchell. (RIGHT) Bruhn presenting the Dance Magazine Award to Nureyev, 1973. Photo: Louis Péres. (OPPOSITE BELOW) Bruhn and Nureyev, 1975. Photo: Rosemary Winckley.

Flower Festival with Nadia Nerina, Royal Ballet, London, 1962. Photo: Dominic.

〔 CHAPTER 13 〕

B RUHN WAS STILL in Copenhagen in the fall of 1959 when he received a letter from the dance critic P. W. Manchester saying that she had bumped into Lincoln Kirstein on the street in New York. Their conversation had turned to Erik Bruhn as a possible guest artist with the New York City Ballet, of which Kirstein was director, together with George Balanchine. The letter went on to say that Kirstein was most excited over this possibility and that if Bruhn were interested she should let him know. The dancer was delighted and promptly answered that he would be overjoyed to dance with the City Ballet, a company he greatly admired, and that he would be thrilled to work with George Balanchine, a choreographer whom Bruhn deemed a genius.

Soon thereafter, a letter reached Bruhn from Betty Cage, administrative director of the City Ballet, inviting him, on behalf of Lincoln Kirstein, to join the company. Bruhn instantly accepted the invitation. He had, of course, danced in various Balanchine works in the repertoire of the Royal Danish Ballet and the American Ballet Theatre, but he had never had the good fortune of working with Balanchine himself. Bruhn was now at the peak of his career and felt that it would be highly challenging to stretch and broaden his art beyond the classics, to give his body the chance to be molded through the aesthetics of this great choreographer.

Bruhn had, in the meantime, learned that Maria Tallchief would also be rejoining the company after a year's maternity leave, and the prospect of dancing with this superb American ballerina made his entry into the New York City Ballet an even more exciting venture. He had had a brief but memorable meeting with Tallchief in 1949, when he had first joined Ballet Theatre and when Tallchief was among its guest artists. The young ballerina was at that time married to George Balanchine but was dancing with the Ballet Theatre because the City Ballet, of which she was a leading member, held only infrequent performances. She had joined Ballet Theatre on tour in Chicago to dance *Swan Lake*, partnered by Igor Youskevitch, and as it turned out, the role of Benno, the Prince's friend, was danced by Erik Bruhn. George Balanchine had traveled to Chicago, both to be near his wife and to supervise her rehearsals.

To the twenty-year-old Bruhn the vision of Tallchief and Balanchine had been dizzying, and the opportunity to dance with Tallchief as the Swan Queen and with Youskevitch as Prince Siegfried was challenging indeed. During that performance, Bruhn remembers being so tense when he had to catch the Swan Queen in his arms that, at the concluding pose, he faltered and both dancers suddenly collapsed in a heap on the stage. Bruhn now roars with laughter at this memory and says, "I think we simply collapsed together because each of us in our own way was so nervous that this seemed to be the only way to end the act!"

Although Maria Tallchief divorced George Balanchine in 1952, she continued to dance on and off with the New York City Ballet until her retirement in 1965. A uniquely gifted dancer of Osage Indian descent, Tallchief had trained with Bronislava Nijinska and at the School of American Ballet, where she received special instruction from Balanchine. From 1942 until 1947 she danced with the Ballet Russe de Monte Carlo, eventually becoming a soloist, and in the fall of 1947 joined Balanchine's company, Ballet Society, which became the New York City Ballet the following year. Since that time, her name has irrevocably been linked with that company. Tallchief created many important Balanchine roles and her performances received high praise from the critics. With her exotic looks and background, her temperament and élan, Maria Tallchief, one of America's great ballerinas, was known to produce fireworks both on and offstage.

At the time Erik Bruhn joined the New York City Ballet, in the late fall of 1959, Tallchief was married to Henry Paschen, the owner of a successful construction company in Chicago, and she had recently given birth to their daughter, Elise. Tallchief was in superb form when she re-entered the company and was delighted at the arrival of Erik Bruhn. She too recalled their first nervous encounter at Ballet Theatre in 1949, and, despite their mishap in *Swan Lake*, had taken account of Bruhn's very special qualities as a dancer and as a person. She found him to be a quiet, reserved young man, and was particularly struck by his blond good looks. She had, in the meantime, followed his career throughout the years and was well aware of his reputation as the most spectacular male dancer of the day.

"When Erik was invited into the New York City Ballet, I was incredibly pleased," says Miss Tallchief. "We had André Eglevsky, but as great an artist as Eglevsky was, I don't believe he was the actor that Erik proved himself to be. Erik was the full artist, actor, dancer. He was a supreme technician and I knew how much he was looking forward to working with George. At any rate, we opened that first season with Balanchine's one-act version of *Swan Lake*, and, I dare say, we were a sensational success."

Indeed, the advent of Erik Bruhn's entry into the New York City Ballet was met with extraordinary interest by the ballet world and when, on December 8, 1959, Bruhn made his debut with Tallchief in Balanchine's *Swan Lake*, the public and New York's dance critics not only acclaimed Bruhn's artistry but hailed the birth of a new and altogether dazzling partnership.

John Martin wrote in *The New York Times* of December 9:

> The *Swan Lake* that opened the program may well have set a record for brilliance. Miss Tallchief was at the top of her form and that is pretty high. . . . With Mr. Bruhn as her partner, she could not conceivably have been either ungracious or unaware. Here is a superb *danseur noble*; it is rarely indeed that the term is so apt. The role of the Prince in this particular piece is only what the dancer makes it, for its opportunities are anything but obvious. Mr. Bruhn places himself in space, as it were, with the utmost precision at all times, and never without both aesthetic and dramatic illumination. . . . How fortunate we are to have him around for the season!

In the following weeks, Bruhn danced in several more Balanchine ballets, each of which he executed with mastery. With Patricia Wilde, one of the company's leading ballerinas, he danced in *Divertimento No. 15*. Assuming the leading male role in this masterpiece, he negotiated Balanchine's quicksilver steps so brilliantly that it moved John Martin to dedicate his entire *Times* review of December 12 to the dancer's phenomenal virtuosity:

> Although Bruhn's solo variation has been danced well by other dancers before now, it had on this occasion the flavor of an entirely new piece of composition. . . .
>
> When he is called upon for multiple air turns, he produces them as a compositional element and not as a feat of virtuosity. He stands nobly, he moves cleanly; he never dissipates the attention in unconscious irrelevances, but makes every point directly, economically and unequivocably. His manner is gracious and warm, and the very fact that he is sparing of his smile makes it all the more ingratiating when it comes.

In the weeks that followed, Bruhn partnered Tallchief in Balanchine's *The Nutcracker* and again the critics described their partnership "as though made in heaven." But Tallchief was not Bruhn's exclusive partner at the City Ballet. As noted, he danced with Patricia Wilde and, as the Poet, in Balanchine's *Night Shadow* (later to be called *La Sonnàmbula*), with Allegra Kent and on other occasions, with Jillana.

On January 20, 1960, the New York City Ballet premiered a program entitled *Panamerica*. This was a tribute to contemporary Latin-American composers and consisted of a series of short ballets choreographed by Balanchine, Gloria Contreras, Jacques d'Amboise, Francisco Moncion, and John Taras. It was for this occasion that George Balanchine created *Preludios para Percusión*, his first original work made specifically for Erik Bruhn. It was a pas de deux which Bruhn danced with Patricia Wilde to the music of the Colombian composer Luis Escobar.

On the surface of things, Bruhn's early tenure at the New York City Ballet would indicate that the dancer was achieving a veritable dream-come-true. His press was glowing and the public roared its approval. This critical praise and the public's excitement would multiply when Bruhn danced with Maria Tallchief. It would seem that everyone was happy—and everyone *was*, except for Erik Bruhn.

Bruhn says: "Almost from the beginning, I sensed that something wasn't quite right about my life with the New York City Ballet. I signed a contract for that 1959–60 season for not very much money, which was perfectly fine with me. I signed simply because it would give me a chance to work with Balanchine. I loved his company and his works. I had seen the company perform as early as 1951 and was tremendously impressed. There were wonderful dancers, and I particularly remember Maria Tall-chief. I mean, Maria's *Firebird* was just incredible. She danced like a million dollars. I had even met Mr. Balanchine and thought he was a beautiful man. Of course, he knew I was Danish and we talked about his early years as guest choreographer of the Royal Danish Ballet in 1929 and 1930. I suppose that's when he developed his fondness for Danish dancers. Anyway, I had also heard that he had come to see me and Violette Verdy perform *Miss Julie* with ABT, and I believe it was as a result of Violette's performance that he asked her to join his company.

"At any rate, when I received my invitation to join the New York City Ballet, I flew from Copenhagen to New York, and there I was—a member of the New York City Ballet! I religiously took company class and renewed my acquaintance with Maria. Very occasionally I would glimpse Mr. Balanchine and he would sort of say hello. I found that pretty strange, but I kept quiet. Mind you, I was never told what I'd be performing with the company, but Maria and I began to rehearse on our own the *Swan Lake* that was supposed to open the season. However, I was never told that I would open the season with Maria, so it was all quite peculiar. Naturally I told Maria how odd it seemed that Mr. Balanchine barely talked to me. Maria told me to say nothing. I said nothing.

"About a week before the opening of the season, Betty Cage called me into her office and said, 'I must talk to you about Mr. B. It seems he feels you're auditioning him.' I was stunned. I said, 'What do you mean?' She said, 'Well, he doesn't know what you want to do here. You see, we know you are a star and that you've danced with Ballet Theatre. Well, here we don't have any stars.'

"I couldn't believe it! I said, 'But *you've* asked me to come here. I signed a contract. I asked for nothing special—no special billing, no extra money!' She agreed but said that we ought to call a meeting—that Balanchine, Lincoln Kirstein, and I ought to get together and talk."

Bruhn had in the meantime met Lincoln Kirstein for lunch and dinner several times. According to the dancer, these informal get-togethers were not entirely pleasant. They seemed to have featured intellectual discussions centering on the art of the dance and Bruhn seldom agreed with Kirstein's opinions. Finally Kirstein stopped inviting Bruhn, and their relationship cooled. Erik Bruhn was made to feel uncomfortable in the company before he even set foot on the City Center stage or danced in a single role. He began to question whether Balanchine had really wanted him in the first place. Perhaps Balanchine was coerced by Kirstein into taking him on. Whatever it was, Bruhn felt deeply shaken by the treatment he received from both Kirstein and Balanchine.

As promised, Betty Cage called a meeting and Bruhn found himself seated in Cage's office facing the two men. "To my utter amazement, Balanchine repeated everything Betty Cage had already told me—that I was a star, that I was used to much more money and big billing, and what did I want to do in his company? I listened to this and was flabbergasted. Lincoln and Betty kept absolutely still. I told Balanchine that since he had ostensibly asked for me, and since I was deeply grateful to have been asked, I didn't understand why he was saying these things to me. I said, 'You are the director of this company and if you don't know what to do with me, then I must leave immediately.' I went on to tell him everything I had told Betty Cage, and made sure that he understood that the sole object of my having come to the City Ballet was to benefit from his genius—that I was tremendously anxious to work with him, and that I loved his ballets. Well, I went on in this vein, when suddenly a big change came over Mr. Balanchine. He suddenly smiled and said that he had misunderstood everything.

"That same afternoon I was asked to learn a whole batch of roles, and it was only then that I was told Maria and I would be opening the season in *Swan Lake*. I mean, we would have barely a week to prepare it. It was madness. Balanchine himself came to rehearse Maria and me in *Swan Lake* and I was working on six or seven other ballets at the same time. Brand-new costumes were being fitted on me by Karinska, whom I got to love. She fitted me personally and took the greatest care with each one of my costumes. This all happened within a span of one week, and I was totally exhausted, but suddenly, the atmosphere had changed completely, and for the first time I felt I belonged somewhere. Opening night came and Maria and I did our *Swan Lake*. Apparently it was a fantastic success and the critics all said, 'Tallchief and Bruhn take over Balanchine's *Swan Lake!*' And that, of course, put an end to our partnership. Mr. B. didn't like that one little bit, and all my troubles began all over again."

Almost from its inception, the New York City Ballet has deliberately set out to be a company that celebrates its repertoire more than its individual dancers. Balanchine has frequently said that the star system is not for him, that it detracts from the works being performed. As the company's chief choreographer, he has always felt that his dancers must place their bodies in the service of the ballets they were performing—and these ballets were almost invariably his own at the time when Bruhn had joined the company's ranks. Balanchine felt that if he were to adopt the star system, the public would come to see the stars and not the ballets. Furthermore, if a star were suddenly indisposed and a lesser name substituted, the public would not come at all, and that was not Balanchine's idea of how to run a company. (Ironically, in 1978, Balanchine engaged Mikhail Baryshnikov, a superstar if ever there was one, to join the company's ranks.)

Balanchine must have had some reservations regarding Bruhn's entry into the company in 1959. There was no question that Bruhn was indeed a star and that the public *did* flock to those performances in which he appeared. Since Maria Tallchief had become a star of the company, despite Balanchine's attitude toward the star system, and while he had more or less accepted this fact (she had after all been his wife), he was loath to accept a partnership that veritably dripped with stardom. (In a curious way, Balanchine never quite minded his female dancers achieving a kind of veiled star status. In later years he would rejoice in Suzanne Farrell's immense popularity and carefully nurtured her career.)

When Bruhn and Tallchief received enormous critical praise for their performance in Balanchine's *Swan Lake*, the choreographer's hackles must have risen. As Miss Tallchief put it: "The moment anything like that happened, George didn't like it. I was Balanchine's star at the time and he didn't want another star dancing with me. He didn't want us to be a couple."

According to Bruhn, most of his subsequent scheduled performances with City Ballet were in one way or another frustrated by Balanchine. Among the works that Bruhn was to have danced during that first season was the third movement of the choreographer's *Symphony in C*. When rehearsals began, Balanchine elected to change the entire movement and this bothered Bruhn, who had already begun to rehearse the original version with Patricia Wilde.

Miss Wilde remembers the circumstances of this episode in vivid detail. "The changes that Mr. B. made in the third movement were very difficult and complicated. The first change was that he wanted Erik to extend his arms in second position and I was to push off that arm and finish a double pirouette after he steps across and then take his other arm. *Very* tricky! Another change he made was in the third section of the third movement. For some reason, he wanted Erik to stand completely still at the back of the stage while I was to do a double tour en l'air into arabesque three times and right in front of Erik, one of the world's greatest technicians. Well, I thought it was pretty silly doing double tours with Erik standing right there watching me. What happened was that as a result of this change I got such a stiff neck that I couldn't do the performance. What's more, Erik didn't do the ballet either.

"I must say in defense of Mr. B. that he *did* want Erik to fit into the company and that Erik wasn't quite used to the hectic pace at which we worked in those days. He just wasn't accustomed to being thrown into new works and it rattled him. There were times when we didn't know whether he was going to dance or not, because Erik would cancel performances. However, I have very happy memories of dancing with Erik, particularly when Balanchine choreographed our pas de deux for the *Panamerica* night. Erik didn't miss a single performance of that, and that's because we were so well prepared for it."

Erik Bruhn says that when he thinks back to his first season with the New York City Ballet, the chemistry between him and Mr. Balanchine just didn't seem to be right. "Things just never seemed to jell between us, and I can honestly say that this was the most destructive and negative relationship I have ever had. What is so unbelievable is that I went back for more!"

Bruhn remained with the New York City Ballet from December 1959 to the middle of February 1960. He completed his season but was clearly glad to leave a situation that had become psychologically debilitating. Still, in dancing for Balanchine, he had broadened his creative range and had experienced working with a choreographer whom Bruhn continued to admire. And Bruhn had loved dancing with Maria Tallchief—the two had developed a rapport that went beyond the stage. As matters turned out, Miss Tallchief, for reasons of her own, also became disenchanted with her position at the City Ballet. She also elected to leave the company at the end of the 1960 season. In a statement quoted by Walter Terry in the *Herald Tribune* she declared: "I can stand being listed alphabetically if I must, but I will not be treated alphabetically." She added that, despite her deep affection for the company, she could not return to it under the prevailing conditions.

At this juncture of their careers, neither Bruhn nor Tallchief could foresee that in 1963 both dancers would find themselves back with the New York City Ballet. For Bruhn, this second visit would prove even more disastrous than the first, and in the meantime, Bruhn and Tallchief, individually and apart, would continue to move from triumph to triumph with various other companies, and the two would enter into a stormy personal relationship which would bring out both the best and the worst in them.

⟦ CHAPTER 14 ⟧

"OUR GREAT dancer is home again and in most splendid form," wrote Svend Kragh-Jacobsen in *Berlingske Tidende* on February 25, 1960. And Erik Bruhn was indeed back in Copenhagen dancing as a guest artist with the Royal Danish Ballet. He was happy to be there, for he had had his fill of the City Ballet and its atmosphere, and he found comfort in his home town and in familiar surroundings. He gave distinguished and dazzling performances in Fokine's *Chopiniana*, partnering Margrethe Schanne; in *Miss Julie* with Kirsten Simone; and in various Bournonville works. With every return to the Royal Ballet, the press and the public vied for adjectives to praise him. The rancor he had elicited in previous years was gone and he now emerged as a figure of unending pride to his fellow Danes. He became a favorite of King Frederick IX, an inveterate ballet lover, and mingled with the aristocracy of the city. As a native son, he had brought glory to his country, for he was at the time the only Danish dancer to have made a major career in other parts of Europe and in America.

Bruhn's return to his family was equally comforting. His mother's business was thriving and she was, naturally enough, very proud of her son. His father was no longer living, and his sister Benthe had left Denmark in 1951 to live in Canada, because, as Bruhn recalls, it seemed impossible for her to find a husband in Denmark. "When she landed in Canada," says Bruhn, "the first thing that happened was that she met a Dane and she married him immediately."

His half sister, Else, now in her forties and still unmarried, was no longer living at home. "I managed not to see Else very often, but sometimes she'd call me in our house in Gentofte, and when she called it always meant that she was in one of her 'up' periods. Unfortunately she was still besieged by nervous spells. But when she was fine, she could be very generous, charming, sweet, and loving."

His sister Birthe had married and lived some miles from Gentofte. Bruhn would occasionally visit her but their rapport was not particularly strong. As for his sister Aase, she too had married and was living away from home, which left only his loving aunt Minna, who continued to share the Gentofte house with Bruhn's mother.

In 1957 Bruhn had purchased the Gentofte house belonging to his mother: "I was traveling a great deal at that time and during those periods when I would be in Copenhagen, I very much wanted a place of my own. At one point, I told my mother that I would be building my own house. She said, 'Why don't you buy *this* house?' I thought about it for a while and then decided that I *would* buy it from her."

Erik Bruhn's development as a person was in many ways predicated by his development as an artist. In a sense, Bruhn the artist shaped Bruhn the man. Indeed, according to the outside world, the artist was so pure, so perfect, so flawless that the human being was expected to live up to the same godlike image. Those who claim to know Bruhn well are ready to concede that Bruhn's high artistry was a matter of professional achievement, intelligence, and plain hard work. Clearly, Bruhn the man had his faults like everyone else and some of them could be decidedly unattractive. Moody by temperament, Bruhn had the capacity of making people suffer, if only to test their friendship. He could say cruel things and, whether he meant them or not, he occasionally alienated those close to him. A streak of irony and mocking contempt might temporarily sour a relationship and the objects of such sarcasm might be hurt or confused if not downright angry.

Any number of Bruhn's close friends have been subjected to such treatment, but in most cases they have come to realize that his provocations are often the result of some inexplicable quirk that causes him to lash out at others. Many people find Bruhn an extremely difficult man to know because of his apparent aloofness. He does not immediately make himself accessible to strangers, but will often give the impression of coldness and detachment. He does not suffer fools gladly and will not engage in casual chitchat. Bruhn operates on instinct, and in discussing other people he will frequently allude to the word "chemistry." He might say: "The chemistry between us just didn't work." Or, "I guess we had the right chemistry." If the chemistry works, Bruhn is instantly happy. It also helps if the friends he makes have a sense of humor. Bruhn loves a good laugh—and frequently at his own expense. He likes unexpected turns of phrase and it amuses him if an outrageous situation should befall him or others.

In the company of close friends he is as open and candid about himself as he is about others. When he is relaxed, he can regale his friends with endless stories about people he has known or situations he has been in. At such times, there is nothing distant about Erik Bruhn. He can communicate a great sense of intimacy and has the capacity for feeling himself close to those around him. Because Bruhn travels extensively, he has made friends and acquaintances in various parts of the world. In Denmark, he is a great celebrity, but he has only a handful of close friends. The Danish actress Susse Wold is a woman of great charm and beauty, perhaps as celebrated in Denmark as Bruhn himself. The daughter of a famous comedienne, Marguerite Viby, Wold trained at the Royal Theatre in Copenhagen and has appeared successfully in both dramatic and comedy roles.

She has known Erik Bruhn for over fifteen years. "Of course, everybody has heard of Erik Bruhn here in Copenhagen. What I heard was that he was extremely arrogant and stand-offish. When we met I discovered that exactly the opposite was true. He was warm, friendly, and completely charming. We met at a party just before he was to join Mr. Balanchine and the New York City Ballet. Almost immediately we got into a discussion and we laughed a lot. Well, when he was about to leave for America, he told me to write to him. And so I did. He answered immediately and we had a correspondence. Sometimes one can get to know a person very well through letters.

"Erik was rather pleased that I didn't know too much about dancing. I mean, I don't have the slightest idea if somebody's feet are right or if a jump is high enough. . . . I just can't tell those things. What I *could* tell about Erik is that he was a great actor. Just to see him portray the role of James in *La Sylphide* was to know what acting is all about. He projects the characters he portrays with tremendous feeling. It's an energy that comes from within and it's quite apart from his technique as a dancer. And, of course, his stage presence is unbelievable.

"I think Erik is one of the strongest people I've ever met. He has enormous courage. Yet, there are many things he's afraid of, but he does them anyway. I'm talking about the way he uses his talent. It's one of the things that keeps him alive—this courage to do things he fears, because when everything goes too easily for him he does not feel sufficiently challenged. He makes difficulties for himself, in order to overcome them.

"Erik has very dramatic ups and downs. When he is down, he is *really* down. At those times he doesn't try to overcome it, but just collapses. Then, when he starts to come up, it's like a new beginning. I have seen Erik be very unhappy and become unsure of himself, both as a person and artist. He would then question his very existence. He would consider it idiotic to be a dancer—putting on makeup, going on the stage, and throwing himself around. At these times he would say, 'Is this what life is really all about?' I've seen him like that and although we are very close friends, I've never been able to get him out of those moods.

"I think he's the kind of person on whom you cannot put a single color, because the color always changes. Erik changes according to the people he's with. Also, he is not the same person tomorrow as he is today. Sometimes he scares people by his directness, but that's his way of trying to make contact. He's not the kind of man who likes to talk about the weather. Erik and I have been through quite a lot together and I think we can call ourselves true friends."

Bruhn considers his friendship with Susse Wold an important one. He says that they have a kind of inner rhythm that makes their relationship mutually satisfying. "When I first met Susse she was going through a very rough period, and I think I was of some help to her during that time. I have a lot of fun with Susse and I kid her a lot. As she is very much of a public figure in Denmark, she is constantly in the news, and some of the things people write about her are quite outrageous. At any rate, throughout the years, our friendship has deepened and I know that if ever I needed her she would be there."

Also of special meaning is Bruhn's friendship with Ingrid Glindemann and the man with whom she shares her life, Lennart Pasborg. Miss Glindemann is a dancer with the Royal Danish Ballet and also happens to be the head of the Dancers' Union of the company. Lennart Pasborg, an unusually handsome young man, has a degree in medicine, although he is not a practicing physician. The couple have a three-year-old son—a remarkably bright child whose affection for Erik Bruhn knows no bounds. Ingrid and Lennart live in a comfortable apartment, not far from the Royal Opera House in Copenhagen, and whenever Bruhn comes to the city he spends many evenings with them. On such evenings, Bruhn might play all sorts of rough-and-tumble games with their little boy, who gleefully climbs all over him. Indeed, Ingrid and Lennart are "family" to Bruhn and their friendship means a great deal to him.

There are other good friends in Copenhagen and with each of them Bruhn shares a special rapport. Susse Wold has said that Bruhn changes according to the people he is with. This may be so, but generally speaking he follows a code in which instinct and integrity play a large role.

Nevertheless, most people find Bruhn to be something of an enigma. The great character dancer Niels Bjørn Larsen, once ballet master of the Royal Danish Ballet and currently director of the Tivoli Pantomime Theatre, has known Erik Bruhn since he was a child at the ballet school. He and his wife, Elvi Henriksen, a pianist at the ballet school, consider Bruhn to be a man apart.

"Erik is not only a soloist on the stage but in life as well," says Bjørn Larsen. "He is a very friendly person, but he is really two people. There is the outward man and there is the inner man, whom no one will ever know. Erik is tremendously egocentric . . . and he has that Mephistophelian laugh. It's a bit sinister, that. I would also say that, in a strange way, Erik is better at taking than giving. He has a way of bringing you near him and making you feel close to him, and then, suddenly, he will make you feel like a stranger."

Miss Henriksen echoes these sentiments and adds, "He is very much a man alone. I think he leads a very lonely life. I believe he is not a happy man. He has position, money, and success. But it is not enough. Something is still missing. Perhaps it is because he demands as much of himself as he does of others. I feel that his fate is always to be alone."

The Danish critic Svend Kragh-Jacobsen has also known Bruhn since he was a young student at the Royal Ballet School. He has written monographs on the art of the dancer and has traveled far and wide to report on Bruhn's performances.

Commenting on their relationship, the critic says: "We have a very strange friendship, Erik and I. But who knows Erik? All I can say about him is that he is a man of great integrity. On the other hand, he is rather fond of making trouble for himself. If he is not in some kind of trouble, he will be very quick to create some. The most astonishing thing about his career is that after he had gone out to prove to himself and others that he was a great classical dancer, he was able to switch gears by appearing in highly demanding character roles such as Jean in *Miss Julie* and Don José in *Carmen*. When he did that it was a revelation. I remember when he performed in *Miss Julie*, he had the look of a shark. Sometimes he has that look in private life. He looks as though he could bite someone and go right through the bone. I have been around a long time and discovered that many dancers are really very silly. Erik is not among them. Basically he is a very intelligent and very sensitive person. As a dancer, he was unique. We will not see the likes of him for many, many years."

When people call Erik Bruhn a private person, they have good reason. He is not given to wearing his heart on his sleeve. He is particularly private when it comes to his romantic involvements. Sonia Arova attests that it was difficult for him to show his emotions and yet she is sure that they ran very deep.

Indeed, as his fellow Dane, the dancer Peter Martins, once said: "We Danes may seem very cool on the surface, but inside we're like a volcano."

Like most people, Bruhn is a great believer in the reciprocal intensity of the moment. He does not measure the length of time in which a relationship has evolved but rather the degree of passion involved. He has decried the fact that his own passions have all too often been one-sided. Often, his feelings could not be returned. Conversely, it pains him when he himself cannot respond to someone who may have developed a strong attachment for him. "It so seldom works out just right!" he says, wistfully.

Bruhn is a person who does not like to be emotionally overwhelmed by others. As he puts it, "I generally run when I begin to feel that someone starts getting too possessive. I have loved people on many different levels. But some people fall in love with me, and when they do, there is nothing which is enough for them. When I feel that happening, I have to get out. This is not a mysterious streak in me, it's simply a matter of survival. I suppose it must be difficult for those people, but I've had involvements in which I give them this and I give them that, and it's still not enough. It's possible that I give them everything except the very thing they want, and that is *all* of me. The fact is, I can only give all of me to the person I *want* to give all of myself to. A case in point was my involvement with Maria Tallchief."

〚 CHAPTER 15 〛

W HILE THEY were dancing during the 1959–60 season at the New York City Ballet, it became increasingly clear to Erik Bruhn and Maria Tallchief that they not only formed a perfect artistic partnership, but were deeply drawn to one another offstage. Like his first love, Sonia Arova, Tallchief was a dark, intense, and volatile woman. She loved having fun and she loved to laugh. She was a superb dancer and as a person was perhaps the more flamboyant and the more aggressive of the two. She was extremely outspoken and, as the City Ballet's first ballerina, decidedly demanding. Although married to Henry Paschen, it appeared that her attraction to Erik Bruhn was more than a passing fancy.

Their joint departure from the City Ballet at the end of that first 1959–60 season may have been indicative of Tallchief's desire to continue her personal and professional relationship with Bruhn outside the confines of a company which both found progressively constricting. Although Bruhn returned to Denmark and Tallchief remained in America, the two would be reunited during a countrywide tour planned by American Ballet Theatre, which had now resumed operations. Indeed, after he had fulfilled his season with the Royal Danish Ballet in February 1960, Bruhn returned to New York and to ABT, which was to give a brief season at the Metropolitan Opera House before the tour.

Erik Bruhn's appearances with Ballet Theatre at the Metropolitan Opera continued to find him in top dancing form. He repeated his triumph in Birgit Cullberg's *Miss Julie*, which he now danced with the

French ballerina Claude Bessy, who had been brought to the company as a guest artist. Also, during that season, Bruhn repeated his role of the Lover in Antony Tudor's *Jardin aux Lilas*. Nora Kaye danced Caroline and, oddly enough, the reviews described Bruhn as not entirely at ease in the Tudor style.

Everyone in the company was looking forward to the six-week tour that would take them to Moscow, Leningrad, Tiflis, and Kiev. Under the auspices of the President's Special International Program for Cultural Presentations, administered by the American National Theater and Academy, ABT would make a visit to the Soviet Union in September—the first American ballet company to be so honored.

In Europe Maria Tallchief became Bruhn's principal partner. In Moscow, the company danced at the Stanislavsky Theatre and in the audience were such renowned ballerinas as Galina Ulanova, Maya Plisetskaya, Olga Lepeshinskaya, Raisa Struchkova, the Russian choreographer Leonid Lavrovsky, pedagogue Asaf Messerer. Most impressive of all was Nina Petrovna Khrushchev, wife of the Soviet leader and, as *Time* magazine put it, the most powerful balletomane in Russia. The company brought Balanchine's *Theme and Variations*, which received a lukewarm reception; Agnes de Mille's *Rodeo*, which drew much laughter and applause; Jerome Robbins' *Fancy Free*, which was deemed less a ballet than a piece of vaudeville; Antony Tudor's *Jardin aux Lilas*, which was appreciated for its poetic atmosphere; and the Black Swan pas de deux, danced by Bruhn and Tallchief, whose performance proved a total triumph. Indeed, the Bruhn-Tallchief partnership seemed to have roused the Russian public into a frenzy.

Their reviews could not have been more spectacular. *Time* magazine wrote: "Maria Tallchief and Erik Bruhn in the Black Swan pas de deux, which the Russians know by heart and perform with shattering ease, was the triumph of the evening. The applause which followed their dizzying leaps and spins was thunderous."

There was no question that Erik Bruhn and Maria Tallchief had conquered the Soviet public and the critics, and that their partnership was sealed during this important tour. At this time a singular honor came to Bruhn. He was approached by Gosconcert, the official Soviet organization in charge of culture with foreign countries, inviting him to be a guest artist with the Bolshoi Ballet during a forthcoming season. The invitation was extended to cover a period of one full year. Bruhn accepted with pleasure and Gosconcert informed him that they would be in touch with him through the Soviet embassy in Copenhagen regarding contractual arrangements.

Another event of note—one that Bruhn was not aware of—took place when American Ballet Theatre was invited to witness a performance of *Swan Lake* given by the Bolshoi Ballet in Moscow prior to their own opening. The American dancers sat in the audience surrounded by police and Soviet officials, who did not permit fraternization between the Russian audience and the Americans. Among the Russians was a twenty-two-year-old dancer of the Kirov Ballet by the name of Rudolf Nureyev. He had seen photographs of members of the American company and eagerly sought out Erik Bruhn. As a student of the great Soviet teacher, Alexander Pushkin, Nureyev was told by Pushkin himself that one of the greatest classical dancers of the day was a Dane named Erik Bruhn. And now Erik Bruhn was sitting nearby though, much to his chagrin, Nureyev was not permitted to speak with him. What was worse, Nureyev would momentarily be leaving Moscow to dance in East Germany with a Soviet variety troupe, thereby depriving him of the opportunity of seeing Bruhn dance during the ABT performances.

It would seem that the young Nureyev had already been far too friendly with visiting foreign companies, among them the American troupe of *My Fair Lady* and the National Ballet of Cuba. Inquisitive in every way, he had befriended members of these companies, much to the displeasure of the Soviet authorities. (It is entirely possible that Nureyev's departure for Germany was deliberately timed to coincide with the ABT tour in the Soviet Union.) Though Nureyev never saw Bruhn dance in Russia, he was determined to have a record made of Bruhn's appearances, and a close friend agreed to film some of the Danish dancer's performances with an eight-millimeter camera. The impact of seeing Bruhn dance, even on film, was staggering. Nureyev told the British writer John Percival: "It was a sensation for me. He is the only dancer who could impress me out of my wits. When I got back to Moscow, he had been dancing there, and one of the young dancers said he was too cool. Cool, yes—so cool that it burns."

It was during the American Ballet Theatre tour in Russia that Erik Bruhn realized his relationship with Maria Tallchief was beginning to assume a seriousness he found both overwhelming and distressing.

"You know, when Maria and I were dancing with the City Ballet,

George Balanchine stopped us from dancing together several times," says Bruhn. "Later, in a strange way, I myself stopped our partnership. Frankly, we had gotten too involved, and I somehow couldn't stop it. Toward the end of the Russian tour, things got out of hand. Maria suddenly announced to me that she had decided to divorce her husband and would marry *me*. When I heard this, I said no. At the end of the tour, it became clear to me that in order to put an end to the situation, I would have to break with Maria. She became frantic and impossible. I simply couldn't handle it and told her that I no longer wanted to dance with her, talk to her, or ever see her again."

For her part, Maria Tallchief had her own reasons for being dismayed with Bruhn during the Russian tour. "Just before we were to open in Moscow, Erik said he had hurt his back. He announced that he could not rehearse the Black Swan pas de deux with me and he was flat on his back in his hotel room. I was petrified at the thought of doing the Black Swan in Russia, because I felt I was bringing coals to Newcastle. I mean, I had danced the Black Swan with Erik only once or twice before, and I needed to rehearse. Well, Erik just couldn't bring himself to do it. So, I asked Royes Fernandez to help me. Finally, on the day before we opened, Erik appeared at the theater. It was a freezing-cold day and I continued to be petrified. We had one rehearsal and then, the next night, we went on. Erik had gotten out of bed and never danced better in his life. He was a sensation. I, on the other hand, was unbelievably scared! I don't know how I got through the performance!"

Turning to her personal feelings toward Bruhn, Tallchief says: "There is no doubt that I was in love with Erik Bruhn. I mean, who could not fall in love with Erik? When you dance with him it is impossible not to. Those blue eyes and the noble Greek-god face! Not only that, but he was a great partner, and I do mean great! The trouble is, Erik *lets* you fall in love with him and then . . . good-bye! He's a very elusive man. Erik comes to the brink of things and then, suddenly, something stops. Take his relationship with me. We were ready to do *everything* together. We could have had a ballet company of our own. People asked us to do things all the time. Perhaps Erik didn't want the responsibility. It's not that Erik is afraid or does not believe in himself, it's just that he has some inner quirk about success and about people. What is it? Basically, he is a desperately lonely man. He always was and he always will be."

At the conclusion of the six-week tour in Russia, the break between

Bruhn and Tallchief seemed final—at least where their personal relationship was concerned. However, both knew that in April 1961 they would be appearing together for a season with American Ballet Theatre at the Broadway Theatre in New York, and no amount of personal conflict could separate a partnership that had been hailed as among the most exciting in the world.

Some weeks after the Russian tour, Bruhn returned to Copenhagen to fulfill his dancing obligations with the Royal Danish Ballet. Tallchief had returned to America. By October 1961, Erik Bruhn was settled back into his Danish life. He had six weeks of rest and lived happily in Gentofte, well taken care of by his aunt Minna and his mother. He took company classes and was scheduled to appear in various works, including a new production being mounted for the Danes by the French choreographer Roland Petit, entitled *La Chaloupée*. Already in the Danish repertoire was Petit's hugely successful ballet, *Carmen*, which he had originally created for his Ballets de Paris in 1949. Petit had himself danced the role of Don José and his wife, Renée Jeanmaire, had created a sensation as Carmen. In Copenhagen, *Carmen* had proved to be the 1960 box-office hit. The young Danish dancer Flemming Flindt scored an immediate success as Don José. Carmen was danced by Kirsten Simone, whose interpretation was considered only slightly less memorable.

Bruhn had gone to see a performance of *Carmen*, and found it impressive, particularly Flindt's remarkable interpretation. As it turned out, Flemming Flindt was about to take several months' leave of absence. Niels Bjørn Larsen, then the company's ballet master, was concerned about Flindt's imminent departure and was particularly distressed over the fact that Henning Kronstam, who was to have replaced him in the role, had decided against doing so. As *Carmen* was the season's largest drawing card, Bjørn Larsen was at a loss as to whom among his dancers could vividly portray such a role. On an impulse he approached Erik Bruhn, asking him whether Don José might interest him. Bruhn had, after all, made brilliant use of his dramatic abilities in *Miss Julie*, and *Carmen* might just prove an equal challenge. To Larsen's delight, Bruhn accepted the role, although he worried that Flemming Flindt would not be around to teach it to him, and it would be several weeks before Petit himself would come to Copenhagen to stage his *La Chaloupée*.

"Of course, I was the most unlikely person to portray Don José," says

Bruhn. "I was blond and bland-looking for the role. But I thought that with some careful makeup and dying my hair it could probably work. I had one week to learn the role. There was a black-and-white film with Flemming in it, but you could hardly see what he was doing. Bjørn Larsen, who tried to help, couldn't really remember all the steps. I did the best I could and performed the ballet with Kirsten Simone."

The reviews of *Carmen* with Bruhn and Simone were nothing short of sensational. As in *Miss Julie*, Bruhn had transformed himself from a danseur noble into a magnetic and riveting dramatic actor, who, even in repose, illuminated a character at once subtle and complex. Even Kirsten Simone had expanded and deepened her characterization in dancing with Bruhn. But *Carmen* was Bruhn's ballet, and as a result of his performance in it, he was awarded one of Denmark's highest theatrical tributes—The Theater Cup—given once a year by the country's leading critics of drama, opera, and ballet.

When Roland Petit arrived in Copenhagen early in 1961 to set his *La Chaloupée*, which would star Bruhn and Marianne Walther, he saw Bruhn in *Carmen*.

Bruhn remembers being apprehensive about dancing the role of Don José, with Petit sitting in the audience. "After the performance, Roland came back to see me. I told him what a difficult time I had had learning the steps. Roland smiled and said, 'Erik, you didn't do *one* step as I choreographed it, but I thought you were magnificent! Keep it that way!' "

Petit's *La Chaloupée* was premiered at the Royal Theatre on February 18, 1961. The ballet deals with a bank robbery. The leader of a gang of robbers falls in love with a seamstress who, as it turns out, is the banker's daughter. Love converts the gangster, who forces his gang to return all the money. He himself enlists in a regiment, and all ends happily with his marrying the banker's daughter. The score, written by Maurice Thiriet, was a derivation on a rather banal Jacques Offenbach waltz entitled "La Chaloupée" (known in America as "The Apache Dance"), from which the ballet derived its title.

Writing from Copenhagen, for the *Herald Tribune* of March 12, 1961, the American critic Lillian Moore reported: "What Erik Bruhn does with the role of the gangster is little short of miraculous. He has found an entirely new way of moving, staccato, tense, jaunty, exaggerated and entirely divorced from his natural lyric style. The leaps are sharp as knife thrusts

and the incredible pirouettes have even more speed and precision than
usual, although they begin with no discernible preparation and finish with
split-second accuracy."

The year 1961 had begun in glory for Erik Bruhn. At thirty-two, he was
undisputedly the world's leading male dancer. His artistry was unrivaled.
No other male dancer of his generation could equal the brilliance and
seamlessness of his technique, and no one could match the refinement of
his style, whether it was in the prince roles of the classics or in the dramatic roles that he had by now made his own. Whenever and wherever he
danced, adulation came his way. Erik Bruhn had won the admiration of an
international public and earned the awe and respect of his peers.

The international press had long considered him a phenomenon. Every
major publication in Europe and in America offered him the sort of accolades reserved for artists of genius, and in May 1961, when Bruhn returned
for his New York engagement with American Ballet Theatre, *Time* magazine devoted a major article to the dancer's art. Under the headline of
DANSEUR NOBLE, it reviewed Bruhn's career in glowing terms:

> Trained in Denmark, Bruhn leaped to fame in 1955, when he appeared in
> *Giselle* with Alicia Markova, in a performance that dancer-choreographer Ted
> Shawn recalls as "one of the two greatest performances I've ever seen." Back
> home Bruhn, 32, is the idol of the Royal Danish Ballet, where he has brought
> new life to the classic roles reserved for a *premier danseur noble*. His technical
> credentials include a fine dramatic sense and an ability to leap with a high-
> arching grace, to turn with cat quickness and fluidity on the ground or in mid-
> air, to project emotion with vivid movements of arms, legs and body. But
> Bruhn long ago became aware that "technique is not enough," and he is re-
> markable for the feeling of tension he can convey by his mere presence. Poised
> and trim, he somehow rivets an audience with the promise of action before he
> has danced a step. . . .
>
> As Bruhn soars ever closer to his apogee, he spends restless nights reviewing
> roles in his mind. He has surprisingly little of the vanity that goads most per-
> formers; he does not want audiences to pay, he says, "only to see me jump."
> Furthermore, he would rather "be bad in a good ballet than be great in a bad
> ballet."

To survive in the face of such overwhelming adulation—to face the re-
sponsibilities of having to live up to the constant artistic perfection that

was expected of him—began to prove more of a burden than a source of inspiration. The pressures put upon him by the two major companies with which he was now appearing on a regular basis and by the managements of the various companies with which he appeared as guest artist would often plunge him into a deep depression. There was a constant self-questioning and a strange self-doubt as to his true merits as an artist. At this moment of his career, no one would dare offer Bruhn any constructive criticism. As Bruhn puts it: "When you've become a box-office name, your fellow dancers are afraid to say anything. And even more, directors or managers never say anything—so long as the house is full. So, everything falls on you."

[CHAPTER 16]

B RUHN'S appearances with American Ballet Theatre during April 1961 found him reunited with Maria Tallchief, who during this season made her first appearance with Bruhn in the title role of Birgit Cullberg's *Miss Julie*. It was her first major venture into the dramatic sphere and she readily gives credit for her success in the role to Bruhn.

"Whatever success I had was due to Erik. He coached me completely. Actually, I had learned the steps from someone who had danced it before, but it was Erik who told me *how* to dance it and who gave me the subtle shadings which made the difference in whether you knew what you were doing or not."

John Martin in *The New York Times* of April 25, 1961, found Tallchief remarkable: "It would seem that Miss Tallchief has found a fresh field for herself and a new world to conquer." Bruhn was again praised as the sinister valet.

The two repeated their triumph in the *Swan Lake* pas de deux and were paired for the first time in Grand Pas Glazounov from *Raymonda* staged by Frederic Franklin. This tour de force was premiered that season and proved to be spectacularly successful.

Halfway through the American Ballet Theatre season, Bruhn returned to Copenhagen, where he participated in the Royal Danish Ballet and Music Festival.

The Bruhn-Tallchief partnership was resumed in July, when the two dancers were invited by Ted Shawn to appear at the 1961 Jacob's Pillow Festival. They danced the *Flower Festival at Genzano* and repeated their *Swan Lake* Act Two pas de deux, again to glowing reviews. But if their partnership on stage was nothing short of perfection, their personal relationship was again riddled with tension. At one point, matters came to a head and Bruhn remembers a particularly serious quarrel that culminated in his decision to end the partnership once and for all.

"The last thing that Maria said was, 'All right, I'll find a new partner. There is a Russian that has just defected. He is in Paris and I'll find him. *He*'ll be my new partner!' I told her, 'Good luck and go away.' I was happy it was over, because this thing we had together was going to destroy us. It couldn't work."

Bruhn returned to Copenhagen and Tallchief went to find her Russian.

During the previous month—on June 17 to be exact—the world press reported the defection of Rudolf Nureyev from the Leningrad Kirov Ballet, then appearing at the Paris Opéra.

In one of its "Letters from Paris" *The New Yorker* magazine succinctly summed up the event: "At Le Bourget Airfield last June, Rudolf Nureyev of the Leningrad Kirov Opera Ballet escaped from the rest of the Soviet troupe with whom he had appeared at the Opéra here. Paris ballet circles consider that in this defection Russia lost its most phenomenal young male dancer, and that the West gained the strangest, and uncontestably the most influential personality—as well as the greatest technician—since Nijinsky, to whom he is the first ever to be so compared."

Indeed, with Nureyev's defection, the ballet world would never be the same again. In Paris, he almost immediately joined the International Ballet of the Marquis de Cuevas and became an overnight sensation. This was not merely because of his phenomenal technique and magnetic stage presence but also because no Russian performer had ever before dared to single-handedly defy the Soviet authorities by seeking asylum in the West. The publicity surrounding Nureyev's defection was staggering. Everywhere he went, he was photographed and interviewed. It was perhaps the first instance since the advent of Nijinsky in which a ballet dancer engaged the imagination of the general public. People who had no interest in the dance were suddenly talking about Nureyev. It is safe to assume that his exceptionally photogenic good looks had a great deal to do with his instant celebrity, for Nureyev's appearance was just as singular as his act of defiance. The long, unruly hair, the high cheekbones, the blazing eyes, the flaring nostrils, and the trim, handsomely proportioned body all provided fuel for the cameras of the media. Reporters followed his every move, and were particularly quick to note that Nureyev was everyone's image of the romantic ballet star—exciting and unpredictable. Although his English was far from perfect he managed by word as well as deed to stir up excitement.

The ballet cognoscenti pounced on the Soviet dancer just as quickly as the media had. All of Nureyev's performances in Paris were instantly sold out. Far more informed than either the press or the general public about the dance, balletomanes were quick to note that Nureyev's formidable assets—his thrilling panther-like leaps, his blazing stage persona—far outweighed an occasional lack of polish. There was no question that Nureyev, at the age of twenty-three, had arrived!

It has been said that among the reasons Rudolf Nureyev escaped to the West was his wish to work with Erik Bruhn. Alexander Pushkin's remarks about Bruhn's great artistry, and the film that Nureyev's friend had taken of Bruhn during his appearance in Moscow were evidence enough that Nureyev could learn a great deal from Bruhn. In point of fact, however, Nureyev was eager to learn from everyone, and he became an avid observer of every aspect of culture the West had to offer.

But Erik Bruhn *was* a special case. No two dancers could be more dissimilar in temperament or style. The finesse of Bruhn's style and the symmetry of his line, his grace and nobility, and his power to move an audience by the sheer beauty of his movement were all qualities that Nureyev could indeed profit from. The raw energy of the Dionysiac Nureyev might be tempered by contact with the Apollonian Bruhn.

Several months after parting from Erik Bruhn, Maria Tallchief was in Deauville with her daughter and the child's nurse. While she was in Deauville, the de Cuevas Company performed there with Nureyev and Rosella Hightower heading the company. It was Tallchief's first view of the Russian dancer whom she had angrily told Bruhn would be her new partner. She was deeply impressed and arranged to take company class with the de Cuevas Ballet. She soon made Nureyev's acquaintance and they established an immediate rapport. During the course of their many conversations, Nureyev told Tallchief how eager he was to meet Erik Bruhn and how anxious he was to work with Vera Volkova, whom he knew to be teaching at the Royal Danish Ballet.

"I told Rudy that Erik was in Copenhagen just then, as, of course, was Volkova," recalls Tallchief. "I told him that as soon as he was free we could both go there. Well, Rudy had a television engagement in Frankfurt and would not be free for several weeks. I decided to go to Germany with Rudy to watch the taping. From Frankfurt I called Erik—he couldn't have been more surprised!"

Erik Bruhn himself remembers the circumstances of Tallchief's fateful telephone call. "When that call came from Germany, Maria had already known that I had arranged for her to dance with me at the Royal Danish Ballet. This was not anything I really wanted to do, because Maria and I were through. But Niels Bjørn Larsen, who had heard of our successful partnership, was after me to bring Maria over and present her to the Danish public. Well, I pulled myself together and wrote a very formal letter to Maria, on behalf of the company, inviting her to dance with me. I made it very clear that we would rehearse and that we would dance. However, we would *not* see each other otherwise. It was at this point that she called to accept my invitation and also told me that she had found her wonderful Russian dancer. When we spoke on the telephone, I asked her whether she would respect my conditions. She said, 'But of course!' She then said that Rudy would like to say hello. So, Rudy said hello—and that was that."

Tallchief and Nureyev arrived in Copenhagen three weeks earlier than expected. "I remember being at home," says Bruhn. "The phone rang again. It was Maria saying that she and Nureyev were having a drink at the bar of the Hotel Angleterre and wouldn't I like to come and join them? It was late afternoon and the place was very dark. I greeted Maria and there sat this young dancer casually dressed in a sweater and slacks. I sat down and looked at him more carefully and saw that he was very attractive. He had a certain style about him . . . a kind of class. It was not a natural elegance, but somehow it worked. He did not speak very much, probably because his English was still not very good. It was something of an uncomfortable situation because of my relationship with Maria. She and I covered it up with lots of unnatural laughter. Rudik mentioned much later that he had hated the sound of my laugh. Anyway, it was all I could do to get through that hour we spent together."

The Danish press lost little time in discovering that Nureyev was in Copenhagen and, as everywhere else, he was hunted by reporters. The dancer eluded them as best he could. His object was to observe Bruhn in class and at rehearsals, and to work privately with Vera Volkova. Maria Tallchief spent as much of her time with Nureyev as possible, staying out of Bruhn's way, except during those times when they worked together. The ritual of work would find Nureyev taking company class in the morning, working with Vera Volkova in the afternoon, and attending performances of the Royal Danish Ballet in the evening.

Bruhn remembers those early classes with Nureyev. "Not many people would address Nureyev. He seemed very strange to the Danes. To me, he seemed less strange. In class Rudik would always be in the first group and always in the middle—that is very Russian. I would stick to the second group and always stand in the back—that is very Danish. One time Rudik came up to me and said, 'Why don't the Danish people respect you more? You are such a great dancer and you are so respected in Russia.' I told him, 'What do you expect them to do—crawl on their hands and knees when I come around?' You see, in Russia they have certain rules about the hierarchy of dancers, and Rudik wasn't used to seeing me being treated like everyone else. In the beginning that's more or less all we would do—take class.

"Then one day Maria said that Rudik could give a marvelous class and wouldn't I like to take one? Well, he gave us a Russian barre and in the middle of it I had to stop, because it was extremely hard on my muscles. It wasn't the steps or the exercises, but the timing involved. Later on, as we got to know one another, I would give classes to him, and he seemed to take to them very well."

Bruhn concedes that the trio was a highly complex one and as time neared for Bruhn and Tallchief to make their joint appearance with the Royal Danish Ballet—they were dancing *Miss Julie* and the *Don Quixote* pas de deux—the situation exploded.

"We were rehearsing onstage," says Bruhn. "Rudik was watching. During a break, Rudik came up to me and told me he wanted to have lunch with me alone—without Maria. He said he had to talk to me. He then

went to Maria's dressing room and told her he would be having lunch with
me. As I understand it, she had a fit, and I think a little violence occurred.
The reason I'm saying this is because the craziest scene ensued. Maria ran
out of her dressing room, Rudik went running after her, and I ran after
both of them! Just at that moment, the entire company was coming out of
class and at least fifty people witnessed these three mad people chasing one
another around the Royal Opera House! I might add that they pretended
they saw nothing. Well, it all ended that I canceled my lunch with Rudik,
because Maria had threatened to leave. We had not yet danced together
and just to make her stay I gave up all my conditions, so she wouldn't take
off. Finally it all calmed down, we gave our performances, and the three of
us even had dinner together."

Bruhn's performances with Tallchief at the Royal Opera went off as
scheduled. The reviews were particularly glowing for Tallchief. The ballerina remembers being at Bruhn's house when some of those reviews came
out. As they were in Danish she recalls that someone read them out loud,
translating them into English. "One of the reviews may have upset Erik,"
says Tallchief, "because it said something like, 'As Miss Julie, Miss Tallchief was so great that she seemed to overshadow even the great Erik
Bruhn.' I always wondered how Erik felt about that. It's possible that
when Erik heard that review, he may have decided to stop dancing with
me. Whatever it was, we did manage to remain friends anyway—although
our personal relationship in Copenhagen was extremely shaky."

"Whatever Maria and Rudik had going for them I don't really know,"
says Bruhn. "What I do know is that whatever Maria was trying to get
herself into or out of was not working yet. In retrospect, I can see that it
was not an easy time for her, and it wasn't an easy time for me. It was certainly a confusing time for Rudik. Well, it took several years for us to recover from our Copenhagen experience. Finally Maria returned to
America and Rudik stayed on."

It was while Nureyev was in Copenhagen that Vera Volkova, with
whom he had been taking private classes, received a telephone call from
Margot Fonteyn in London. The ballerina had heard about the phenomenal young Russian and wondered whether Volkova might know of his
whereabouts. She was organizing a gala in aid of the Royal Academy of
Dancing and wanted Nureyev to appear in it. Volkova informed Fonteyn
that Nureyev was in Copenhagen at that moment and she suggested it

would be simpler if he talked with her directly. This Nureyev did, and it was agreed that he would go to London and make arrangements for the gala.

Upon Nureyev's return from London, Bruhn invited the Russian dancer to live in his house in Gentofte since it would save Nureyev a great deal of money, of which he had little. Bruhn's mother found the visitor less than congenial.

"My mother knew nothing of Rudik except what she had read in the papers," recalls Bruhn. "Anyway, I showed him to his room, which had a trapdoor in it. My mother was not there at the time. But when she came home, I said, 'I would like you to meet Rudolf.' They shook hands through the trapdoor—and it was oddly symbolic. These two people had what seemed to be a violent reaction to one another. It was like lightning. Mother was a Scorpio and Rudik was Pisces . . . so you can imagine. She just never got to like him. It just never worked. It was a chemical reaction."

The two dancers were now seen everywhere together. Mostly, however, they took class. Again, Bruhn recalls these classes with particular pleasure. "I set all the classes we took. We never spoke to each other during class. We never corrected each other. In the center we did our combinations separately and we could see that we were executing them differently. He had his schooling and I had mine. I was obviously not going to make him do a combination the way I did. I was watching with great curiosity how he would take the same steps and how different it would look. It was like speaking the same language, using the same words, but expressing oneself with a different accent and intonation.

"There were times when we *did* argue. Rudik would be watching the Danish dancers in Volkova's class and criticize things. He kept saying, 'That's wrong . . . it's not Russian!' I told him that the Russian school was not the only one—that there was the Danish school as well. I told him that it might not be what he liked but that it wasn't necessarily wrong. Later, we would experiment together, trying to approach steps in different ways, and, little by little, I would try to do them his way and he would try to do them my way. That's how we began to take from each other. It was not a matter of copying or imitating but of trying these things within the context of our own individual schooling. I never tried to influence Rudik, but in a way he influenced me. And he helped me through his incredible force and vitality. He was raw and, of course, he was so young. I, on the other hand, being ten years older, was merely polishing my technique.

"Yet, with all my acclaim as being the West's leading male dancer, I had reached a dead end. Seeing Rudik move was an enormous inspiration. It was through watching him that I could free myself and try to discover that looseness of his. Before Rudik, I had very little competition in the West, and it was only with Rudik's arrival on the scene that I really felt stimulated.

"While Rudik stayed with me, there were many rumors about us. People thought that our being together so much of the time, laughing together and being nice toward each other, discussing things and working together, didn't seem altogether sincere. They thought we were putting on an act. This kind of attitude persisted—even after Rudik became more famous. Well, that never bothered us. Some people even said that Rudik came out of Russia for the express purpose of 'killing me,' and how could I put up with it? I never believed that, of course. Only once did I use that against him and that was when we had an argument. I got very mad and said, 'You just came out to kill me!' When he heard that Rudik got so upset, he cried. He said, 'How can you be so evil?' I know it was a vicious thing to say, but somehow I had to throw that at him, and I don't even remember what the argument was about. But you see, people have always speculated about us or tried to put ideas into our heads. Actually, for the first four or five years of our friendship, there was a mutual inspiration. I know that he would always say to everyone that I inspired him far more than he inspired me. But that was not so. I gained as much from him as I hope he gained from me."

The Russian dancer's association with the de Cuevas Ballet was still in effect, but the company was not performing during this period. Nureyev's engagement at the London gala arranged by Fonteyn at the Drury Lane Theatre would be his next dancing engagement—his first appearance on a London stage. For three months, however, the two dancers lived together in Copenhagen.

During this period, a letter arrived for Erik Bruhn from the Soviet embassy in Copenhagen. Bruhn expected to hear about his Bolshoi engagement, for he had made plans to spend at least a year dancing with the company. When he opened the letter, he found that it was in Russian, a language he did not know. He casually asked Nureyev to translate its contents and to his amazement learned that the Bolshoi had changed its plans and that his appearances would have to be postponed. Bruhn thought the matter over and felt that a wait would somehow intrude on his future plans. Ultimately he chose to decline the Bolshoi's invitation.

"It did not immediately dawn on me that the postponement may have been the direct result of my association with Rudik. But as Rudik was staying in my house, and as we were seen together so often, it is entirely possible that we may have been followed by the KGB. Suddenly this became a big problem, and Rudik and I both decided that it might be best to leave Denmark for a while.

"As luck would have it, I received a call from London. It was Anton Dolin inviting me to be a guest in a group he was putting together for a two-week season there. He told me that I would be partnering Sonia Arova. Well, I hadn't seen Sonia in ages and knew that she had gotten married to Job Sanders, but that they were now divorced. I decided it would be nice to see Sonia again, and I accepted Dolin's offer. Sonia then called me and we arranged to rehearse in Paris, where she was then living. Rudik agreed to come with me.

"We took a train and I noticed that Rudik looked terrified. He wasn't sure whether he was carrying the proper papers that would permit him to cross the border. He was afraid that someone might try to grab him. He was pale and petrified by the thought of being kidnapped and being taken back to Russia. Actually Rudik went around with this fear for several years. Eventually we landed in Paris without incident, and we both breathed a sigh of relief."

When Bruhn and Sonia Arova spoke on the telephone to make their rehearsal arrangements in Paris, the ballerina invited him to stay in her apartment. "Erik told me that he would not be coming alone. And so I made a reservation for him and Rudolf in a small hotel. I met them both at the train station. I had of course heard about Rudolf Nureyev. When they got off the train, Rudy eyed me in a very strange manner. Later I asked Erik why he had done this, and he said that I reminded Rudolf of Maria Tallchief—it was the first time anybody had ever said that.

"Anyway, I was very happy to see Erik again. It almost seemed as though we had again found that magical touch we had had when we first met. And it would be wonderful dancing with him again. The hotel Rudolf and Erik stayed in was very inexpensive, very close to my apartment, and we saw each other constantly. Erik and I began rehearsals for the Dolin London performances. We would be dancing the *Flower Festival at Genzano* and the *Don Quixote* pas de deux. Rudolf came to our rehearsals. I remember him sitting there very quietly and watching like a hawk!"

The brief Paris stay found Erik Bruhn more relaxed than he had been in a long time. Seeing Arova again was pleasant and he was particularly happy that they were now simply good friends. Also, for the first time, he began to relate more fully to Rudolf Nureyev.

"In Paris I could finally relax," says Bruhn. "All the tension with Maria in Copenhagen had gotten to me. Basically, I was in such a state that I was not able to appreciate Rudik. It was not until we were in Paris that I finally had a chance to sit back and look at him. I had been looking but not actually seeing. Suddenly I saw!"

The rehearsal period over, the three dancers traveled to London, where Bruhn and Arova performed with the Dolin troupe at Golders Green Theatre and at the Streatham Hill Theatre in October 1961. During one of these performances, Dame Ninette de Valois, the founder of the Royal Ballet, sat in the audience. A woman of great vision and personal magnetism, Dame Ninette had led the British company to greatness. After having seen Bruhn dance, she elected to invite him to become a guest artist with the Royal Ballet for the season. Coincidentally, the Gala for the Royal Academy of Dancing, at which Nureyev was to make his London debut, would also take place in November.

The gala was one of the most anticipated dance events of the year. London audiences had been hearing about the Russian defector for months and they were waiting to see for themselves whether all that had been written and said about him were true. Sir Frederick Ashton choreographed a special solo for Nureyev entitled *Poème Tragique*, set to music of Alexander Scriabin. In addition, Nureyev would partner Rosella Hightower in the Black Swan pas de deux.

Erik Bruhn remembers that night. "It was a sensational evening. Seeing Rudik on the stage was a shock. He had a tremendous presence and it was inspiring. I must confess that I was not taken with his Black Swan—something was still missing. But the Ashton work was superb. Rudik had told me how delighted he was to work with Ashton and I could tell that Ashton was inspired by him. Ashton used him beautifully and I wish there had been a film made of that performance. Anyway, that was the first time I ever saw Rudik dance."

As a result of this memorable gala, Rudolf Nureyev was invited by Margot Fonteyn to dance with her in a forthcoming *Giselle* with the Royal Ballet at Covent Garden, and this event was to be the beginning of their legendary partnership.

〖 CHAPTER 17 〗

IN DECEMBER 1961 Erik Bruhn and Rudolf Nureyev conceived the idea of presenting themselves with two partners in an evening of solos, pas de deux, and pas de quatre. It would give the two dancers the opportunity to dance together on the same stage, as well as to choreograph works for themselves and each other. They discussed possible partners and finally decided on Rosella Hightower and Sonia Arova. The plan was to rehearse for four weeks at Hightower's school, Le Centre de Danse Internationale in Cannes, after which they would give two performances in Cannes and two more in Paris.

Bruhn and Nureyev began thinking about repertoire. The Danish dancer chose to choreograph a plotless work to a Toccata and Fugue by Bach and a concluding set of Spanish dances to popular Spanish music, which he called *Fantaisie*. Nureyev's contribution would be a pas de quatre to music of Glazounov's *Raymonda* and the pas de deux from *The Nutcracker* and *Don Quixote*, both of which he would dance with Hightower.

Sonia Arova was delighted to be asked to participate in this unusual presentation and recalls the two months during which Hightower, Bruhn, Nureyev, and she worked together: "Rudy, Erik, and I took an apartment together in Cannes facing the sea, and every day we went to rehearse at Rosella's school. It was a very productive time for us all. Erik's piece based on Bach was diabolical and Rudolf's excerpts from *Raymonda* for the four of us were equally demanding. Erik and I did *Flower Festival* plus the original *Raymonda* pas de deux. It all ended with a sort of Spanish potpourri created by Erik in which I walked in with him, then Rudy flirted with me and I went off with him, and Rosella stayed with Erik. We then all finished dancing together. It was exhausting!"

On January 6, 1962, the foursome gave their first performance in a theater in Cannes and repeated it a few nights later. They then traveled to Paris to give two performances, on January 12 and 13, at the Théâtre des Champs Elysées. These events drew packed houses, but the critical reception was mixed. One dance critic from London's *Dance and Dancers*—Marie-Françoise Christout—was particularly offended: "The recital may have been of more interest to the sociologist than dance critic. It resolved itself into something in three more or less equal parts—dancing, hysterical applause from a roaring mob, and intervals. That such artists should lend their talents to this type of circus enterprise seems utterly regrettable."

Regardless of the criticism, the enterprise left the four dancers limp with exhaustion. To make matters worse, Bruhn had injured his ankle during one of the Paris performances, and could barely finish the performance on closing night. Indeed, the foot injury turned out to be relatively serious and, as a result, Bruhn had to cancel an engagement in America, an NBC television appearance on the "Bell Telephone Hour," during which he was to have danced the *Flower Festival* pas de deux with Maria Tallchief. Bruhn felt that NBC might accept the services of Rudolf Nureyev in his stead, and Sonia Arova, who was flying to New York, was delegated to suggest the substitution, which was, not surprisingly, accepted promptly. Nureyev was elated, although apprehensive about dancing in the unfamiliar Bournonville style, so Bruhn decided to go to New York to coach him in this difficult pas de deux. When Tallchief and Nureyev made their appearance, television audiences throughout America had their first glimpse of the Russian star.

Following their New York stay, Bruhn and Nureyev flew to London. The time was nearing for Nureyev to make his Royal Ballet debut on February 21, 1962, partnering Margot Fonteyn in the first of a series of *Giselles*. At the same time, Erik Bruhn would also be joining the company as a guest artist. During their stay in London, Bruhn and Nureyev rented an apartment together. Several of their appearances with the Royal Ballet would find them dancing the same roles—*Giselle, Swan Lake, Sleeping Beauty, Les Sylphides,* and the *Don Quixote* pas de deux. As everywhere else, the Russian dancer was the object of extraordinary publicity.

This barrage of publicity may have been a contributing factor to Erik Bruhn's sense of discomfort during his tenure with the Royal Ballet. Another may have been the fact that he was not entirely happy with the partner chosen for him by Ninette de Valois—the ballerina Nadia Nerina.

While he was aware that Nerina was one of the Royal Ballet's major dancers, he did not consider their partnership ideal. "I had to learn to like dancing with Nerina, and we developed a fine relationship. In fact, we were acclaimed together for our performances. I must say that the only work I liked dancing at the Royal Ballet was *Giselle.* I hated *Sleeping Beauty,* and I took it upon myself to make some changes in the choreography, something that did not sit very well with Michael Somes, who taught me the role. But performing with the Royal Ballet was something of a drag. I mean, I wanted a zipper changed on the top of my costume, and they had to go and check with Madame de Valois. It was ridiculous. All my requests were finally agreed to, but it was a hassle."

What may have riled Bruhn further was the matter of ballet critics making comparisons between performances given by him and Nureyev. He considered it unfair and tiresome. The two dancers tried to make light of the situation.

"Of course, with Rudik on the scene, and with his creating such an incredible sensation, the press had a field day. And the fact that we were appearing together as guest artists was further grist for the mill. I mean, they saw us together and they watched us like hawks, and it was as if they had placed bets on which of us was going to survive. Rudik kept feeling guilty about the press overlooking me, and he was very considerate. That was enough for me. The rest I could not control. It was never the press that disturbed our friendship. Our ups and downs had to do with the relationship itself. But it was annoying and irritating to see how small and mean the press was, and how much it enjoyed trying to disrupt our lives.

"Still, there were times when we had a lot of fun together. I remember how we were both trying to learn to drive in London. Rudik had a car sent from France but neither of us knew how to drive it. So, one day, the two of us were trying to teach each other how to drive and, of course, we didn't know what the hell we were doing. Every time Rudik was at the wheel I was such a nervous wreck that I would have to open the door and throw up. When *I* was driving, the same thing would happen to him. The car looked like it had been beaten with a hammer. People would scream at us and call us killers.

"We told Margot about our so-called driving lessons and she was completely appalled. She thought it was horrible that we were driving around the city without a license. Well, she knew someone at the Automobile Association and arranged for us to have an instructor who would take us for a drive and who would then give us a license. Needless to say, we were both terrified. It was worse than going on the stage. I told Rudik that he should drive with the instructor first and if *he* managed to get a license, then I would brave it too; but if he didn't, then I wouldn't even try. Well, he was out for ten minutes and came back and said he had his license! So, I had to go next.

"I sat next to this man and I was at the bottom of a hill and he told me to drive to the top of it before entering traffic. I hadn't mastered that at all. So I told him to get out of the car and go to the top of the hill and stop the traffic, because I was sure I was going to hit all those cars. The man just looked at me and said, 'Have you read the Highway Code?' I thought he was referring to some Agatha Christie novel. I said, 'No, I haven't. I never read detective stories.' You can imagine his expression. Anyway, it was a nightmare—especially when he asked me to park the car. I told him I would rather not, because I would either end up much too far from the curb or right on top of the curb. The instructor was a very nice man and, for some reason, I got my license too."

Bruhn and Nureyev were deep in rehearsal for the Royal Ballet season—Bruhn with Nadia Nerina and, later on, Nureyev with Yvette Chauviré.

Nadia Nerina observed the two friends during their three-month stay with the Royal Ballet: "Nureyev was not so well known as a dancer in London," she said. "I mean, he had created a sensation at the gala and in *Giselle* with Fonteyn. But most of the publicity really centered on his defection. I must say, there was a staggering amount of it, and no dancer had ever before gotten that kind of attention, including Erik. You see, Erik's name was supreme in the ballet world, but it was not totally known to the general public. And, of course, he hadn't defected. At any rate, Erik and I became very good friends and we had a great time together. Since he was Nureyev's friend, my husband, Charles Gordon, and I would often invite them for weekends and dinner—we were a frequent foursome.

"I must admit that it was something of a problem when Nureyev began appearing at all my rehearsals with Erik. There we were, working on our roles, when Rudy would start pointing things out to Erik, telling him what was good and what wasn't. The trouble was that Rudy was forcing his personality on Erik and it made Erik nervous. You must understand that Erik was always very cool and collected, and would come to rehearsals prepared in his mind as to what he was going to do. He was very organized and he would always appear meticulously dressed for our rehearsals. On the other hand, Rudy would come in looking like a ragbag and slop about. Their personalities were totally different. Finally I had had enough. I began to realize that Rudy was having a bad effect on Erik. He was unsettling him. I made up my mind to tell him that it would be better if he would leave us alone. I remember his looking at me rather like a dark cloud. I said, 'I'm sorry, Rudy, I am not going on until you leave this rehearsal room.' Well, he left rather sheepishly and when he closed the door behind him, I could still see him with his nose pressed against the door window watching us. Ultimately, he did not return to the rehearsals.

"What was so awful was that Erik became progressively more upset. I'll never forget him saying to me after he'd been with us for two months that he was not a classical dancer. I remember replying that I had never heard such a bunch of rubbish in all my life, and that he was the greatest classical male dancer I had ever seen. I did not wish to interfere with his personal life, but it was obvious that he was extremely upset. After a while, Sonia Arova appeared on the scene and the three of them, Sonia, Erik, and Rudy, formed a kind of a trio, which seemed altogether too complicated for me. Finally my husband and I did not see too much of them."

The performances of Bruhn and Nerina during that 1962 season at the Royal Ballet were hailed by the critics, despite Bruhn's reservations about his British partner and despite his emotional state. On March 27, he and Nerina performed in *Swan Lake*.

Nerina and Bruhn next appeared in *Giselle*, and once again the critics raved, although Bruhn was now beginning to be compared to Nureyev, who had danced Albrecht earlier on in the season with Fonteyn. In the May issue of *Dance and Dancers*, Peter Williams opened his review by stating, "The memory of the recent Fonteyn-Nureyev *Giselle* lingers, and what is more it seems likely to overshadow most performances in this ballet for some time to come. It was possibly this shadow that dimmed down the Nadia Nerina–Erik Bruhn performance in the same work on April 3, even though so much of what they did was excellent and perfectly right. Bruhn is the kind of artist upon whom any male dancer can safely model himself. To copy Nureyev could easily bring disaster. . . . The telling simplicity of Bruhn's playing in the first act of *Giselle* is exemplary—not a gesture wasted, not a second out of character. There was none of the wild rapture of Nureyev, yet he remained completely true to the spirit of romanticism."

On May 3 a very special event took place at the Royal Opera House. For an annual benefit gala in aid of the Royal Benevolent Fund, Erik Bruhn was invited to stage excerpts from August Bournonville's ballet *Napoli.* The company had never before performed the Bournonville classic, nor had its dancers been previously trained in the Bournonville technique. The evening, which included several other works, turned out to be a notable success. Bruhn himself partnered Nerina in the *Flower Festival at Genzano* pas de deux, and Antoinette Sibley, Graham Usher, Georgina Parkinson, Merle Park, Bryan Lawrence, and Lynn Seymour danced the pas de six. Bruhn seemed to have conveyed the Bournonville style to the English dancers with unusual clarity, for they danced with all the fleetness and bravura it called for.

Dame Ninette de Valois remembers the event. "Erik Bruhn is regarded by the dance world in England as the greatest and most noble example of the Danish school. I recall with pleasure his appearances with the Royal Ballet and the visit that he made about seventeen years ago when he mounted on our company some famous Bournonville dances. Among the performers was a very young recruit from the Royal Ballet School, whose potential was quickly spotted by Erik. The young man eventually emerged as Anthony Dowell. . . . We ask Erik very often to pay our school a visit. Perhaps one day we will have the good luck to get him."

As distinguished as the gala and the Bournonville excerpts were, the greatest accolades came to Bruhn. But even as Bruhn's performances were being praised, Nureyev's appearances with the Royal Ballet received greater attention. He was, after all, a new quantity and the public and critics alike were eager to see him in action. As the season progressed, reviewers felt obliged to comment on the presence of both these stars, for it was indeed unusual for two such remarkable artists to be sharing roles on the Covent Garden stage. What is more, it was rare for the Royal Ballet to engage guest artists at the time Bruhn and Nureyev danced with them. All in all, Londoners were experiencing a head-spinning dance coup. Indeed, so sensational was the presence of Bruhn and Nureyev during that 1962 season that even the American press considered it worthy of coverage. Walter Terry of the *Herald Tribune* had come to London to report on the season and sent back an article which opened with, "A beatnik and a prince have taken London by storm."

But perhaps one of the most fascinating glimpses into the Bruhn-Nureyev presence in London came from critic Clive Barnes. Barnes had been on the scene writing for the London *Times* and the *Daily Express*, and was not yet living or working in America.

"It was quite a traumatic experience for them," he says. "My wife, Patricia, and I got to know Erik but hardly knew Rudolf. Indeed, no one knew Rudolf. It takes a very long time to get to know him. He doesn't trust you for five or six years and that's just for starters.

"I am not at all sure that the Royal Ballet realized that Erik and Rudolf were living together. It took them a long time to understand that relationship. Anyway, Rudolf and Margot created a sensation in *Giselle*. Erik was dancing with Nadia Nerina. The competition was fantastic, but at this time they were very, very different dancers. To some extent Erik was caviar to the general. I mean, every dancer and certainly the elite critics knew that Erik was the world's greatest male dancer. In a way, Erik was a kind of cult hero. He was not at that time a superstar. Interestingly enough he gained that status *after* Rudolf.

"Erik hoped very much to be taken on by the Royal Ballet and to be a member of the company, but this did not happen. It was a decision made by Ninette de Valois and Frederick Ashton and it was a very cool decision. They decided to have only one great foreign dancer, and Rudolf was more useful.

"I remember Erik coming around and we did an interview with him for *Dance and Dancers*. It was just at the point when that decision had been made and Erik was shattered. He looked ash-gray. I had never seen him look so much like the Prince of Denmark. Erik was very hurt and he felt very rejected. He had virtually given up Ballet Theatre for this and he didn't want to go back to Copenhagen on a permanent basis. He felt his international career was shattered. He could not understand, because he felt the Royal Ballet was absolutely right for him. It was an opportunity to learn all those wonderful Ashton roles, which were ideal for him. Of course, Ashton could have said, 'I want to do a ballet for Erik Bruhn.' But Ashton didn't, and in fact he only created one major role for Nureyev and that was *Marguerite and Armand*. Erik was hurt and it must have been a difficult time for him."

It is safe to say, in spite of his remarks to Barnes, that Bruhn's appearances with the Royal Ballet in London were not to his complete satisfaction. The three months spent with Nureyev in London deepened their relationship, although it seemed steeped in emotional upheaval. It was a matter of temperament. The volatile young Tartar, with his high-strung impulsiveness, his quick-to-flare temper, his often abrasive treatment of others, and his very obvious admiration of Erik Bruhn, must have jarred and jolted the reserved Danish dancer. The onslaught of Nureyev's feelings, the passion that seemed to guide him, must in some way have frightened Bruhn. But he was not willing to be dominated or smothered by even so exciting a personality as Rudolf Nureyev. There is no question, however, that Bruhn's emotions were touched—so much so that he himself needed to escape the very intensity he had elicited.

Bruhn claims that in some mysterious way the two dancers were predestined to meet and he likened their meeting to two comets colliding and exploding. "What happens with me is that I collide with things. There is a meeting or a collision and it is inevitably momentary. If I try to sustain it as something permanent, it doesn't work. The initial collision is attractive and exciting, but I have to follow my instincts about it and my instincts invariably guide me into many different directions. Rudik has always claimed that I was an example of freedom and independence—that I would always do exactly what I wanted without regard to others—and it may be so. Well, in those early years that's what happened between Rudik and me—a collision and an explosion which could not last. If Rudik had wanted it otherwise, I'm sorry. Still, we remain friends and we have continued to go through a great deal together, and on many different levels."

With Mona Vangsaa in *Coppélia*, Royal Danish Ballet, 1948. Photo: Rigmor
Mydtskov.

(BELOW) In *Coppélia*, American Ballet Theatre, 1971. Photo:
Martha Swope. (OPPOSITE ABOVE) With Sonia Arova in *Coppélia*,
Bell Telephone Hour television production, 1963. Photo: Fred Fehl.
(OPPOSITE BELOW LEFT) *Coppélia*, American Ballet Theatre, 1968.
Photo: Fred Fehl. (OPPOSITE BELOW RIGHT) With Carla Fracci,
Coppélia, American Ballet Theatre, 1968. Photo: Fred Fehl.

(ABOVE) With Allegra Kent in *Night Shadow*, New York City Ballet, 1959. Photo: Fred Fehl. (BELOW) *Divertimento No. 15*, New York City Ballet, 1959–60. Photo: Fred Fehl. (OPPOSITE) In Bruhn's own production of *Romeo and Juliet* with Carla Fracci, American Ballet Theatre, 1966. Photo: Martha Swope.

(OPPOSITE ABOVE) With Natalia
Makarova in *The Miraculous
Mandarin*, American Ballet Theatre,
1971. Photo: Fred Fehl. (OPPOSITE
BELOW) With Makarova in *Les
Sylphides*, American Ballet Theatre,
1971. Photo: Fred Fehl. (RIGHT)
Goeren Gentele. Photo: Aftonbladet.
(BELOW) Curtain call with Carla
Fracci, 1971. Photo: Louis Péres.

(OPPOSITE) With Natalia Makarova in John Neumeier's *Epilogue*, American Ballet Theatre, 1975. Photo: Kenn Duncan. (ABOVE) *Las Hermanas*, American Ballet Theatre, 1975. Left to right: Bonnie Mathis, Lucia Chase, Bruhn, and Marcia Haydée. Photo: Beverley Gallegos. (RIGHT) Bruhn in his straight dramatic role as the Samurai in *Rashomon* with Susse Wold, Allescenen Theatre, Copenhagen, 1974. Photo: Lillian Bolvinkel.

(RIGHT) Bruhn in *Jardin aux Lilas*, 1976. Photo: Jack Vartoogian.
(BELOW) With Gelsey Kirkland in Antony Tudor's *Jardin aux Lilas*, American Ballet Theatre, 1976. Photo: Jack Vartoogian.

〖 CHAPTER 18 〗

FOLLOWING his London engagement with the Royal Ballet, Erik Bruhn joined the Royal Danish Ballet on tour in Florence, where he had committed himself to dance two performances of *La Sylphide*. Nureyev, anxious to learn more about the Bournonville style, traveled with Bruhn to Italy to watch him rehearse as well as perform.

"Of course, Rudik was now firmly ensconced with the Royal Ballet in London," Bruhn says, "and he and Fonteyn had become the new great partnership. Still, he took time off because he wanted to see all the different things I was doing. At that time, I saw a lot less of his dancing than he did of mine. At any rate, he saw those *Sylphide* performances and then flew back to London."

At the invitation of John Cranko of the Stuttgart Ballet, Bruhn went to Germany. The company had been under the direction of Nicholas Beriosoff, but in 1961 John Cranko, a choreographer with London's Royal Ballet, had taken over as director. When Bruhn came as guest artist, the Stuttgart Ballet had been under Cranko's guidance for a year, but he had already begun to make notable changes with marked success and, before his untimely death in 1973, would eventually lead the company to international stature. In July 1962 Cranko mounted a Stuttgart Ballet Festival, for which he had invited a roster of international dancers: in addition to Bruhn, there were Yvette Chauviré from Paris, Georgina Parkinson from the Royal Ballet in London, Erika Slocha and Karl Musil from the Staatsoper Ballet in Vienna, and Rudolf Nureyev. There would be several premieres, notably *Les Saisons* and *Daphnis and Chloë* by Cranko.

Bruhn and Georgina Parkinson danced in *Daphnis and Chloë*. The work proved an immediate success.

Indeed, Bruhn considers *Daphnis and Chloë* one of his major achievements. "Of the few ballets specifically created for me, I would say that *Daphnis* was certainly my favorite. John used me in a way that employed my specific talents. He somehow knew exactly what I could do and in some ways it was almost too much. I think that the ballet was only successful when I danced the role. John found qualities in me that just can't be taught and that cannot be analyzed. It was amazing, because I didn't particularly enjoy exposing my facility—the tricks—but he loosened me up and gave me a freedom that scared me. The fact was that, even *I* had difficulty in duplicating myself. I did only two performances of *Daphnis and Chloë*. The first night was a miracle and the second horrified me. I simply could not repeat myself and it was a very strange sensation."

A contributing factor to this odd circumstance was a mounting tension that seemed to be surrounding him in Stuttgart. Bruhn had just gone through an emotionally chaotic period in London, and in Stuttgart he seemed to be experiencing even more inner chaos. A gala was to take place during the Festival Week at which Bruhn was scheduled to dance. As the time neared, Bruhn announced that he was ill and could not appear. "I felt this tension growing, first of all within myself about *Daphnis*, and then the general bad atmosphere that pervaded when Rudik and I were together—taking class together, being seen together, and all that. People were provoking us. Jokes were being made, and it just got to me. I was working and I did not want to be intefered with or interrupted. Anyway, the intrigues were just too much. I declared myself sick and went to bed. People said I was playing a game. Kenneth MacMillan, who was having one of his works performed, and John Cranko came into my room and didn't believe I was sick. I threw them out, got up, got into my car, and left Germany. I left without saying a word to anyone, including Rudik.

From Stuttgart Erik Bruhn drove to Copenhagen, though on the way he developed spasms in his back and it took him a week to get there. He was scheduled to perform in September at the Tivoli Gardens with Sonia Arova. It was the one hundredth anniversary of this famous garden theater and Bruhn had decided to choreograph a special pas de deux. This gala event would be attended by the king and queen and Bruhn looked forward to participating. Once more Nureyev appeared on the scene. He wanted to see the gala and Bruhn invited him to stay in his house, along with Sonia Arova. When Arova arrived, she complained of knee trouble. As it turned out, she had torn some ligaments around the kneecap, and a doctor advised her to rest for at least a week.

Arova remembers Bruhn choreographing their pas de deux on himself and Nureyev. "We were frantic, because the performance was a week off. I couldn't move and Rudy very kindly offered to take my place in the rehearsals. I sat there with my leg propped up trying to learn it by just watching. Anyway, I finally got better and, with several injections, managed to perform the pas de deux with Erik. It turned out to be a wonderful work and the performance went very well."

The house in Gentofte was teeming with strong personalities. There was Bruhn's mother, Sonia Arova, and Rudolf Nureyev. (Bruhn's aunt Minna, his beloved *Moster*, had died six months earlier.) Arova, who flew to Paris three days after her performance with Bruhn, noted that Bruhn's mother was not in the best of health. She also recalled that the two friends were having a stormy time of it.

Bruhn too was aware of his mother's ill health. "My sisters and I urged her to get herself examined by a doctor—something she hated. Finally she went, and they found a blood clot. They told her she must go to the hospital the next day. The clot was then in her leg, but was apparently moving upward. She kept saying she didn't want to go to the hospital and absolutely refused to go. So we put her to bed and I decided to move next to her room in case she needed me. Then, after a few days, the doctor examined her again and found that the clot was beginning to move into her lungs. There was no time to lose. It was arranged that she would enter the hospital that very evening. Just that night, Rudik and I were supposed to have dinner with Vera Volkova. I told my mother we would cancel the dinner, but she said I didn't need to—that my two sisters would take care of her, and go with her.

"So Rudik and I went to Volkova's. After a while, the phone rang. It was one of my sisters saying that the ambulance had just come to the house, but before getting into it, my mother had fainted. She said they were on their way to the hospital. I thought I had better get there quickly and left Rudik at Volkova's. When I got to the hospital, my sisters had already left. I asked to see my mother and they ushered me into a room and to my shock I saw that she was lying there covered up with a sheet. I was told that she had died only a short while before. I later found out from my sisters that Mother had died in the ambulance on the way to the hospital. They were just going to phone me when I arrived at the hospital. Well, it was traumatic, but when I removed the sheet from her face, her expression seemed very peaceful. Later, the doctors performed an autopsy and discovered that she also had had cancer. However, it was the blood clot that killed her. She died three months before her seventy-first birthday.

"When I got home from the hospital, I called Volkova and told her what had happened. Rudik immediately got on the phone and said he would come home right away. When he got there he was extremely thoughtful. What was very difficult to face was the fact that I was scheduled to dance *Carmen* the very next night. Of course, I could have canceled. But I remembered my mother saying to me that whatever happened, I was to do my performance—it was her wish. And so, on the night after my mother died I gave a performance. I danced with Kirsten Simone. Rudik came to see us. I only got through it because my mother had given me the strength to do it. At any rate, Rudik was scheduled to leave the next day, but he decided to stay on an extra few days to help me through the difficult time of being alone in the house. This is something I shared with Rudik and it has bound our friendship. I mean, he could have just run away. But he didn't."

Among the close friends Erik Bruhn had made in New York was Christopher Allan, whom the dancer met while he was performing during the 1957–58 season at American Ballet Theatre. Allan had worked as a press representative for the company and was introduced to Bruhn by Violette Verdy, for whom Allan had a particular fondness. After Christopher Allan left ABT his firm, Allan, Ingersoll & Weber, became representatives for well-known film stars and the company eventually had offices in New York, Los Angeles, London, Paris, and Rome. A bachelor, Allan was considered one of the kindest and most generous of men. From the first, he insisted that whenever Bruhn was in New York he was to consider his apartment on East Sixty-sixth Street a second home.

An inveterate balletomane, Christopher Allan loved to discover young dancers. In 1962 he had traveled to Milan, where he attended a ballet performance at La Scala. Dancing that evening was a young ballerina named Carla Fracci. Allan was struck by Fracci's talent and beauty, grace and superb technique. Her vivaciousness and charm were altogether captivating, and Allan was certain that his friend Erik would be enchanted by her. Upon his return to New York, he contacted Bruhn in Copenhagen, telling him of his discovery. Bruhn told Allan that he had, in fact, seen Fracci dance in London in Dolin's *Pas de Quatre* and had adored her in it. When Allan further suggested that Bruhn introduce Fracci to America, Bruhn instantly agreed. Allan next made arrangements with NBC for Bruhn and Fracci to appear together on the "Bell Telephone Hour," and it was decided that the two dancers would perform excerpts from *La Sylphide*. In mid-October, Bruhn was in New York rehearsing with Fracci for their television appearance on October 22. Bruhn credits Christopher Allan with having introduced him to a partner with whom he would make ballet history, for the television appearance found the two dancers in instantaneous harmony.

Fracci remembers that first encounter. "It sometimes happens that there is an immediate understanding between two people and that is what occurred between Erik and me. My English was practically nonexistent. But we did not have to speak. It was an amazing thing, because it seemed as though we had known each other forever. Things functioned perfectly from the outset. It was like love-at-first-sight—a love that intensified on the stage. What I experienced with Erik was this love, respect, and tenderness. Of course, I am speaking of the love that happens between two dancers during performance. Offstage we did not fall in love, but we did become the greatest of friends."

As it happened, the television appearance coincided with the Cuban crisis in America, and the audience watching Bruhn and Fracci were subjected to several interruptions with newscasters giving the latest developments on the political situation. Most of Bruhn's solo was lost, as were several other variations. Still, Ann Barzel writing in *Dance Magazine* found the telecast extraordinary: "Bruhn danced with the noble bearing and fastidious technique for which he is famous. Miss Fracci danced marvelously. She bounded lightly and her footwork was beautifully accurate. The close-ups revealed she is a beauty."

The meeting of Bruhn and Fracci through Christopher Allan cemented the friendship between the two men. Allan undertook to be Bruhn's official representative; he negotiated certain contracts for Bruhn's American appearances, and eventually became the dancer's general and generous factotum for many years.

The year 1962 also found Erik Bruhn and Sonia Arova making a two-month guest appearance on tour with the newly formed Australian Ballet, under the artistic direction of Peggy Van Praagh. They would dance Van Praagh's new full-length production of *Swan Lake, Les Sylphides,* the *Don Quixote* pas de deux, and *Coppélia,* with Bruhn making his debut in the role of Franz. Their reception in Australia was rapturous. Their final performance in January 1963, held at Her Majesty's Theatre in Adelaide, was memorable: "The audience roared, the dancers in the wings applauded and Mr. Bruhn and Miss Arova together, applauded both the audience and the rest of the company. Later, the Australian prima ballerina, Kathleen Gorham, presented Miss Arova with an opal and Mr. Bruhn with a silver boomerang on behalf of the Australian Ballet," reported the *Adelaide Advertiser.*

As was his custom during those years, Rudolf Nureyev liked to be present at as many Bruhn performances as possible. True to form, he had flown from London to Sydney and stayed a week. Arova, Nureyev, and Bruhn were constant companions, visiting the sights, swimming together, and generally enjoying each other's company.

Following his Australian engagement, Bruhn flew to New York and was approached by Lucia Chase to resume his association with American Ballet Theatre. He had been away from the company for three years and had traveled all over the world as a guest artist with other companies.

Bruhn felt that Chase was unwilling to make certain concessions. "Her conditions were the same as they had been in previous years. I wanted to have more control over where, when, and with whom I would dance. But she offered me the same amount of money as before and I found that quite insulting. I'm sure Lucia thought I was being very grand, but I had been dancing everywhere with great success and her offer was simply not acceptable. So, I did not return to ABT. Instead, I went to Milan, where Carla Fracci and I danced our first *Giselle* together at La Scala." It was during this second meeting with Fracci that their partnership flowered. Their *Giselle* was magical and both dancers came to the realization that in each other they had found an ideal.

"To dance with Carla was to have fulfilled a love affair—a love affair consummated on the stage," says Erik Bruhn. "Of course, I have had great satisfaction from dancing with other ballerinas, but this was something new. We did not recognize what we had when we first danced together in 1962 on that television appearance. I mean, we met, we danced, we parted. But when we danced that *Giselle* in Milan in 1963, we were both ready for what happened between us. The moment was there and we were both prepared for it."

Carla Fracci is of the same mind when it comes to remembering the occasion: "There are really no words to explain it," she says. "It was something we felt. Everyone who saw us understood that there was a great truth and beauty in the partnership. It has certainly marked me for life."

Upon completing his engagement at La Scala with Fracci, Bruhn returned to Copenhagen, where he participated in the annual Danish Ballet Festival. Also at this time, two major honors came to Erik Bruhn. In Denmark, he was made a Knight of the Order of Danebrog. In Paris, he was awarded the Nijinsky Prize.

With the death of his mother, Bruhn now lived alone in the Gentofte house, which he proceeded to renovate. Brand-new appliances were fitted into the kitchen and bathrooms. The main upstairs bedroom now boasted a balcony overlooking the sumptuous garden, and the basement contained a laundry room and bathroom. Most of the furniture in the house was newly bought, since Bruhn's sisters had divided most of the contents among themselves. Only a few choice pieces were retained by Bruhn. The large living room, with its French doors leading to the garden and its windows fitted with mauve, yellow, and green stained glass, had various built-in alcoves forming comfortable denlike spaces. Objects and precious mementos gathered by Bruhn during his travels now fill the house. Two precious Oriental carpets, gifts from Nureyev, cover the floor of the living room. On the walls hang rare prints and paintings. Two Goya prints and several Japanese prints are also gifts from Nureyev. The dining room is furnished in modern Danish style, and on one sideboard stand four candlesticks created by the Danish designer Bjørn Winblad, each of which bears one of the dancer's names—Erik, Belton, Evers, and Bruhn. The garden is relandscaped.

Running this beautiful and comfortable two-storied house on a quiet, tree-lined street was Bruhn's devoted housekeeper, Ella Schram. The dancer had known Ella since he was a boy. She would come and help with the household chores, as indeed had her own mother-in-law, when the Bruhn family was still together. Bruhn now considers Ella Schram his family, and has a very particular affection for this charming and energetic woman. "After my aunt and mother died, I asked Ella to take care of things for me," he says. "At first she only came a few days a week, but later, as our friendship grew, she would come almost every day. When I was not in Copenhagen, she would look after everything. And when I was there she would come and prepare meals for me. We would sit and have breakfast together and talk for hours. For me she represents the family that I never had and still don't have. I am devoted to Ella. And when I travel we correspond. I don't know what I would do without Ella."

Mrs. Schram speaks of Bruhn almost as a son. "Erik never tells me what to do. And he never treats me like a servant. He trusts me completely. I don't live in his house, because I am married and have my own home. When Erik is in Copenhagen, he usually sleeps late and then he wakes up, has breakfast, and goes straight to the Royal Theatre to take class. Often, he goes to see friends or has people over. Usually he cooks for himself, but if he brings people home I do the cooking. He is not very particular about food and generally eats very little.

"I am like a mother to Erik and he confides in me. Ours is a relationship beyond the usual type. He depends on me to a certain extent, but I hope he doesn't depend on me psychologically—that would be too much. I have often wondered why Erik doesn't sell this house and live in the country. But something is holding him here and, of course, it's where he was brought up. He has been very kind to me. One time he even took me to New York and I saw him dance at the Metropolitan Opera House. In the evenings we would always dine together in New York.

"Erik is not a typical star. I mean, he is neither conceited nor snobbish. People say that Erik is a lonely person, but I don't believe this is true, because things are always happening to him. Of course, I worry about him, not so much about his personal affairs, as about his career. I'm talking about the injuries. I always worry that he will fall and hurt himself. But somehow, even when he is injured, he doesn't stop for a minute. All I can say is that he is just a very warm human being. And I love him like a son."

During his stay in Copenhagen in 1963, Bruhn worked with some of the youngsters in the Royal Danish Ballet School. He took particular pleasure in teaching and had done so off and on each time he found himself performing at the Opera House. Among his students during the late fifties, he took note of the potential talents of two youngsters who would eventually rise to prominence: Peter Martins and Peter Schaufuss.

Peter Martins, now a principal dancer with the New York City Ballet, remembers that Bruhn was an important influence. "Erik influenced not only me but a whole generation of dancers in Denmark, as well as all over the world. His influence was far greater than Nureyev's. I mean, Rudy had enormous influence in many other ways, but what dancers took from Rudy is not what they took from Erik. When Rudy came out, we looked at him and said, 'Look at this Russian animal, this maniac. How fascinating! Maybe we should let our hair grow! Maybe we should act like him.' But with Erik it was different. He had enormous concentration and strived for the utmost and the impossible—he never gave in. When I think of Erik, I think of an empty studio and this pale man, dressed in black, standing at the barre all by himself. There would be no pianist, no tape recorder. It was just him and a towel over the barre. That is Erik to me. Always working to perfect himself. Strangely enough, he probably never got there in his mind.

"Of course, at the Danish Ballet School, there were some inside jokes about Erik among us students. One of them was that Erik didn't dance that often in Denmark because there was not enough money—the Danish Royal Ballet couldn't afford him. To us, Erik represented wealth. I mean, he would come home wearing these extravagant fur coats. There were big cars and fancy things. We all assumed that he was ripping off the Danish theater every time he danced, but nobody knew for sure. The joke among us kids was that every time Erik arrived, the management would turn off the heat in the hallways to save money. Whenever it was freezing at the school, we would say, 'Erik is home guesting.' The kids today now say that about me."

Peter Martins also recalls his debut at the Royal Danish Ballet at the age of eighteen. "Frank Schaufuss, Peter's father, had choreographed a ballet for Erik called *Garden Party* to music of Glazounov. There was a couple in white and a couple in black as the leads. Erik and Anna Laerkesen danced the white couple and a young boy, Aage Poulson and Inge Olafson were the black couple. At the time, Aage Poulson was the boy on his way up. Well, the day before the premiere of the ballet, Aage was ill and Frank Schaufuss came to me and asked whether I could do Aage's part. I said that I could do it, but that to dance on the same stage as Erik Bruhn was terrifying. I mean, it was mind-boggling. But I did it, and it went rather well, and Erik was wonderful to me. He treated me like an equal.

"I remember the time when Erik and Nureyev were together here in Copenhagen. This was very soon after Rudy's defection. Here was Erik, our great idol, with this mad Russian. We looked at Rudy and we thought, Why is he bringing in this number? To us stuck-up Danes he seemed like someone who couldn't really dance, because to us dancing was only one thing, and it never varied. I mean, if someone didn't do the positions perfectly—then he was a bad dancer. Immediately we resented Rudy. How dare he, this Russian peasant, come in here and think he has something to show us, and how dare Erik bring him in! Of course, some of us thought differently. I realized that these two guys had something to offer. I recall very clearly how Erik would do a class full-out and Rudy would stand at the barre and watch. When Rudy would execute the steps and try to copy Erik, he just couldn't do it; that was a schooling Rudy knew nothing about. What was so interesting was that when they both came back a few years later the situation was reversed.

"When I came to America I saw much more of Erik than I had in Denmark. Curiously enough, I never wanted to get to know Erik too well. He was too much of an ideal. But in New York, Christopher Allan, who was a great friend of Erik's, brought us together. I used to say to Chris that Erik was impossible to get to know. Chris was funny. He said, 'Yes, he is impossible and you're impossible too. You are both made of the same ice, and neither of you wants to melt.' At Chris's parties Erik and I would usually end up talking together until three or four in the morning. I was, of course, very interested to hear about why his appearances with the New York City Ballet didn't work. Balanchine does not like to talk about it, but I think he admires Erik a lot. I personally think that Erik's timing was off for Balanchine's choreography when he joined the City Ballet, back in 1959. I believe he was about thirty and that's a late age to join. For a punk like myself—I joined when I was twenty-one—it was a lot easier.

"I have always been aware that people would say I danced just like Erik Bruhn. I remember being horrified when Clive Barnes once wrote: 'Peter Martins dances more like Erik Bruhn than Erik Bruhn.' It was like getting a cold shower. Yes, I was aware of this comparison, but I was also a victim of it. I happen to have had the same training as Erik and I move like Erik, and there was a certain resemblance. But I always felt that I was being punished for this. Oddly enough, the greatest moments Erik gave me were when he didn't dance on stage, but just stood there or just sat there. Erik put standards in my head and taught me something without saying a word. He taught me that someone could go on stage and take command of the audience without dancing one step. To me, those are the great dancers. And he did it better than anybody else. Then, when he *did* dance it was as close to perfection as anybody could get."

Peter Schaufuss, then a member of the National Ballet of Canada, was equally moved by Erik Bruhn and, like his contemporary, Peter Martins, would eventually join the City Ballet.

"I think I knew Erik's face before I knew his name. My parents, Frank Schaufuss and Mona Vangsaa, were both principal dancers with the Royal Danish Ballet. They would bring me to the theater and it was like a big family, and Erik was part of it. Erik was like a brother or an uncle to me, and our friendship was a very natural thing. When Erik would come and teach class he would work with me and give me steps, and he saw that I was eager to learn. We all wanted to be like Erik Bruhn, because he was the greatest male dancer in the world. Erik was responsible for the great changes in male dancing that took place. He pioneered the art of the male dancer.

"Erik set the example of a dancer wanting to leave home and explore the world. My leaving Copenhagen had a lot to do with this. And I've become a much better dancer for it. I think that all the male dancers who left Denmark owe it to Erik. He was the first to open our eyes and minds. He showed us that it was possible to risk everything by leaving. I left because I trusted his experience."

Peter Martins, Peter Schaufuss, and later Adam Lüders and the young Ulrik Trojaborg, all graduates of the Royal Danish Ballet School, would make their future careers in America and elsewhere. Indeed, all four have danced with the New York City Ballet, and Peter Martins, Adam Lüders, and Ulrik Trojaborg have since made this company their primary dancing base.

Erik Bruhn's tenure with the New York City Ballet during the 1959–60 season had ended unhappily, but when he received a second invitation from Betty Cage, Bruhn was still intrigued by the notion of dancing for Balanchine. To be sure, he responded to Cage's letter by saying that he would return to the company for its 1963–64 season on the condition that George Balanchine himself extend the invitation to him personally.

"I was in New York at the time and told Betty Cage that I would have to hear it from Balanchine's own lips. Well, Mr. B. took me out to lunch and couldn't have been friendlier. He said he wanted me back and that he planned to create new works on me. Finally, I agreed—and back I went."

Despite her own negative feelings regarding her previous treatment at the City Ballet, Maria Tallchief also found herself returning to the company, and the presence of Bruhn may have been a contributing factor to this decision. Thus, in spite of their highly complex personal relationship, the two dancers were once more reunited in a company that had, after all, provided them with uncommon artistic fulfillment. As it turned out, this re-entry into the New York City Ballet would cause Erik Bruhn even greater distress than had his first experience there.

[CHAPTER 19]

O
N OCTOBER 3, 1963, Erik Bruhn turned thirty-five. He was at the midpoint of his career and continued to enjoy unprecedented success whenever and wherever he danced. At thirty-five a male dancer's capacities begin to diminish. The strength and stamina start to fade and it is one of the ironies of the art of dance that just when an artist enters into intellectual and creative maturity, his body begins to fail him. But even so, none of Bruhn's powers seemed to have decreased. On the contrary, his physical, artistic, and intellectual powers merged, producing performances of even more astonishing depth and clarity.

For years, he enjoyed excellent health and whatever occasional injury or physical discomfort he suffered was quickly overcome. A strong sense of self-preservation, abetted by his high sense of discipline, found him in consistently superb form. Like all dancers, he followed the rigors of daily classes, which maintained his stamina and kept his muscles limber.

But in the winter of 1963, when Bruhn rejoined the New York City Ballet, he began to show strange symptoms of an illness that he could neither account for nor understand. Onstage his performances continued to be superlative, and he showed no strain or discomfort. He repeated his early triumphs in *Divertimento No. 15*, *Swan Lake*, *The Nutcracker*, *La Sonnàmbula*, among other Balanchine works. He negotiated the difficult Balanchine steps with radiant precision, and no one watching him dance could suspect that when he stepped off the stage, sharp pains in his stomach would suddenly besiege him.

At first Bruhn paid little attention, assuming that the pains were the result of exertion. When these same stabbing pains continued to recur, however, he became concerned. He consulted a doctor and was told that there seemed to be no cause for alarm. X rays indicated nothing unusual and he was advised to rest and to eat more carefully. Yet the pains persisted, and Bruhn began canceling a number of performances.

This first encounter with an unaccountable physical illness confused the dancer and he blamed this sudden onslaught of pain on his basic unhappiness at the City Ballet. "I don't know why I put myself back into a situation that I knew just couldn't work," says Bruhn. "It wasn't the dancing that bothered me. It was the atmosphere of the company and my relationship with Balanchine."

There was apparently ample reason for Bruhn's unhappiness. There is probably no male dancer who has not wanted to perform in George Balanchine's 1928 masterpiece, *Apollo*. This enduring work, originally created for Diaghilev's Ballets Russes and first danced by Serge Lifar, has become one of the seminal ballets of the twentieth century. Every major male dancer looks to *Apollo* as the apotheosis of the neoclassical style, and its choreography, with its sublime symmetry and wondrous compositional flow and architecture, has offered the male dancer an unequaled sense of challenge and achievement.

Erik Bruhn had no doubt envisioned dancing this work set to the Stravinsky score and quite rightly felt himself eminently suited for the role of Apollo. Indeed, throughout his career, Bruhn's admirers have longed to see him dance this role, feeling that he would probably emerge as his time's greatest Apollo. Shortly after Bruhn's re-entry into the City Ballet, Balanchine told him that he would dance *Apollo* during the season. He indicated to the dancer that he felt certain his interpretation would be the definitive one. And Balanchine announced that he would teach the role to Bruhn himself; Bruhn was elated. A date was set and rehearsals began.

"To be taught Apollo by Balanchine himself was, of course, the most exciting thing I could think of. He told me that he would work with me alone on a certain Sunday—that the three girls in the ballet would not be present, and that he would demonstrate all their variations himself. Well, to be with Balanchine alone was something incredible. It was the one and only time that Balanchine and I had a real rapport. During the session he said, 'You are *the* Apollo!' I remember his coming into the studio with a very bad cold, looking as though he were falling apart. But in the three or four hours that we worked together, he was transformed. It was as though he had just invented the ballet all over again, and the years seemed to drop off him. What was so fantastic was that he danced every part himself, including all the Muses. He and I danced the pas de deux and it was glorious. After working for hours he said, 'You've learned the part. You know it!' And that was quite true, because he was such an incredible teacher.

"Anyway, this was Sunday. Monday would be a dark night. On Tuesday I looked at the call-board and saw that Balanchine had scheduled me to dance in *Apollo* that night, *without* a rehearsal! I was shocked. I went to the company manager and said that I couldn't possibly dance in the work. I was told that Balanchine said I knew the ballet. I thought it must be a joke. Finally I told the manager to tell Mr. Balanchine that I would dance Apollo that night on the condition that Balanchine himself would dance with me onstage—exactly the way he had in the rehearsal room. I was not about to go on that stage and see those three girls for the first time without having rehearsed with them. Well, Balanchine refused to give me that rehearsal and I didn't get to dance the ballet. It was another instance of what I was going through with the company, and it was the worst thing that happened between me and Balanchine. And, of course, to this day I have not danced Apollo."

Disappointment mixed with anger found Bruhn increasingly at odds with Balanchine and with his stay in the company. But he continued to dance, partnering Tallchief, Melissa Hayden, Allegra Kent, Patricia Wilde, and Mimi Paul, among others. He had signed a contract and was determined to honor it. And yet, as the weeks progressed, the mysterious pains in his stomach would appear with greater and greater frequency. Something was definitely wrong.

"I remember dancing *Swan Lake* with Melissa Hayden," says Bruhn. "When I got home after the performance I was sick all night and thought I would die. The next morning, I went to see Betty Cage to tell her that I must quit. I said I was sick and couldn't stay. When Betty told Balanchine of my decision to leave the company, he turned as white as I was gray. I went to see him and somehow I couldn't control myself and said, 'I am sick and I think it is because of you.' He said, 'Let's sit down and talk about it.' He began to recommend a wonderful doctor and said that if it should be cancer of the stomach in its early stages, it could be arrested very quickly. For some reason I got furious. I told him, 'Mr. Balanchine, if I do have cancer, it has nothing to do with you. But if I do *not* have cancer and I am sick because of you, then I'll sue you!' Well, it turned out that I did not have cancer and maybe it was not because of Balanchine that I was sick. But I do think that it was the chemistry between Balanchine and me that gave me so much trouble."

Erik Bruhn left the New York City Ballet only a few weeks into the season. As he put it, "I danced a few more performances and then I again went to Betty Cage and said, 'I'm leaving this company and I do not understand how anybody can survive here.' "

The pains experienced during his brief stay with the City Ballet did not go away. Clearly, it was not the company or Balanchine that could be held responsible. Still, it is certain that they did not help matters.

Commenting on this odd turn in his state of health, Bruhn states: "Sometimes the pains were unbearable. I went to doctors and most of them told me it was nothing serious. I myself was convinced that these pains were brought on by emotional stress. And for that there were no pills. I remember seeing a woman doctor who told me that if I were not careful I would actually induce a *real* illness out of my unconscious mind. Well, all I knew was that these stomach pains were real enough. There were days when I could barely get out of bed. I would dance and everything would be fine, and suddenly *there* were the pains. It was unbelievable and I lived with that for nearly twelve years! And yet, in all those years, I continued to dance. How I did it I'll never know!"

Bruhn had never danced at the Paris Opéra, but in the spring of 1964 he made his debut there. It was the ballerina Claude Bessy, with whom he had danced at American Ballet Theatre, who extended the invitation.

"I had danced *Miss Julie* with Claude Bessy and it worked very well," relates Bruhn. "When she invited me to come to Paris and dance *Giselle* with her, I agreed, although I felt that she was somewhat too tall for the part, and I could not quite see us doing it together. But, she arranged for me to meet with the director of the Paris Opéra Ballet and I confessed to him privately that I felt I could not do *Giselle* with Claude. I told him that I could only do it with Yvette Chauviré, whom I had met in London when she danced with Rudik at the Royal Ballet. I knew that Chauviré was a superb Giselle, and it seemed right for me to dance with her. The trouble was I had to break the news to Claude, and it came as a shock to her. However, I promised her I would return another time and dance with her in Skibine's *Daphnis and Chloë* and the *Don Quixote* pas de deux."

Bruhn had not danced *Giselle* for a period of two years. He was now ready to rethink the entire work and it was decided that Chauviré would come to Copenhagen, where they would rehearse together.

"We talked and worked and we enlisted Vera Volkova to help us reinterpret our roles. Rudik was around again and the three of us took class together. Chauviré and I felt that we should try our *Giselle* in Berlin before presenting it in Paris. The Berlin experience was very helpful; it gave us a chance to establish a close rapport on stage. We did two performances in Berlin and then went to Paris."

Yvette Chauviré, for years adored by the French public, was thought to be one of the greatest Giselles of her time. In dancing the role with Bruhn her artistry was matched by an equally great Albrecht. Their appearances at the Paris Opéra were a triumph. "There are times when meetings are providential: the meeting between a goddess of the dance such as our own Yvette Chauviré and the Danish *danseur noble* will remain in our memory for a long time," wrote Jean Laurent, a noted French critic.

Other reviewers were no less moved, and the two artists found their partnership acclaimed by an audience known for its hypercritical reactions. Still, there were some critics who, having heard that Bruhn was highly instrumental in refining Nureyev's own technique, had referred to Bruhn as Nureyev's teacher.

"I found myself reading reviews which claimed that Erik Bruhn, Nureyev's teacher, was dancing for the first time at the Paris Opéra. Well, what was a teacher doing dancing *Giselle*? As it turned out, Rudik came to Paris to see us. He was not present at the first performance but was there for the second one.

"For some reason, Rudik seemed somewhat down. He avoided the press and said that he didn't want to see anyone except me. When we were together he seemed more relaxed and we had a good time. One night we decided to go to Maxim's. It was just the two of us. Of course, the minute we entered, everybody knew who he was and nobody knew who I was. Anyway, we ordered some Russian caviar and they brought in this huge bowl and put it in front of us. We were hungry and ate the whole thing. You can imagine what the bill came to! We could barely scrape up the cash between us to pay for it. At any rate, during that dinner at Maxim's, Rudik was very quiet about my *Giselle*. It seemed strange that he shouldn't make some comment about it. Finally, as we talked, Rudik told me that he and Margot had been asked to dance *Giselle* in Australia, but that he wasn't sure whether he would accept the engagement. Then he said: 'After seeing you do it here in Paris, I don't think I can dance *Giselle* anymore.' So, it must have affected him quite a lot, and perhaps that's why he didn't bring it up sooner. I told him that he must accept his Australian engagement and that if he felt like it, he should rethink and rework his interpretation of the role, and I believe that's what he did."

In May 1964 Bruhn participated once again in the Royal Danish Ballet's Festival season, dancing Don José in Petit's *Carmen* and creating a leading role in Frank Schaufuss's *Garden Party*, during which the young Peter Martins made his unexpected debut. Then, true to his word, Bruhn returned to the Paris Opéra that June and danced with Claude Bessy in Skibine's *Daphnis and Chloë* and the *Don Quixote* pas de deux. He had also arranged to repeat his *Giselle* with Chauviré at the Festival in Nervi, Italy—but his pains had returned, and the Nervi engagement was canceled.

Bruhn's peripatetic schedule next led him to New York, where he had been invited by Rebekah Harkness to appear as guest artist in her newly formed company, the Harkness Ballet. It was a company of high intention but poor management. A wealthy patron of the arts, Rebekah Harkness had sponsored various dance tours abroad and it was now her wish to form a company of her own.

To that effect, Mrs. Harkness engaged George Skibine as artistic director and hired a number of first-rate dancers, including Marjorie Tallchief (Maria's sister), Lawrence Rhodes, Helgi Tomasson, Richard Wagner, Brunilda Ruiz, and Lone Isaksen. She asked choreographers such as Brian Macdonald, Alvin Ailey, Donald Saddler, Stuart Hodes, and Michael Smuin, among others, to create new works for the company. As ballet masters, she engaged Vera Volkova, Alexandra Danilova, and Leon Fokine. Composers writing specifically for the company included Carlos Surinach and Vittorio Rieti. This impressive roster of artists was joined by Erik Bruhn, who came to Mrs. Harkness's estate at Watch Hill, Rhode Island, to begin rehearsals with the company.

"When I arrived at Watch Hill, I was in very poor shape," remembers

Bruhn. "I had had a terrific bout of stomach pains after my Paris appearances, and had thought I would really have to give up dancing once and for all. But Mrs. Harkness was very nice—she was always nice to her dancers—and somehow I managed to pull myself together. I was to dance with the company's prima ballerina, Marjorie Tallchief, who had been a ballerina with the de Cuevas Ballet, the Paris Opéra Ballet, and had also appeared with great success with the Bolshoi Ballet. Unfortunately, I did not establish the kind of dancing rapport I had with her sister, Maria. Still, she was a very fine dancer."

That August 1964 Bruhn worked productively and happily. The stomach pains had temporarily left him and the beautiful seaside landscape was conducive to his sense of well-being. During that period he began choreographing a new work on the company entitled *Scottish Fantasy*. At the same time, Stuart Hodes began to create his brilliant and disturbing ballet *The Abyss*, in which Bruhn would dance a leading role. He also rehearsed a series of Bournonville works staged by Vera Volkova under the title *Bournonville Suite*.

As the Harkness Ballet would not make its official debut in Cannes until February 1965, Bruhn had several months to himself. In October 1964 he received an invitation to dance with the Royal Swedish Ballet in Stockholm, a city he had not visited since the Royal Danish Ballet had performed there in 1951. Bruhn had had no contact with the company and did not know what to expect when the invitation came to him. It was Goeren Gentele, director of the Royal Swedish Opera House, who extended the invitation to Bruhn and it included a request that in addition to dancing with the company, he would also do some teaching.

"The arrangement was that I would spend six weeks in Stockholm," says Bruhn. "I only remembered one ballerina with whom I felt I could dance there, and that was Gerd Andersson. Other than that, I knew nothing of the company. Well, when I got there I was appalled. I was to dance *Giselle* but when I got to Stockholm I found out that Gerd Andersson was pregnant and they suggested another dancer, whom I did not consider suitable. Finally, I insisted they bring Kirsten Simone from Denmark. We began to rehearse and I immediately saw that the company just didn't know what it was doing. I stopped all rehearsals, went to Gentele, and told him I would have to cancel my engagement because I would look ridiculous dancing with amateurs. He cajoled me out of it by telling me that he himself would rehearse the company. I had the feeling that Brian Macdonald, who had just arrived as artistic director of the ballet company that year, was not very happy in Sweden, and therefore was not yet leading the company in any positive direction—and it also looked as if he wanted to give his own ballets priority. In other words, the classics had been totally neglected. Kirsten Simone and I finally did dance *Giselle,* and I also began to teach at the school, but I knew that the Swedish ballet was in big trouble."

After his stay in Stockholm Erik Bruhn undertook a project which he had been looking forward to for some time. The National Ballet of Canada, under the direction of Celia Franca, was anxious to mount a production of *La Sylphide,* and Franca, long one of Bruhn's champions (the two had met and danced together with the Metropolitan Ballet in England in 1947), felt that the obvious person to do this was Erik Bruhn.

When this attractive invitation came his way Bruhn had, in fact, been in New York staying with his friend Christopher Allan. Franca telephoned Bruhn and she told him that her company was very poor, that they couldn't afford to pay him much, but that they were extremely anxious to have the best possible *Sylphide.*

"I was a bit taken aback," says Bruhn, "because producing a ballet like *Sylphide* scared the wits out of me. Could I do it? Could I be fair to Bournonville and his tradition? Finally, I thought, Why not? I accepted and, as it turned out, I enjoyed the experience tremendously. I went to Toronto and was faced by a company that had no notion of what Bournonville was all about. But I managed to work with the dancers and while they looked nothing like the Danes—how could they?—they somehow responded to my direction and to my ability to demonstrate the style without stifling them. It was a happy time for me and I thought that the company, under Celia's direction, was really first-rate. Anyway, I mounted *La Sylphide* and danced James with Lynn Seymour—who came in as a guest artist from London's Royal Ballet—and she was wonderful. Rudik also flew in from London to watch rehearsals and I could tell that just by watching us he was learning the ballet in his mind."

La Sylphide was Erik Bruhn's first major staging of an important classic. Although he had mounted several Bournonville excerpts, notably for the

London Royal Ballet Gala in 1962, he had never before produced a Bournonville work in its entirety. The production opened on December 31 and Fraser Macdonald, writing in *Dance News* of February 1965, called the staging and Erik Bruhn's performance an unqualified triumph.

At the O'Keefe Center in Toronto, Bruhn danced the opening performance with Lynn Seymour as the Sylph and Celia Franca as Madge the Witch, and was also scheduled to appear on the next evening, January 1. During this second performance, he injured his knee but, despite great physical pain, he managed to finish the ballet. When the curtain fell, he was rushed to a physician and was told he could not dance for several days. The following night the role of James was danced by Earl Kraul and on January 5, Rudolf Nureyev, on only two days' notice, made his unexpected debut as James in *La Sylphide*.

"It was the most beautiful James that I have ever seen him do," recalls Bruhn. "He was simply brilliant." Indeed, Nureyev's critical reception was sensational.

On the following evening, January 6, Erik Bruhn was well enough to resume dancing and this performance, danced with the fine Canadian ballerina Lois Smith, proved an even greater triumph than the previous ones. Some have suggested that in the wake of Nureyev's extraordinary success on the previous night, Bruhn may have wanted to show his superiority in the role. Be that as it may, this particular performance received twenty-five curtain calls. There was no question that at thirty-six, Bruhn was as impeccable as ever and still at the very height of his powers. The critics continued to marvel at his genius.

When Bruhn appeared with the company in Montreal on January 26, the *Montreal Star*'s Sydney Johnson wrote: "It was no surprise to find Mr. Bruhn's technique simply electrifying, but the memory one carries away is not so much what he does but the poise, authority and assurance with which he does it. Every step and every gesture seems to be an essential part of the character's performance and Mr. Bruhn finishes even the most complicated step so neatly and effortlessly that for the second or two between *enchainements* one is more conscious of James the Scot than Bruhn the virtuoso."

When he undertook the staging of *La Sylphide*, Erik Bruhn could think carefully about the work's dramatic content. His analysis and interpretation of it became the standard for subsequent productions.

❲ CHAPTER 20 ❳

I T WAS NOW time for Erik Bruhn to rejoin the Harkness Ballet in their
debut performance in Cannes on France's Côte d'Azur. The company's
reception could not be called enthusiastic. Writing in the New York
Herald Tribune of February 22, 1965, Peter Brinson wrote: "In the casino
at Cannes, last night, a new American ballet company was born to Mrs.
Rebekah Harkness and her Rebekah Harkness Foundation. The infant,
smaller and frailer than a difficult labor had led one to expect, will need
careful nursing before long life will seem assured. At the moment it is
doing only moderately well."

For the occasion, Erik Bruhn presented his *Scottish Fantasy* and appeared in Stuart Hodes's *The Abyss*. He traveled with the Harkness for
three months and considered the experience enjoyable, though not memorable: "They needed a name that was known in Europe and that's why I
went along. Actually I had a very good time, because Mrs. Harkness saw to
it that her dancers were well looked after. She gave marvelous parties and
there were many laughs."

Following this tour Bruhn once more danced in Copenhagen for the
Sixteenth Annual Royal Ballet and Music Festival. This time the dancer
received a very special award: he was elected by the Students' Association
of Denmark to join its roll of honor. This highly prestigious association is
composed of deans and professors of Danish universities. A testimonial
banquet was given for Erik Bruhn and a laurel wreath was placed upon his

brow—the very first time that a male dancer had been so honored. Following the festival, Bruhn was to have appeared in Germany, but a station wagon ran over his foot and the engagement had to be canceled. By August he was able to fulfill an engagement with the Australian Ballet at the Baalbek Festival in Lebanon.

He then returned to the Royal Danish Ballet and began rehearsing for the company's third tour to the United States. He would dance *Miss Julie*, *Carmen*, the *Don Quixote* pas de deux, and *La Sylphide*, all with Kirsten Simone. It was during this tour with the Danes that Bruhn experienced what could be called something of a career crisis. It came in the form of a deep self-questioning.

He told one reporter: "I've reached a critical time in my life. It's been a lonely tour this time. If you know something and you have difficulty making others understand, it makes for loneliness. I find it difficult to be with the Royal Danish Ballet for long periods of time. We Danes have lapsed into complacency, because of our great sense of the past. I understand it, because I'm Danish. But they don't understand me. I thrive on differences, on complication. America gave me that. You can't go back. And I've run out of companies. After this tour I've nowhere to go. I just don't know what I will do. You're hungry, you're greedy for something, you don't know what, you just go and look for it."

When the Danes wound up their tour at the New York State Theater, its critical reception was divided. Most of the critics continued to extol the company's great Bournonville tradition and praised its excellent dancer. Bruhn, now thirty-seven, received glorious notices despite his inner feelings. But there was a minority report on the company's emphasis on its past.

"Something is rotten in the state of Denmark's ballet," said *Newsweek*. "The Royal Danish Ballet have become dancing curators of a museum of the Danish dance that dates back to 1748, and which is dominated by the nineteenth-century works of August Bournonville. But the Danes, by revering his every step, have turned it into a gravestone."

The Danes themselves may have come to realize their need for putting some new life into their company. They would not abandon their Bournonville tradition but would expand their repertoire to include more modern works. Its director, Niels Bjørn Larsen, had announced his retirement that year and it was rumored that Erik Bruhn was offered his post. If so,

Bruhn must have declined, because the future of the company was placed in the hands of Flemming Flindt, one of the Royal Danish Ballet's most distinguished young dancers and choreographers.

By the end of its American tour at the end of 1965, Flemming Flindt assumed his post. He said: "Ballet is a youthful concern. We have an enormous responsibility to the past. But I know that we must not be tied down to it. I am already looking for new choreographers. We must have our own time."

After having completed his guest appearances with the Danes, Erik Bruhn had no future plans. Then, during the early part of 1966, he received an invitation from the Rome Opera House to spend three months with its ballet company, staging new works, dancing, and teaching. Bruhn had no previous experience with Rome and knew little of the company. Nevertheless, he resolved to accept the invitation and proceeded to stage three works—La Sylphide, Swan Lake (Act Two), and a new pas de deux of his own creation, Romeo and Juliet, to the Prokofiev score, which he premiered with Carla Fracci.

"It was an unbelievably strenuous time for me," remembers Bruhn. "There were moments when I threatened to leave because the Rome Ballet was in such poor shape. I danced and I shouldn't have. I taught and it was like pulling teeth. The experience left me completely drained and I couldn't wait to leave. When it was over, I had five or six weeks off and left to take a holiday in Cannes. I was there for two or three days, when suddenly I got violently ill. That same awful stomach problem returned. I stayed in bed for two weeks, and the doctors took all sorts of tests but could find absolutely nothing wrong. When I felt better, I returned to Copenhagen and consulted with more doctors. They all claimed that the pains were a result of too much work. They said that the reason I became ill in Cannes was that all the hard work I did in Rome had stuck in my bones and when I finally relaxed in Cannes, the strain just burst out. In other words, I had been bottling up too much tension."

To live with the sudden onslaught of pain would be Erik Bruhn's lot for several years to come. His friends were naturally concerned, and Bruhn himself was plunged into many periods of depression, for no doctor could diagnose the pains when they came. This inexplicable phenomenon preyed on his mind and when the pains became unbearable he would shut himself up in his room and allow no one near him. Often he contemplated retiring from the dance forever; after all, everyone he had consulted had blamed his pains on physical strain. Perhaps it *was* the dancing that caused it all, and yet, in the act of dancing, no pain was present. Then, surely, it must all be in his mind! He must be suffering from some sort of psychosomatic illness. Were he to enter analysis, the problem might disappear. Far in the back of his mind, however, Bruhn was certain that his stomach pains were the result of some physical malfunction. But what was it? No one could tell him. Bruhn now lived for those periods that did not find him in agony. Since the pains were so unpredictable, the solution was to continue working, and hope for the best.

With his successful staging of *La Sylphide* for the National Ballet of Canada, the company now asked him to mount a brand-new *Swan Lake*. Bruhn was intrigued. He had liked working for the Canadians, and Celia Franca, the company's director, was a good friend. He had enjoyed living and working in Toronto and felt that the atmosphere would be conducive to productivity. Again, all these factors might reduce the possibility of a recurrence of pain. Bruhn thus traveled to Canada and embarked on a production that would prove highly controversial.

As it happened, Rudolf Nureyev had staged his own version of *Swan Lake* in 1964 for the Vienna Staatsoper Ballet. At that time, Bruhn and Nureyev had discussed *Swan Lake* in detail. In fact, according to Bruhn, Nureyev asked him to collaborate on his production. The two dancers ultimately did not see eye to eye on the work's interpretation. Still, Bruhn had gone to Vienna to watch Nureyev work. Bruhn liked many of Nureyev's musical choices, including Tchaikovsky's original Black Swan music, which he would later adopt for his own version.

"Rudik claims to this day that everything I used in *my Swan Lake* I stole from his production," says Bruhn. "Well, that simply isn't true. There are certain similarities here and there, but my choreography is quite different. It's true that Rudik chose a beautiful piece of music to indicate the character of the Prince in the first act, which is a slow solo variation. Yes, I did that too, but again my choreography is very different. The fact is, I took my version a bit further than Rudik did.

"I think the most unorthodox change I made was of turning the role of Von Rothbart, usually portrayed by a man, into a woman—and I called her the Black Queen. I wanted to equate the Prince's relationship to Von Rothbart with that of his mother, the Queen. Well, everybody, including

Rudik, got very upset over this major alteration, because the whole ballet was now seen on Freudian terms. I didn't think there was anything wrong with that. I did not change the relationship of the Prince and the Swan Queen. I only made the public a bit more aware of the Prince's psychological character. In a way, the critics had something new to chew on, because whenever *Swan Lake* is performed, Von Rothbart is usually not mentioned. Suddenly, with that character having been turned into a woman, *everybody* had something new to write about."

The premiere of Erik Bruhn's *Swan Lake* took place on March 27, 1967, at the O'Keefe Center in Toronto. Lois Smith danced the Swan Queen and Earl Kraul was Prince Siegfried (whom Bruhn merely identifies as the Prince). Subsequent performances were danced by the young Martine van Hamel, who had won a first prize at the Varna International Ballet Competition in 1966. Her partner was Hazaros Surmejan. There was no question, however, that when Bruhn himself danced the Prince with guest artist Anna Laerkesen, the production assumed the depth Bruhn had envisioned.

Predictably, the production's critical reception found various critics at odds with Bruhn's conception of *Swan Lake*. Ralph Hicklin, writing in the May 1967 *Dance Magazine*, stated: "This *Swan Lake* has the major advantage that it puts blood into the veins of the Prince, who becomes, as character and dancer, something more than the cardboard *porteur* and supporter that one is accustomed to. What could be more predictable when the choreographer is one of the great virtuosi of his day? . . . Von Rothbart has given way to a character known as the Black Queen (mimed with malevolence by Celia Franca). This change in sexual balance inevitably alters the shape of the Swan legend. . . . All is not well yet with *Swan Lake*. The narrative needs some clarification, particularly in the last act; for the Black Queen is still something of a cipher. In all its essentials, however, Bruhn's *Swan Lake* is fine dance, fine drama, and in his artistic collaborator, Desmond Heeley, Bruhn has been extremely fortunate: I have never seen a Swan Lake set and costumed with so much feeling for atmosphere, for gothic romanticism, and for the exigencies of dancers' bodies."

Bruhn himself contends that he was inspired to conceive his version of *Swan Lake* after seeing a Paris production during the mid-1950s done by the Soviet choreographer Vladimir Bourmeister for the Stanislavsky Ballet. Bruhn claims that it was the first time he had seen the Prince as more than just a partner, and it was then that he resolved to create a Prince that was

actively involved in the story from beginning to end. He does admit, however, that he never quite developed or justified the character of the Black
Queen: "I might like to develop the role further in the future, but I will
not change it back into a male role."

Bruhn's *Swan Lake* proved a great financial success for the Canadians.
When it opened at the O'Keefe Center, the box-office returns came to
$93,400—a record for the National Ballet. The work remains in the com-
pany's repertoire to this day.

When, in 1963, Erik Bruhn partnered Carla Fracci in their first *Giselle*
at La Scala, Milan, it became clear to him that in Fracci he had found a
ballerina of exceptional brilliance and beauty. Not since his appearance
with Markova in 1955 had Bruhn experienced such an affinity with a
dancer—such ease and freedom. While Yvette Chauviré's Giselle had
enormous warmth and true distinction, it lacked the youthful trembling
and caressing sensitivity that Fracci gave the role. Following their performance together in Milan, Bruhn kept Fracci in mind for future appearances,
and when in 1967 he resolved to return as guest artist with American Ballet Theatre, he chose to make Fracci his principal partner.

"Lucia Chase had been after me for several years to rejoin ABT,"
Bruhn says. "Finally, I gave in on the condition that she engage Carla as
my new partner, and it was during this period that our partnership really
blossomed."

Thus, during the early summer of 1967, American Ballet Theatre offered a pairing that would indeed go down in the annals of ballet history:
Bruhn and Fracci appeared in *La Sylphide* and *Giselle* and the critics were
enchanted.

Clive Barnes, writing in *The New York Times* of May 22, 1967, stated:
"Miss Fracci, as the Sylphide who prettily lures a young Scotsman to leave
his fiancée and fly with her to the woods, was like a romantic lithograph
come to life. Her curled arms, smiling face and delicate feet, were all the
very picture of Victorian grace, and she seemed as fragile as a leaf, as in-
tangible as the air. Mr. Bruhn is the man chased by the furies, hunted by
destiny. From beginning to end, he is a man of tragedy, a man whose
tight-drawn face suggests a past, and whose eyes seem haunted with a fearful intuition of the future. His dancing was magisterial—there is no dancer
alive with more style, more grandeur and more passion."

When Bruhn and Fracci appeared in *Giselle*, Patricia Barnes, writing in

London's *Dance and Dancers* of August 1967, called Fracci a born Giselle: "She was tender and vulnerable in the first act, ethereal and ghostly in the second. Her *bourées* skim across the ground with a fleetness and delicacy I have rarely seen equaled, and she dances with a tender intensity as if every moment she is pouring her strength into the now exhausted Albrecht, willing him to live. Bruhn's taut and tortured Albrecht perfectly complimented Fracci's trusting and sweet Giselle . . . he appears to work on a role all the time so that it gains in stature at each successive performance."

Bruhn's partnership with Carla Fracci would last, on and off, for five years and the two would create as similar an impact as had Nureyev and Fonteyn.

It is interesting to note that Erik Bruhn has never danced with Margot Fonteyn, a fact that has astonished the ballet world, for these two artists would surely have created their own particular magic. Speaking about this curious happentance, Bruhn stated that in 1963 an opportunity arose for Fonteyn, Nureyev, Fracci, and Bruhn, and six other dancers to undertake a special tour. The idea was to offer a repertoire that might find Bruhn dancing with Fonteyn and Nureyev with Fracci. As it turned out, according to Bruhn, Fracci did not seem to fit into the scheme of things and it appeared that Fonteyn was reluctant to include her.

Because Bruhn had wanted Fracci, he backed out of the venture. "Margot never said anything bad about Carla, but I think there was room for only one ballerina on this tour. Anyway, this might have been my chance to dance with Fonteyn, but it was not to be, and perhaps it's just as well. Margot has never been an easy person for me to know. She is so extremely ladylike in every situation, that it makes me feel slightly uncomfortable. But the real fact of the matter is that Rudik adored Margot and they were so wonderful together that I did not want to threaten that relationship in any way. Mind you, Rudik was quite anxious for me to dance with her, because he thought we were absolutely ideal. I found that very flattering, but told him that we were perhaps *too* ideal and that without a sense of contrast the partnership might come off as extremely boring. You see, it was the contrast that caused the spark between Rudik and Margot, and I think that Carla and I had that same spark. I think that Margot and I are too much the purists—our lines are too similar, and, in a way, I have the feeling it wouldn't have worked between us."

Another missed opportunity for Erik Bruhn was a closer association with the British choreographer Antony Tudor, whose works were in the repertoire of American Ballet Theatre. Bruhn seemed to be an ideal Tudor dancer. His great acting ability would have brought authority and a new dimension to the various Tudor roles. But, again, Bruhn felt uncomfortable dancing Tudor. He had appeared as The Lover and later as The Man She Must Marry in the choreographer's *Jardin aux Lilas,* and had also danced in his *Romeo and Juliet* as well as the French partner in *Gala Performance.* It is possible that the two men did not share the "chemistry" needed for a good working relationship. Bruhn claims that Tudor's major output centered on creating great leading roles for women, but that his male characters were never as fully developed. Too, he deemed Tudor a man capable of highly abrasive treatment toward his dancers, and was loath to be subjected to it himself. Still, whenever he worked with Tudor, the choreographer's handling of Bruhn was never less than cordial.

"Tudor and I have never been close," says Bruhn. "But I did enjoy the experience of working with him. What I didn't enjoy was dancing his roles. I loved watching his ballets, but as a performer I did not find them satisfying. I must say, I had one rather wonderful experience with him and that occurred in Toronto. I remember we were staying in the same hotel, and Tudor invited me and a friend to come to dinner, which he said he would cook for us himself.

"It was the strangest thing, because I had really only known him as a vicious man who would attack everybody. He would reduce dancers to tears. On that night, however, I never saw a more beautiful man. He was so open, so sensitive. I got to see that other Tudor—the one that few see. I thought to myself, This must be a very vulnerable man to have to make himself so hard during rehearsals. Perhaps that difficult veneer is a form of protection. Anyway, that evening was a revelation."

Bruhn and Fracci did not always dance together during that 1967 season with American Ballet Theatre. He repeated his role in *Miss Julie* with Veronika Mlakar and danced the *Don Quixote* pas de deux with Lupe Serrano. Fracci danced in Tudor's *Jardin aux Lilas* and *Romeo and Juliet,* among other works, with various other partners. That same season, Bruhn and Fracci were invited to participate in a television program being prepared by NBC, which would be shown on September 22. This was a "Bell Telephone Hour" devoted to *The Many Faces of Romeo and Juliet.* This color program included excerpts from Shakespeare's play, acted by Claire Bloom and Jason Robards, various musical works based on the theme, and operatic arias sung by Anna Moffo and Sandor Konya. Carol Lawrence and Larry Kert repeated their roles from the 1957 musical *West Side Story* and Fracci and Bruhn performed Bruhn's own *Romeo and Juliet* pas de deux.

The early part of 1967 was a happy and productive period for Erik Bruhn. He was less besieged by his still mysterious stomach ailment. He danced better than ever, and his work at American Ballet Theatre not only cemented the Fracci-Bruhn partnership but intensified his relationship with Lucia Chase, who now considered the Danish dancer as the company's most compelling and valuable star.

Henceforth, Bruhn would return to ABT with regularity, as indeed would Carla Fracci. But New York would not claim Bruhn's time exclusively. All too soon, he would have to make a quite serious decision—one that would broaden his scope as an artist, as well as bringing into play all his resources as an administrator. It was a role he had never before attempted—that of artistic director of a large ballet company.

〖 CHAPTER 21 〗

GOEREN GENTELE, the general director of the Royal Swedish Opera House, offered Bruhn the post of artistic director of the Royal Swedish Ballet in 1964, when the dancer had appeared in Stockholm as a guest artist. The invitation was precipitated by Bruhn's dismay with the Swedish dancers, whom he considered to be below the standards of dancers appearing in other major ballet companies. Bruhn had disliked dancing with the company, but in Gentele he had found a sympathetic friend. The two men had discussed the future of the company and during an exchange of ideas Gentele felt that Erik Bruhn would be the perfect person to give the Swedish dancers the discipline and creative impetus he knew they lacked.

It took Bruhn three years to reach a decision. In the meantime, he had returned to Stockholm to dance with the Swedes in 1966 and in the early part of 1967. It was during the latter engagement that he and Gentele resumed their discussions and, shortly thereafter, Bruhn resolved to sign a contract as director of the Royal Swedish Ballet.

The Royal Swedish Ballet flourished under Gustavus III, during the latter part of the eighteenth-century. At the time, its choreographers were Antoine Bournonville, father of August, and Marcadet. Filippo Taglioni became the ballet master in 1818 and his daughter, the famed Maria, appeared as guest artist, as did August Bournonville. The company went into a sharp decline during the second half of the nineteenth century but recovered somewhat when Michel Fokine and his wife, Vera, came to the company in 1913. The Fokines did not remain in Stockholm long enough to make any real impact on the company's artistic evolution and once more the Swedes foundered. Several ballet masters were appointed between 1929 and 1950, at which time Antony Tudor became director. He was succeeded in 1953 by Mary Skeaping, whose central aim was to cultivate the classics. The company's modern repertoire was enlarged through the engagement of such choreographers as Birgit Cullberg, Ivo Cramèr, and Birgit Åkesson. Tudor returned to the company from time to time and other choreographers such as Massine and Balanchine had their works mounted in Stockholm. While the Swedish ballet had every opportunity to flower, it never quite achieved the distinction of its neighbor, the Royal Danish Ballet. Sweden's forte would ultimately be felt in the fields of opera and cinema, while the Danes, through Bournonville, would claim lasting recognition in the field of dance.

In October 1967 Bruhn settled in Stockholm and began to reorganize the company. (Between 1964 and 1966 it had been under the artistic direction of Brian Macdonald.) Gentele called a press conference to announce Bruhn's appointment and when Bruhn was asked by the press what his plans were, he told them that he had none.

Says Bruhn: "I'm afraid I did not endear myself to the Swedish press. I told them that I wasn't at all sure whether I could get the Swedish dancers to dance. I felt that they didn't know *how* to dance. I also told them that the first thing I would do would be to totally reorganize their school."

And it was the school that Bruhn concentrated on first. While working with the National Ballet of Canada, he had befriended Betty Oliphant, once co-director of the Canadian company and at that time director of the Canadian National Ballet School. He found her teaching methods superlative and felt she would be a highly valuable asset to the Swedish school. He invited Oliphant to teach there on a guest basis. It was not an easy task, because Betty Oliphant met with resistance and was considered a threat to the other teachers. Nevertheless, she remained for two months and helped train not only the students but the ballet teachers as well.

"Betty Oliphant produced a miracle," says Bruhn. "At the end of the first year, we had a student performance that made everyone sit up. We also held auditions for the school and hundreds of people showed up, so we had an excellent pick of young hopefuls, which also improved matters.

In other words, before turning to the company itself, I placed all my energies into putting the school in order. I felt that was the most important thing. In the middle of all this, I fell ill again, and it may have been the tension of all that work."

Betty Oliphant recalls this period. "It was very difficult to start with, because I was the one who was going to change the way the school had been set up. Unfortunately Erik was in the hospital at the time and it would have been good to have had him around, if only for moral support. There simply was no organization, but you see, democracy does not work in a ballet company, and I found that the dancers in Sweden were very aggressive. I also felt that Erik was treated quite badly there. The press was particularly venomous."

When Bruhn emerged from the hospital, he concentrated all his energies on working with the company itself. He had thought of mounting a large, full-evening work, in order to have almost every dancer in the company active in one production. To that end, he invited Rudolf Nureyev to come and stage his version of *The Nutcracker*. It would, in fact, be Nureyev's first attempt at reworking this classic. Bruhn recalls that Nureyev worked in something of a panic, because of the large number of people involved and, possibly, because upon his arrival Bruhn himself was out of the city, dancing in Oslo.

"By the time I came back," says Bruhn, "Rudik must have lost his temper once too often, because someone in the company accused him of trying literally to strangle one of the dancers. They had even called in the police! Well, I think that was probably exaggerated, but it is true that Rudik was very rough on the dancers and sometimes unnecessarily so. But Rudik *had* to be rough, because the company was just too lethargic, and somebody had to shake them up. I supported him all the way, and the result was that Rudik's *Nutcracker* proved a huge success."

Bruhn's agreement with Gentele was that he could take time off to dance elsewhere and, during this period, he went to Chicago, where he appeared with Ruth Page's company in performances of her version of *The Nutcracker*. His Sugar Plum Fairy was the Swedish ballerina Gerd Andersson. He also fulfilled a guest engagement in Houston, Texas.

When he returned to take up his duties with the Royal Swedish Ballet he felt the duties were becoming progressively more difficult to execute with any real conviction. "More and more, I felt that Sweden was too much for me. I did not really know if I could solve their problems. I was driving myself very hard, because not only did I have to discipline the dancers but I had to keep myself in shape as well. At any rate, I would tell Goeren Gentele that I was killing myself and that I was getting sick and that I didn't know if I could really change the company. But, somehow, he always persuaded me to go on. You see, he was the most charming man and he had a way of giving me courage. I don't know how I managed, but it ended that I remained director of the Royal Swedish Ballet for over four years!

"Little by little the company got itself on its feet and in the end there was a wonderful spirit. Gentele gave us more performances and, finally, we had a better box office than even the opera. During my third year there I invited Jerome Robbins to come, and he mounted his *Les Noces* on the company and he seemed to be extremely pleased by the way the dancers performed it. In fact, the company gave this work when it visited Paris and Jerry received a gold medal for best choreography and the Swedish ballet received a gold medal as the best foreign company to have appeared in Paris that year. So it seems I did something right. I might add that I also invited José Limón to present his *The Exiles, There Is a Time, Missa Brevis,* and *The Moor's Pavane,* and asked Kenneth MacMillan, Antony Tudor, and Glen Tetley to mount works on the company."

Gerd Andersson, one of the Royal Swedish Ballet's most gifted ballerinas, remembers Erik Bruhn during those years. "As far as I can remember, Erik was loved by everyone with the exception of a few. But you see, people expect so much of a director, and there were times when he was not entirely clear about his position or his intentions. He did not always know what he wanted and that upset and confused us and him. I know for a fact that the dancers all felt that Erik respected them. I think that one of the most important things he accomplished in Sweden was to establish an efficiently run ballet school. Also, he brought many important people to Sweden—marvelous dancers and choreographers—and we should all be grateful to him for that.

"Of course, my greatest joy was dancing with Erik. Unfortunately, while he was director here, he chose not to dance with us very often. But when he had come as a guest artist in previous years, he and I danced the *Flower Festival* pas de deux and *Giselle.* These were among my greatest dancing experiences."

Certainly, the closest friends Bruhn had made in Sweden were Goeren and Marit Gentele. It was Goeren's warmth and encouragement that brought the dancer back to Sweden time and again and Bruhn felt that Gentele's wife, Marit, and their three daughters were like a family to him.

Marit Gentele, an unusually beautiful and intelligent woman, remembers Bruhn's difficulties with the Royal Swedish Ballet. "The moment he tried to change things, people rebelled. Erik had to fight for so much! He had to fight the people who had spent their whole life in the company and who believed in what they were doing. Some of these people had to be replaced and naturally resented him. It takes stamina and steely nerves to hold out for what one wants. Well, in the end, all of the criticism directed at Erik was turned to praise. But before that could happen, there was a great deal of unpleasantness, and the newspapers were absolutely awful to him. Somehow, he could *not* win, and it took him several years before the tide changed. All I know is that whatever was good about the company was a direct result of Erik's hard work and inspiration.

"Goeren and I adored Erik. He was the most delightful guest. We would often bring him out to our house, which was outside Stockholm. He was especially fond of our daughters, Beatrice and Cecilia. We had so much fun together. We would talk and laugh for hours and hours. Of course, I have seen the other side of Erik too—the one that can turn in a second and become extremely hostile and cold. If he feels that anyone comes too close to him or threatens him in any way, he can become violently defensive. Somebody once said to me, 'Do you know what temperament is? It is total calm!' That's how I think of Erik, because he has the ability to control the machinery . . . to look totally calm when inside he might be boiling. You can see that same temperament at work on the stage. At any rate, I can't say that Erik was totally happy in Sweden. He would often get ill and suffer from bad stomach pains. Also, he was not around all that much, because he was dancing a great deal with other companies. But during those four years, we formed a very deep friendship, and that friendship came to mean a great deal to me at a later time."

If Bruhn's stay in Stockholm was marked by personal and professional difficulties, it did not seem to harm the Royal Swedish Ballet. During 1968, for example, Bruhn told Lydia Joel in *Dance Magazine*, "I care very much indeed that my tenure will produce quality." And it was quality that was produced during the Royal Swedish Ballet's first festival, held at the Royal Swedish Opera House during June of that year. Bruhn mounted his production of *La Sylphide* with Gerd Andersson as the Sylph and Nils-Åke Håggbom as James. The company also danced Kenneth MacMillan's *Concerto* with high praise going to Kerstin Lidström, as well as Nureyev's *Nutcracker*. The press was friendly, but questioned Bruhn's absence as a dancer during the festival. His answer was: "I find it very difficult to be both performer and director. As a dancer I am egocentric—as director I am the opposite—aware of everyone else's needs. I do hope to make some appearances here in the future, but not on a regular basis."

And he did perform. He fulfilled engagements with American Ballet Theatre and thus much time was spent in New York and on tour with the American company. Furthermore, he had contracted to write a mongraph for *Dance Perspective* at the invitation of its editor, Selma Jeanne Cohen. This project was to have been a collaboration with Lillian Moore, with whom he had earlier written *Bournonville and Ballet Technique*, published by Dance Horizons in 1961. But Miss Moore died in 1967 and the *Dance Perspectives* monograph, dedicated to her memory, had to be written by Bruhn alone. Entitled *Beyond Technique*, and profusely illustrated by Fred Fehl's superb photographs showing Bruhn in various roles, the publication centered on Bruhn's interpretation of the many ballets in which he had performed throughout the years.

With ABT, he partnered Carla Fracci and, for the first time, a young and highly promising dancer named Cynthia Gregory. Gregory had entered the company in 1965, after having danced for several years with the San Francisco Ballet. She was a tall and regal-looking girl, who at first found it difficult to assimilate herself into a company that had few roles to offer her. Shy, but eager to learn, Gregory would eventually rise to stardom, becoming one of America's greatest ballerinas. She first met Erik Bruhn in 1966, at the time when Harald Lander was a guest choreographer with ABT, mounting his version of *La Sylphide*. He chose Gregory for the role of Effie and Bruhn danced James.

"I was terrified, because I felt not at all suited to the role of Effie," remembers Miss Gregory. "And Lander was difficult to work with. Erik, on the other hand, couldn't have been more helpful. He gave me my first insight into the meaning of pantomime, because Effie is essentially a pantomime role. He would tell me to think of pantomime as if it were a song—as though I were singing rather than acting, and taking breaths and leaving time for the gestures. He was teaching me the way Danish dancers handle pantomime, and it was the clearest possible way of doing it. I will always be grateful to Erik for that important lesson.

"In 1968, I did my first *Miss Julie* with Erik. That was an incredible experience. Lucia Chase did not feel I was right for the role, but Erik insisted. When we danced it, it gave me the chance of a lifetime. And to be partnered by him was absolutely mesmerizing! I mean, when he looked at you he *really* looked at you. And when he grabbed you he *really* grabbed you. And when he threw you he *really* threw you. So, during that first *Miss Julie* I had to be on my guard all the time, because it was all so *real.* Later we danced *La Sylphide* together, and this time I was the Sylph. Carla Fracci could not be there at the time, and again Erik chose me for a performance we did in Chicago. It was really Erik who gave me my big chance at ABT. No one else there thought of me for those roles. Without Erik I would not have moved ahead as quickly as I did, because he built up my confidence and said I inspired him. I took that as an enormous compliment, because he was already such a great dancer and could have danced with anyone. On another tour, Erik and I danced *Coppélia.* Of course, I was very nervous. I remember when we rehearsed together, I kept stepping on his feet or bumping into him, and I would be terribly embarrassed, because I seemed so clumsy. One time, I stepped on his foot rather badly, but dramatically it seemed to work. He said, 'Cynthia, next time don't step on my foot quite so hard, but let's keep it in, because it works.' "

Bruhn remembers with pleasure his work with Cynthia Gregory. He was attracted to her blossoming talent, although he realized that there were areas in her dancing which were still too tentative and that she needed to be given more confidence. "I felt that with work she would bloom. With Cynthia, I was drawn to what her body told me—and what it told me was that she had tremendous potential. But for me, a body is never enough. There has to be a person inside the body and I think I drew out the person. That's why I thought of asking her to dance *Miss Julie* with me. It would make her stop hiding. It would give her courage and confidence. I knew that Cynthia had the possibility of showing great dramatic qualities. At any rate, I'm happy to have been of some help to this beautiful dancer. She has certainly proven herself to be an exceptional artist."

During the time that Bruhn danced with Gregory, he also came into contact again with Harald Lander, who, at the time, was staging various works for the company. It had been many years since Lander brought Bruhn to public notice when he was ballet master of the Royal Danish Ballet, but the shadow of the disturbing "Lander Affair" had always somehow haunted Erik Bruhn. He had, after all, been part of the anti-Lander group in 1951.

Bruhn had always thought of righting his relationship with his early mentor. "Naturally, I was apprehensive about meeting Harald again," recalls Bruhn. "But then, when ABT toured in Holland we met. He had every reason to ignore me, and I was very nervous. Well, he arrived with open arms and a few nights later, we had dinner together. He said, 'One can't go on one's whole life being bitter about the past.' This was a generosity I hadn't expected, because *I* could not have opened out my arms to him. I wanted to, but somehow couldn't. So it all ended well, and we remained friends until his death in 1971. During that particular tour I taught Toni Lander the role of *Miss Julie*, which she danced with Glen Tetley. She was fantastic in it, as was Glen. Later I danced with Toni myself in *Miss Julie* and we had a splendid rapport."

In 1968 Erik Bruhn and Carla Fracci traveled to Spain, where a West German company, Unitel, contracted to film the ABT production of *Giselle*. This would be the third film presentation of the ballet, the first having been a condensed black-and-white version starring Alicia Markova and Anton Dolin. The second, made in England in 1956 by Paul Czinner, was a full-length Bolshoi Ballet version with Galina Ulanova and Nikolai Fadeyechev.

The Bruhn-Fracci *Giselle* would become a lasting contribution to the dance world, for it preserved on film the memory of both dancers at their height. Superbly produced by Joseph Wishy, this David Blair production of *Giselle* included Bruce Marks as Hilarion, Toni Lander as Myrtha, and Eleanor d'Antuono and Ted Kivitt dancing the Peasant pas de deux. The Adolphe Adam score was exceptionally well conducted by John Lanchberry leading the Berlin Opera Orchestra.

The year 1968 was a busy one for Erik Bruhn. Along with his duties at the Royal Swedish Ballet, he paid his annual visit to the Danish Ballet Festival in Copenhagen and also continued to dance for American Ballet Theatre. A notable event that took place at ABT was the world premiere of Enrique Martinez's version of *Coppélia*, which was unveiled by ABT on

December 24, 1968, at the Brooklyn Academy of Music. Bruhn and Carla Fracci as Franz and Swanilda were an immediate success.

In 1969 Bruhn was no less active. In Stockholm, he mounted a new version of *Giselle* which premiered on February 28. With a new orchestration by John Lanchberry and sets and costumes by Desmond Heeley, the production proved a triumph. As was his wont at the Royal Swedish Ballet, Bruhn did not perform in most of his productions and on this occasion the cast was headed by Gerd Andersson as Giselle and Nils-Åke Håggbom as Albrecht. If Bruhn did not dance in Stockholm he would do so in Oslo, as well as in London, where he participated in the Royal Ballet Benevolent Fund Gala at Covent Garden, partnering Fracci in excerpts from Act Two of *La Sylphide*. There were also performances with American Ballet Theatre and, in April 1969, Bruhn and Fracci were honored by that year's prestigious Dance Magazine Award. The third recipient was the American dancer and choreographer Katherine Dunham.

These annual awards, highly nostalgic events, have in recent years been sponsored by the magazine's publisher, Jean Gordon, and its editor-in-chief, William Como. On this particular occasion, April 5, the awards were held at the Colonnade Room of the Essex House in New York City. Bruhn looked particularly handsome in his elegant suit and tie and it seemed incredible that he had turned forty. Looking at Katherine Dunham, he must surely have recalled how at eighteen he had seen this great artist performing in London and must have remembered how inspired he had been by seeing Dunham and her company dance. He would gaze at Carla Fracci and recall his first meeting with her in 1962, when he realized she would be his ideal partner. And he looked at Toni Lander, who had been asked to present the award to him, recalling her as a promising young student when he himself was beginning to make a name for himself at the Royal Danish Ballet School.

Toni Lander came to the podium and made the presentation. "Erik was, from the day he saw daylight, born to dance. He had everything that was required to be a dancer—physique, technique, talent. From the day he took his first step in the ballet school it was obvious to everybody that here was the great hope of Danish ballet. Whatever he did became beauty and perfection. . . . He is always the perfect cavalier to his ballerina and he has that certain way of presenting her onstage so that she looks absolutely gorgeous; and because of this perfection as a partner, he is probably one of the few male dancers who has partnered almost every ballerina. We can surely all say thank you to him for one thing or another in our careers. . . . As the years have passed, Erik has been testing all kinds of styles, adding new forms to his own vocabulary, while bringing so much of himself to other people."

Antony Tudor then made the presentation to Carla Fracci. He said that her dancing evoked in him nostalgia like "bluebells in the rain," and he singled out her concentration, her perfectionism, and the mysterious sense of being possessed which existed in her performances.

Turning forty, which Bruhn had done on October 3, 1968, is a moment of crisis in any dancer's life and particularly in a male dancer's life. Bruhn's remarkable career had made age a matter of scant importance. If he suffered—which he often did—few people knew about it. His technique remained flawless, and his acting ability grew in depth. He continued to astonish everyone by the beauty of his appearance—a face that was only now showing some tiny lines, and a body that still retained its tautness and aristocratic elegance. Bruhn's performances were examples of rare artistry and this artistry was slowly but surely producing a legend.

"I recall turning forty," says Bruhn. "You don't like to think about turning forty, but you know very well that there will be things you can no longer do. When I was thirty-nine I knew that it would be the last time I could take on the challenge of the *Don Quixote* pas de deux. I knew I couldn't make it what I wanted it to be. It is not an easy time. You panic. Whether you talk about it or not, it is with you day and night. It influences your whole being and personality, because at that age dancing becomes harder—not easier. We begin to lose power and when you feel that happening, you become frightened—there's no way you can hold on to it. You can make only so many changes in your performances, but then you have to replace them with something just as valuable—and that's very hard.

"I remember when Rudik turned thirty-nine. He was in a panic. I remember his saying that it would probably be the last time he would dance *Swan Lake*. Of course, he went on, but at a price. I have often spoken with him about his dancing so incessantly. He says that if he didn't dance that much he would lose belief in himself. Every dancer has to make up his own mind on how to face the moment when he must slow down.

"Actually, no one can tell us to stop. If we go on beyond the age when things become more difficult, it doesn't really matter, because even if we lose face our achievements have already been recorded in history. Look at Margot. What could she possibly lose by continuing to dance? She proved herself a long time ago and doesn't need to prove herself anymore. As for Rudik, he can always choreograph or teach—and so can I. At any rate, turning forty was certainly not easy. . . ."

⟦ CHAPTER 22 ⟧

I N EARLY December 1970 the New York press learned that Goeren
Gentele, head of Sweden's Royal Opera House, would become general
manager of the Metropolitan Opera in 1972. The news came as a shock
to the New York opera world. Little was known of Gentele and he was decidedly a dark horse—a veritably unknown figure to replace the extremely
visible Sir Rudolf Bing.

Bruhn was no less surprised, but he was extremely pleased when Gentele told him personally that he would be going to New York and taking
over the Metropolitan. Then and there, Bruhn resolved to leave Sweden
with him. Gentele's formal appointment would not begin until 1972 and
the plan was for him to leave Sweden in 1971, in order to familiarize himself with the Met's operations. Bruhn would call a halt to his own post that
same year. When he made his departure plans known, the Swedish Ballet's
management offered Bruhn the post of "Adviser." The dancer declined,
feeling that without Gentele he could not remain in Stockholm.

Bruhn had, in the meantime, continued dancing and among his various
engagements of 1970 was what he called his "last performance" in Denmark. This occurred on November 6 and the farewell occasion proved
memorable. He performed in La Sylphide with Anna Laerkesen, for which
he received a standing ovation, and the king of Denmark himself sent him
a garland of flowers. It had been twenty-five years since Bruhn had made
his debut as a sixteen-year-old boy at the Tivoli Gardens in 1945, and the
dancer felt that he had more than fulfilled his obligations to the Royal
Danish Ballet.

American Ballet Theatre once more called upon Bruhn for guest appearances with Carla Fracci in *Giselle* and *Coppélia.* Bruhn had also given some thought to restaging *La Sylphide* for the company, a project that would take place during the spring of 1971. The dancer was looking forward to returning to ABT, as he had not danced with the company for two whole seasons because of a neck injury and also because he continued to suffer recurrent stomach pains. Indeed, Bruhn had been in a low state of health and spirits for several long months and had again contemplated retiring from the dance.

One piece of news that reached Bruhn during his period of inactivity was the defection to the West of Natalia Makarova in London in September 1970. The ballerina had been dancing with the Leningrad Kirov Ballet at the Royal Festival Hall when she resolved to seek asylum in England. Makarova would be the second major Kirov dancer to have defected. (Oddly enough, American Ballet Theatre was performing at Covent Garden in London that same season and Bruhn would have been a part of it had he not been injured.) Soon after Makarova's defection, she was invited to make her American debut with ABT, which coincided with Bruhn's own return to the company.

"I was quite excited to learn about Makarova's coming to the West," recalls Bruhn. "She may not remember this, but I first saw her dance during the Varna Competition in 1965. During that year I was vice-president of the competition. We awarded her the gold medal and we knew that she was a fantastic dancer. Anyway, I was delighted to hear that Natasha was joining ABT. But before I knew any of this I was in Copenhagen recovering from my neck injury. When I felt better, I called Lucia Chase to tell her that I would join the company for the seventy–seventy-one season. I also put in a call to Carla in Italy, telling her that I could dance with her—if she was available. She told me that she had made other arrangements and could not, in fact, dance with me in New York until the following ABT season in the spring. I told Lucia that Carla had other engagements and that I would need someone else to dance with. She suggested Natasha Makarova. This would be Natasha's debut in America and it would be her first *Giselle* in this country. Everybody was happy and the press made the announcement that Makarova and I would open the season dancing *Giselle.*

"Almost immediately, I received a telephone call from Carla saying how *could* I do *Giselle* with Natasha! She said *Giselle* was *her* ballet, and only *I* could dance it with her. I told her that she was being absurd, and, besides, she had said she would not be able to come. I could tell that Carla was very upset.

"Natasha and I began to rehearse and two days before the performance I had stomach pains and had to go to the hospital. I did not perform *Giselle* with Natasha for her debut—she danced it with Ivan Nagy. What was so funny was that suddenly Carla appeared on the scene. She had apparently canceled all her European engagements in order to come to New York and dance with me. But I was sick, and she had to dance with Ted Kivitt. When I got out of the hospital, I danced excerpts from *Giselle* with Natasha—the first time I ever danced with her. I remember reading a review of our performance written by Clive Barnes, who said that we had the makings of a very great partnership. I don't think that Carla was too pleased to hear that. Oddly enough, Carla didn't mind my dancing with other ballerinas, but she *did* object to my partnering Natasha. I thought it lacked logic. Carla had been intelligent about everything that we shared together. Clearly, she was jealous."

Carla Fracci remembers this particular season vividly. "I will admit that I was hurt when Erik chose to dance *Giselle* with Natalia Makarova. Of course, Erik needed to dance with Natasha. It was right for him to do so. After all, it was a new experience for him, and it may have been a way for him to refresh it. During that season, after Erik came out of the hospital, he danced two full-length *Giselles* with me. Well, I'll never forget that first performance—it came right after he had danced a full-length *Giselle* with Natasha. When he and I began the ballet, I immediately sensed a certain distance in Erik. This was not the Erik I was used to. Suddenly I felt rebellious and this rebelliousness assailed me with a great force. My feelings were almost brutal. You see, I wanted desperately to recapture that which had always happened between us. I needed Erik to come back to me. I needed to dispel his distance. Well, during the first act I did everything to bring him back and *finally* I did! That evening was absolutely glorious for us both.

"What is so amusing is that when we did our second *Giselle,* it was *I* who felt distant and down. Perhaps it was because I had given so much of myself during our first *Giselle,* so now it was Erik's turn to bring *me* out of it. And he did. There *were* times when we did abandon each other. . . . There were times when Erik made other choices, because, certainly the choices were always up to Erik."

Bruhn elucidates on his need to dance with Natalia Makarova: "Dancing with Carla had reached a point where it seemed as though we were not dancing, but that we were *living* on the stage. There was nothing wrong with that—in fact, it was beautiful. But with Natasha, something new had happened, and it had to do with that Russian schooling of hers. I recognized it immediately, because of Rudik, who had helped me enormously when I needed that total dancer's approach that only the Russians have.

"My European training had maturity and artistry, but I had to go further and I realized that I could only do this with Natasha; I couldn't push the same way with Carla."

In the spring of 1971, Erik Bruhn had staged his version of *La Sylphide* for American Ballet Theatre. Not surprisingly, the work was considered brilliant, as it had when Bruhn staged it for the National Ballet of Canada and the Royal Swedish Ballet. Fracci, who had danced the role before, proved memorable in Bruhn's production, and Natalia Makarova made her debut as the Sylph on July 12, 1971. Bruhn danced James and the two provided balletgoers with a vision of two dancers whose styles differed dramatically, but whose spiritual unity was at all times in evidence.

Makarova remembers this debut with particular joy. "We had many wonderful conversations about *La Sylphide*, and I would say that dancing this ballet, as well as *Giselle*, with Erik was a high point in my career. For me, he was an ideal partner—elegant, refined, emotionally generous. We had a beautiful rapport. There is nothing empty about Erik. Every time we see each other I learn something from him. He has intelligence and sensitivity. Erik would often be around when I would be rehearsing other roles and dancing with other partners. Sometimes he would correct me, and everything he said was just right—precise and full of good taste; but then he is an artist of the first order."

It would seem that with Makarova's arrival, Bruhn was destined to find yet another remarkable partner. They would dance *Giselle, La Sylphide, The River, Coppélia,* and *The Miraculous Mandarin.* But it would be a short-lived partnership. As the season progressed, the dancer felt himself constrained by the onslaught of more stomach pains. He was dancing, and dancing magnificently. As always, the pains would never be present *during* an actual performance, but would assail him before or afterward. This continual struggle with pain caused him to reach a decision he had long been contemplating.

Whether he admitted it to himself or not, Bruhn, at forty-three, felt that despite his ability to deliver immaculate and totally realized interpretations of any role he danced, he would either have to do something about alleviating his pain or retire from the ballet stage. As no doctor had been able to diagnose his ailment, he quite naturally assumed that it was the strain of dancing that brought on his attacks. Were he to stop entirely, they might vanish. Somehow he told himself that if he made a formal announcement of his retirement—if he actually read it in print—and if the ballet world knew that he had irrevocably chosen to stop dancing, then he himself would believe it as well, and with this belief, his illness would disappear.

For the moment, however, he continued to dance with American Ballet Theatre during the 1971 season. The company went on tour and in December played at the Kennedy Center in Washington, D.C. After Washington, the company would be returning to New York and Bruhn was scheduled to make his debut as Colin in *La Fille Mal Gardée.* It was a role he had never danced before—the only major classic Bruhn had not appeared in. He had told Lucia Chase that he would like to dance it with Natalia Makarova as Lise. Carla Fracci was also scheduled to dance Lise and had naturally assumed she would be dancing it with Bruhn.

"I knew that Carla would have trouble understanding my dancing *Fille* with Natasha. I decided not to tell her that I had requested Makarova, but thought of letting Lucia break the news to her. When Carla got the news, she said that she did not mind my doing the opening night with Natasha, but that she expected me to do it with her on the second night. Carla categorically refused to dance it with anyone else. Now these plans all took place in Washington, D.C. Suddenly I felt I had had it. I was in pain and I still had performances to do at Kennedy Center. I did not need these complications with Carla, and one day I called her in to do a barre with me, and gave her a piece of my mind. I told her that I was having a difficult time and that she was making things even more difficult for me. I didn't need that kind of pressure. Carla bust into tears and told me I had misunderstood everything; I said that I had misunderstood nothing. It was a very trying time in our relationship, although I don't think it was a threat to it. I didn't really blame Carla, but it just seemed that no one was making my life any easier."

During that week at the Kennedy Center, Erik Bruhn called Lucia Chase on the telephone and told her that he had decided to retire. He explained to her that he could not go on, that his pains were too severe for him to continue dancing. He said that he would complete his performances at the Kennedy Center, but that he would have to cancel his New York appearances. He would not dance in *La Fille Mal Gardée*, but would fly directly to Toronto from Washington, where he had committed himself to dance a number of performances with the National Ballet of Canada, and go on a European tour with it.

"I told Lucia that I would do my damndest to get through the season with the Canadians and that I prayed I would make it to Paris with them and finish for good. Lucia was very upset and said that I could not possibly end my dancing career with any other company except her own. She insisted that my farewell performance had to be with ABT. I told her that I understood, but that I had signed a contract and that I would have to live up to it. What I didn't tell Lucia was that I had also signed a contract to appear with Fracci in Rome. So it was left like that, and the more I thought about the problems I was encountering with Lucia and Carla, and my commitments, the more depressed I got. No one seemed to care how I was feeling. Of course, we are all egomaniacs and we are all out only for ourselves, especially when we've reached the top. Even in a crisis there is little left over for other people's feelings. Well, I needed some support at this time—not just some, but lots of it. And I didn't get it. It was at this moment that I decided once and for all to get out of this horrible business—at least that is how I felt."

Bruhn concluded his performances at the Kennedy Center. He danced *Coppélia* and *La Sylphide*. Just after his performance of *La Sylphide*, partnering Carla Fracci, on December 29, 1971, he returned to his hotel room and spent the night in agonizing pain. The following morning Carla Fracci went to see him at his hotel to find out how he was feeling.

Fracci remembers their meeting: "I knew, of course, that Erik had threatened to retire on several occasions. I knew that he had been in terrible pain, but what was so amazing was that his performances in Washington were absolutely extraordinary. In *Coppélia* he was simply unbelievable and when we danced *La Sylphide*, he was again miraculous. I remember his telling me after our *Coppélia* that he was feeling so badly that he dreaded going on in *La Sylphide*. But he danced it and his James was perfection.

"That performance on December 29 was fantastic, but I could tell that he felt horrible when it was over. When I went to see him in his hotel room he said, 'Carla, that was my last performance.'

"Of course, I didn't at first believe him. I mean, we dancers are always in pain. A day doesn't pass that we don't suffer with *something*—either it's a foot or a leg, or the neck or the back. But just by looking at him I realized that he really meant it. He said that he simply could not go on dancing, because his pain was too debilitating. It seemed to be a pain of such intensity that there was no arguing about it. Mind you, none of us ever really knew what was wrong with him. All we knew was that there was something wrong with his stomach, and many of us believed that his suffering was purely psychosomatic—that it was all in his mind. When I finally understood that Erik was serious about giving it all up, I went into a state of shock. At that moment I felt that I too would have to stop dancing. Even though I did not dance with Erik exclusively, he had, after all, been my most important partner. And the person who helped me most in furthering my career. I would go back to Italy or wherever, and dance with other partners, but always in the back of my mind was the knowledge that Erik and I would be dancing together at one point or another. Now this would no longer be the case. So, with this terrible news, I wondered what would become of me. How would I continue? Was it all worth it without Erik? Of course, I had to come to terms with this terrible news, because life goes on. Even when we lose a loved one we somehow manage to continue living and, in my case, dancing."

With the conclusion of that Kennedy Center performance of *La Sylphide* with Carla Fracci, Erik Bruhn resolved to cancel *all* of his future engagements. Following his appearances in Washington he returned to New York, where, as usual, he stayed with his friend Christopher Allan. He instructed Allan to draft a formal letter announcing his official retirement. This letter would be sent to Lucia Chase of American Ballet Theatre and to the directors of the Opera House in Copenhagen, the Opera House in Stockholm, the Opera House in Rome, the Berlin Opera, and the National Ballet of Canada in Toronto. The same letter would go to his lawyer, Esther Tonsgaard in Copenhagen, to Carla Fracci, Natalia Makarova, Cynthia Gregory, and to the critics Clive Barnes, Walter Terry, Svend

Kragh-Jacobsen, Mary Clarke of *Dancing Times,* and Peter Williams of *Dance and Dancers* in London.

The letter, signed by Christopher Allan, read as follows:

> Erik Bruhn has asked me to write to you that it is with the deepest regret that he has to announce his retirement. Due to physical illness he must cancel all his engagements. Already a year ago he was advised by his doctors to reduce his activities as a dancer, but saw no possible way of saving himself. As a result, he is now in a situation in which he could damage himself more severely by continuing to dance and with no hope of maintaining the level of performance he demands of himself. As it will be announced officially shortly, he wanted you to have the news before it reached you through other sources. At a later date when he has recovered sufficiently he intends to write you personally to express his profound regrets.

In this letter addressed to Clive Barnes at *The New York Times,* dated January 6, 1972, Christopher Allan added:

> As you know, Erik has three or four times after severe illness brought himself back into peak form. God knows the kind of dedication and determination this must take! His last three performances in Washington even astounded the whole company of American Ballet Theatre and made the return of his illness all the more perplexing. It is probably due to the fact that he demands so much of himself and will never settle for any performance in which he has not tried to better all previous ones. . . .
>
> This has certainly not been an easy decision for Erik. . . . Erik asked I specifically write you because of his personal feelings of warmth for you. He said that if you should choose to print this announcement that is perfectly all right with him as of Saturday, January 8. By that time his letter to all of the various directors in Europe will have been received. He also feels that it is only fair to other dancers that this announcement be made official. Erik is very pleased that Niels Kehlet will be dancing in his place for a number of the performances in the New York season.

When Lucia Chase received Bruhn's official letter of resignation, she was deeply upset and understandably moved. Her association with Bruhn had spanned more than twenty years and, whatever the tribulations, they were far outweighed by the many years of friendship and artistic collaboration. Bruhn had always considered American Ballet Theatre the company which had nurtured and expanded the scope of his dancing career. With ABT he came into international prominence and Lucia Chase considered him an unparalleled artist and a loyal friend.

On January 6, 1972, she responded to his hand-delivered letter and to the personal telephone call she had received from Christopher Allan:

Dearest Wonderful Erik,

Chris has called me with the heartbreaking news and I have read and reread his letter with tears rolling. I can't bear the thought of not seeing you dance again. Every performance I have seen was a gem and in the last two *La Sylphides* in Washington you were at the peak of your incredible form. I was ecstatic and shall never forget them.

But the important thing now is your health—I have been terribly worried about you this past week and would not for the world have you take any further chances. Now you must just get WELL, so that you can enjoy life and things will open ahead for you I know. . . .

All my love and blessings, dearest Erik.

Devotedly,

Lucia

On the following Saturday, January 8, American Ballet Theatre would be opening its New York season at the City Center with a performance of *Coppélia.* This performance was to have been danced by Erik Bruhn and Carla Fracci, but with the announcement of Bruhn's retirement, the role of Franz went to the Danish dancer Niels Kehlet. Lucia Chase persuaded Erik Bruhn to accompany her to the opening. It would be the first time that the public would see the great dancer following the momentous announcement of his retirement.

It was a sold-out house and Bruhn was shaky. He had been in bed all day, but somehow he managed to get dressed and ready for the occasion. When Lucia Chase called for him in her car, he asked that they enter the theater after the lights were dimmed. He did not wish to make an obtrusive entrance. Prior to his going to the theater, he had called Niels Kehlet to wish him the best for his performance. Bruhn felt that the dancer, knowing he was in the audience, would be nervous, and he was aware that this particular occasion might be an emotional one.

Chase and Bruhn entered the City Center theater just as the lights went down. As they made their way down the aisle, Patricia Barnes spotted Bruhn and stood up to embrace him. The audience was undoubtedly on the lookout for Bruhn, wondering whether he would be coming to the performance, and at the sight of him, they rose in a body. The lights had to be turned up again and Bruhn was given a thundering ovation—a vociferous outpouring of love and affection. They realized they would never see him dance again, and this reality suddenly struck home. There were tears in many people's eyes and Erik Bruhn was overwhelmed.

"If Lucia hadn't been there I know I would have fainted," says Bruhn. "The ovation just got to me and I was practically destroyed. Finally everyone sat down and the performance began. I realized it must have been a difficult moment for Carla to come out and dance *Coppélia*, knowing that I would never dance it with her again. In fact, when she made her entrance, I could see tears in her eyes, because she knew I was sitting there. Well, Niels Kehlet, knowing the circumstances of his appearance, somehow danced better than I had ever seen him dance before. He won the house completely. For me, it was an incredible experience and I don't know how I survived that night."

〖 CHAPTER 23 〗

WITH BRUHN'S retirement from the dance in 1971, he felt an enormous sense of relief. It had been a magnificent career; he had achieved what no other Western male dancer had ever accomplished. Respected by his peers and adored by an international public, he savored the satisfaction of having retired at the peak of his career. If he had any regrets he did not voice them. Indeed, for the first time in his life, he felt a contentment such as he had never before experienced. The only shadow facing him was his illness. Now that it was official, now that he would never dance again, would the pains finally leave him?

In New York he had told Christopher Allan that he wished to do away with all signs of his dancing career. There were costumes he had collected that he would donate to the Dance Collection of the Library for the Performing Arts at Lincoln Center. Bruhn recalls how Allan asked for the costumes he had worn in *La Sylphide* and *Giselle*. The dancer was happy to give Allan these souvenirs on the condition that they never be shown to him again. Everything else—his makeup and other stage paraphernalia— was disposed of. Bruhn wanted to be free of anything that would remind him of the dance and of his pains.

"When I got rid of those things in Chris Allan's apartment, I felt even freer. I remained in New York for some weeks, and then decided simply to travel—to go to Europe and to be completely on my own. I thought I would write. I had always wanted to do this, but had never quite found the time. Now I might be able to be more serious about it."

And Bruhn did just that. He was happy and traveled around Europe, wrote a number of short stories, and it was good to be on his own. He didn't think of ballet; he didn't think of performances; he didn't think of his career—all that was now behind him. It wasn't that he would have nothing more to do with the dance. In fact, at some future date, he would perhaps want to teach and even stage some new productions.

"So, there I was, traveling alone, when out of the blue the pains returned. They had caught up with me; only this time there was no one around. I had no sympathy, no consolation. I had not won my battle with pain after all. And everyone had been wrong, because people thought that once I stopped, that would be the end of the pains. It just undid me. I didn't know *what* to do."

Bruhn was plunged into a deep depression and with the weight of the knowledge that the pains might hound him for the rest of his life, he returned to Copenhagen. Once home, many offers to stage ballet performances came his way. Although Bruhn was determined never to dance again, he felt that with the return of his pains, to work again was the only solution. The offer nearest at hand was one that came to him from the Royal Danish Ballet, which asked him to set a new staging of Fokine's *Les Sylphides*. Not wishing to undertake the entire version of this restaging alone, Bruhn enlisted the help of a young dancer whom he had met in America while with ABT. This was Kevin Haigen, a promising seventeen-year-old member of the corps de ballet, whom Bruhn felt to be a gifted young man and whose interest in the classics and quick intelligence appealed to him.

Bruhn and Haigen embarked on their work and Bruhn was entirely pleased with Haigen's enthusiastic and sensitive approach to the ballet. At one point during rehearsals, Bruhn decided once more to consult with his doctors in Copenhagen. This time they placed Bruhn in the hospital for more thorough observation.

"I remained in the hospital for five days," Bruhn recalls, "and, again, was given a clean bill of health by the doctors. They found nothing wrong—except, of course, that I still had the pains. The doctors prescribed Valium and told me it would ease my tension. One night I found myself alone in my house in Gentofte and decided to pour myself a scotch. When I began to drink it, I wasn't sure whether I had taken a Valium or not. I thought I hadn't, so I took one. Then, I had another scotch and the next thing I knew I was sitting on the floor in the basement bathroom unable to move.

"This was how Kevin Haigen found me after he had come back from work at the theater. He was terrified and called my friend Susse Wold. She, in turn, called Bent Mejding, a stage-director friend of hers, and apparently the two came over to my house. I didn't recall anything until early the next morning, when I woke up and saw Kevin, Susse, and Bent looking down at me. It turned out that they had carried me up to my bedroom and when I woke up, there they were. They had called the doctor, who told them I was to be fed lots of coffee. Obviously he thought I was dead-drunk. The truth was I was in agony. That was the first really serious collapse I had ever had."

Just before Erik Bruhn's announcement of his retirement, he had spent a lot of time with his friends Goeren and Marit Gentele, who were now residing in New York. Gentele was deeply involved in the Metropolitan Opera and had been able to settle a musicians' strike threatened for the upcoming season—the first under his management. At dinner one night, the Genteles told Bruhn that they were planning to rent a house not far from New York for the summer months. Gentele would need a good rest before assuming his full duties at the Met, and he and Marit invited Bruhn to be their guest during their vacation. As matters turned out, the Genteles had received a letter from Sweden from their eldest daughter, Jeanette—a child by Gentele's first marriage. It seemed that she missed her family and she urged them to spend the summer in Europe. Realizing that he would spend more and more of his time in New York, Gentele and his wife agreed that a trip with the entire family would be in order. They made arrangements to take a car trip through Italy and travel to Sardinia, a place they had never before visited.

The trip began gloriously. The strange, arid landscape of Sardinia looked beautiful and the narrow, winding roads of the mountains were relatively clear, making the drive both exhilarating and somewhat dizzying. Driving along at a natural speed, and approaching yet another curve, Goeren Gentele suddenly saw an oncoming truck. The truck was veering toward him and in an effort to avoid it, he turned the wheel sharply and the car swerved. But it was too late. Goeren Gentele and his two daughters by Marit—Cecilia and Beatrice—were killed instantly. Marit and her step-daughter, Jeanette, survived.

Marit Gentele recounts the events leading up to the crash and its aftermath. "It was July 18, 1972. I was sitting next to Goeren in the front seat and we were riding along when I saw a shadow . . . that's what it looked like to me. But that shadow was an enormous truck which was approaching us on the wrong side of the highway. I must have gone through the windshield and been thrown out of the car. And that's what must have happened to Jeanette as well. Later, they found out that the man driving the truck was drunk. In fact, he had lost his license for drunken-driving and had just gotten his license back. We were immediately taken to a hospital, and, luckily, Jeanette was not too badly hurt. I, on the other hand, was a mess. Broken bones in my neck, broken vertebrae, bruised muscles, a concussion in my ear, a gash in my hip, a broken shoulder, and a twisted leg. You can imagine. I won't go into my feelings when I learned that my husband and two daughters were killed. Well, they patched me up as well as they could in a small hospital in Olbia, and then arrangements were made to have me flown back to Stockholm, where I entered another hospital. It took me quite some time to recuperate, but eventually I was discharged. Still, there were many things wrong with me—I had to have several more operations and a good deal of plastic surgery. It was at this point that I received a letter from Erik, asking me to come and stay with him at his house in Gentofte."

Erik Bruhn was still in New York with Christopher Allan when the news of the accident reached him. "Chris and I were in the apartment when the phone rang. Chris answered it and after a very long time came to me and could barely speak. I realized that something was wrong, and as he started to give me the news I could see he was shaking. He told me that Goeren, Marit, and *all* the children were dead. I heard what he said but I made him repeat it. I was furious. I wouldn't believe such nonsense. But Chris's expression told me that the worst had happened. Of course, we later found out that Marit and Jeanette were saved, and I was terribly relieved that at least somebody was spared. Almost immediately, I received a call from the Metropolitan Opera House, saying that since I was his only close friend just then in New York, would I come down and speak to the press and face some television cameras. I could have killed them. I was certainly in no condition to talk with anyone. Then, *The New York Times* asked me to write a tribute which they wanted to publish. I couldn't bring myself to do it, because I was in a state of shock. Finally, after three days, I sat down and wrote something."

Erik Bruhn's words in tribute to his friend Goeren Gentele appeared on July 30, 1972. Under a photograph of a smiling Gentele, the tribute read in part:

> You were the man we believed in, who promised to be the person who could fulfill our hopes. I, for one, knew what you could do for ballet. Your ideals, your perspective and your hard-earned professional efficiency always gave me—and as I have witnessed, to many others—a direction, a light to follow, because you made us believe.
>
> I am forever grateful that I have had the privilege of knowing you. I cannot predict what the future has lost, now being without you, but I, like many others, am well aware of what you gave to us while you lived, and that shall remain our inspiration for as long as we are here.

Marit Gentele's physical damage took a long time to heal, but it would be years before the psychological damage would mend. The first step toward that psychological recuperation took place when Marit Gentele was able to travel to Denmark and spend two weeks with Erik Bruhn.

Bruhn was the first friend she could face after the funeral of her husband and daughters in Stockholm.

Bruhn remembers picking her up at the airport in Copenhagen and driving her to his house in Gentofte. "Of course, the drive in my car was a horrible ordeal for Marit. She had not been in a car since the accident. She sat with me in the front seat and never looked at the road once. Her eyes were glued on me. Finally we got home and I decided to sleep in the room next to hers in case she would wake up in the middle of the night and need anything."

Marit Gentele considers those two weeks with Erik Bruhn the greatest help she could have received from anyone. "Erik arranged everything for me. He placed me into physical therapy with a Danish woman, who taught me how to begin moving properly—how to turn my head, how to walk steadily. Little by little Erik and I took two-minute walks just to get me moving again. He was incredible. We talked into the early hours of the morning. I had to face my tragedy and with Erik I felt absolutely safe. I know that had I remained in Stockholm, I would have been hounded by the press and by photographers. Staying with Erik, I avoided all of that. Erik said something so moving to me. He said that I was privileged to have had something that no one else had, and that I should be grateful for that. He made me talk endlessly about Goeren and the two girls, and made me remember all the sweet things about them. He wanted me to retain *those* memories, and by retaining happy memories, I would have that to fall back on. He told me I would be an idiot to fall into a trap of bitterness. He restored my self-confidence. He helped me not to go mad or die of a broken heart. I found this an extraordinary gesture of friendship and loyalty. I think it took tremendous courage and strength of character for Erik, who was ill himself, to take this trouble.

"It wasn't just the way I was feeling, it was also the way I was looking. I was covered with bandages and had bad scars and looked absolutely pathetic. At any rate, very slowly, but very firmly, Erik brought me out of my terrible state. We even began to laugh together. I somehow managed it, hard as it was. After a week, I was able to walk quite normally, and I remember an amusing incident. Erik said, 'Let's take a walk in the Tivoli Gardens.' It was a beautiful day, and we went. When we got there, the place was literally swarming with people on crutches or in wheelchairs. It turned out to be the one day when every crippled person in Copenhagen was given a special outing at Tivoli. We stood there and just *had* to laugh. Erik took me by the arm and said, 'Let's get the hell out of here and have a drink.' When the two weeks were over, I felt I could face the world again. I have come to live with what happened to me. When I think of Goeren and the children, they are not dead and gone—they are just not here. They are *in* me, so they will be alive as long as I am alive. In many ways, Erik was responsible for making me feel this way."

After several months of living in Copenhagen following his retirement, Bruhn came close to despair. His own illness—still a mystery—had worsened, and no one seemed able to help him. It was a difficult and demoralizing period.

Reflecting on his life, his uncertain future, and indeed his own mortality, Erik Bruhn gave vent to some of his innermost feelings. In discursive fashion he verbalized what had been preying on his mind. "People have often casually asked me, 'How are you?' I usually answer, 'The same, only more.' I suppose that's a form of maturity—a state of being yourself. As I've grown older, I've developed the ability to let one mask fall after another, in order to expose my true self. For many years I hid myself, both privately as well as on the stage. Perhaps it was because I was afraid to have people say, 'Is that *all* you are?' Earlier on, I tried to give an illusion of myself to others. But as I've matured, I've tried to gain more confidence so that I can be more myself, rather than just an illusion. Often, I have deceived friends and the public with a façade of reservation and arrogance. It was an image of the great self-sufficient dancer. The fact is, my strongest driving force has been to communicate with others. I have come to realize that to communicate is to share and this has enriched my life.

"When I thought of death, it had always shocked and confused me. My first encounter with it was when I was five years old and saw a little boy being run over by a truck, and the next day he died. No one had explained to me the meaning of death. I have had close friends who have died—Inge Sand, Goeren Gentele and his two daughters, and there were others. It was only recently that I found an explanation of what death meant. I have come to accept it as another form of existence, in the guise of memory. My own death would have meaning to me if I felt that I had given something of value while I was alive. My hope is that I might not die in one of my moods of depression, because then I would not be able to feel anything. Everything would have seemed meaningless—even death. It would be terrible if I were to feel that way, because then I would not be able to accept it as an existence.

"There have been certain moments on the stage where I suddenly had a feeling of completeness. Even disguised as a dancer, I felt like a total being. This has happened perhaps four or five times during my entire dancing career. It was a feeling of *I am.* At those moments, I had that indescribable sensation of being everywhere and nowhere. I had the sense of being universal . . . . but not in any specific form. This experience scared me at first, because one could so easily lose oneself. But it was that very same sensation that helped me to pull through during the toughest periods of my life.

"We who work on the stage have a tendency to only contemplate our navels—to be totally self-involved. At the same time, we are supposed to be all-giving. Many artists think that whatever they do is good enough for anybody. Of course, this is a terrible fallacy. A balance has to be reached.

And that balance is a combination of dream and reality. One of my major struggles has been to retain my sense of reality as an artist, because I knew that if I were only living a dream, then I would lose contact with the real world.

"Thinking back on my career, I had to face many ambiguities within myself. I remember that at my height as a dancer, and when the greatest possible praise would come my way, those would be the times when I would fall into my deepest depressions. And it was at those times that I had to escape—to disappear. I felt an exhaustion and a depression that I could not explain to anyone. I simply had to go off by myself. And when I was alone, I could not talk or listen to anyone. I could not hear a bird that was singing. I could not see the color of a flower. I was alive, but felt nothing. Many years ago, when I was just a boy, I would feel invisible— that time when my mother met me on a very busy street and she didn't see me. I almost touched her and still she didn't see me.

"I have often provoked a conflict with people who were very close to me. I risked losing that person rather than accepting a relationship that would merely be routine. I have done that during love affairs in order to keep them alive. I have risked losing in order *not* to lose. Often I have profited by these risks.

"When I stopped dancing in 1971, people came up to me and said, 'How dare you?' They felt that I had in some way betrayed them, because they had wanted me to continue. It was well meant, because they did not want me to feel forgotten. Of course, we dancers have a tremendous fear of that. I think this is something my friend Rudik suffers from—that desire for recognition on the stage that all dancers are deadly afraid to lose. We all take our nourishment from that mass of people out there, which does not really have an individual identity. But we need them. We are afraid to lose them. And yet we also hate them, because we are so dependent on them. I have known many artists who were unable to cope with the day when they suddenly realized that no one recognized them anymore. It was as if their life were lost. Well, those people lost their life a long time before that! They became too dependent on that mass out there.

"When a star falls, people make a wish. I have only had one wish since I was very young and that was to be able to be strong enough to receive everything that life had to offer me. My one wish was to be strong enough to survive *anything*. People have said to me, 'Why are you such a pessimist?' But, you see, I'm not a pessimist. People said that about my mother, too. But her pessimism was only a pose. In reality she was the most vibrant woman I ever came across. She was a survivor. She was strong and willful, and had a primitive power that did not have a normal sense of logic. But, you see, that primitive force gave us a strong sense of challenge. Some of my sisters could not cope with it. In later years it would be my greatest inspiration, and I *used* that power rather than having it crush me."

In early 1973 Erik Bruhn was living in Gentofte; he had completed staging *Les Sylphides* for the Royal Danish Ballet and also had restaged *La Sylphide* for the Rome Opera. These assignments completed, he received an offer that he found both challenging and intriguing. The Danish stage director Bent Mejding, a close friend of Susse Wold, asked Bruhn whether he might be interested in appearing in a play he would soon be staging. This was *Rashomon*, based on the well-known film by Akiro Kurosawa. The role Mejding had in mind for Bruhn was that of a Samurai, the pivotal character in the play. His leading lady would be Susse Wold. Bruhn was decidedly interested, for he had long harbored a wish to make stage and film appearances which would make profitable use of his acting ability. Indeed, an aspect of Bruhn's art that had never been tapped was his remarkable speaking voice, with its soothing timbre and velvety intonation.

Bruhn accepted the offer and was particularly pleased to learn that *Rashomon* would also include in its cast the extraordinary character dancer Gerda Karstens, who thirty years earlier had given the boy Erik pantomime lessons at the Royal Danish Ballet School. All in all, the idea of appearing on stage as an actor came at a most propitious moment. Bruhn's only fear was the matter of his illness, which might recur unexpectedly and might prevent him from undertaking this or any other assignment.

In the meantime, Bruhn traveled to New York to see his friend Christopher Allan and to present the 1973 Dance Magazine Award to Rudolf Nureyev. On that occasion, William Como, editor of *Dance Magazine*, introduced Erik Bruhn: "Erik is one of the important 'foreign geniuses' who influenced American ballet. At his retirement not long ago, Mr. Bruhn broke our hearts: we were not ready to part with him as a dancer; we will never be."

Erik Bruhn stepped on the podium and his friend Nureyev stood at his side. "I'd like to first thank the editors of *Dance Magazine* for having asked me to present Rudik, today, the award," he began. "It is to me an occasion perhaps even more special than the one at which I myself received the award, because it provides me with an opportunity to express for the first time in public my great gratitude to a friend, the man, the dancer Rudolf Nureyev. To me it often seems like yesterday that I first met Rudolf in Denmark in the fall of 1961. As it turned out, we were to work together for some years following our first encounter.

"At the age of thirty-three, I had passed through various phases in my life as a dancer. I had reached a peak and a certain recognition in the West, but also a personal feeling of stagnation in my work. It was thanks to Rudolf Nureyev and his inspiration at that time that pushed me through a very difficult period as a dancer. . . . . It was not necessarily because of the youth he had then, nor his drive and ambition, which are the ingredients in the career of a professional dancer, that I was affected by knowing Rudolf. It was his burning passion for the art of dance that gave me infinite inspiration and helped me push through a difficult phase of transition as a dancer."

Turning to face Nureyev, Bruhn concluded by saying: "I can only wish you, when you come to need it, a similar inspiration. . . . Rudik, I am proud to present this award to you in recognition of your rare talent and your greatness, which has touched the entire dance world. I salute and congratulate you."

While still in New York, Bruhn learned that some of his *Rashomon* rehearsals would have to take place in Stockholm, where Susse Wold was appearing in a play. He thus made ready to fly to Sweden. As he bade farewell to his friend Chris Allan, he noted that this generally quiet and even-tempered man was in unusually high spirits. It was an elation that Bruhn could not quite make out, and he questioned Allan about it. "It's just that life has never treated me better," said Allan. Bruhn smiled, and told him that he couldn't be more pleased. Still, there was something strange about it all, and Bruhn left the city puzzled over his friend's uncharacteristic behavior.

On arriving in Stockholm, Bruhn felt in poorer shape than he had hoped. Still, he began rehearsing *Rashomon* and, although in pain, worked with enormous concentration. As time went on, the pains worsened.

"I began feeling so ill that it occurred to me that I might as well do the play and die onstage rather than just being carted off to a hospital. It was a nightmare, but we went on with the rehearsals. During the last week in Stockholm my stomach pains were so bad that I was given morphine injections. Finally the doctors there said that I had better return to Copenhagen. They told me to place myself under my own doctor's care and if matters were to improve, I would be able to continue the rehearsals in Denmark after Susse Wold's play closed."

When Bruhn arrived in Gentofte, a pile of mail awaited him. Among the letters was one from Christopher Allan containing all sorts of news and gossip of his activities in New York and it was so high-spirited that Bruhn again felt disturbed. "Chris's letter was so full of life, so incredibly elated, that it didn't sound right to me. A few days later, I answered him saying that I hoped all the good things that were coming his way were making him happy. The fact is, Chris seemed basically very sad and was often depressed—that was his usual mood. I mean, he was the sweetest, most generous man, who would never let anyone pick up a check, who could not take any form of gratitude, whose sole object in life seemed to be to please others. I don't really know what his private life was like, but I suspect that it could not have been very fulfilling.

"Anyway, I answered his letter and to my shock it was returned unopened. I know I didn't make a mistake in the address and I couldn't imagine why the letter had come back. I forgot all about it, when one night the phone rang. It was Lucia Chase. She sounded strange—not the usual merry Lucia—and before she went any further I suddenly said to her, "Chris Allan is dead." She said, "How did you know?" She went on to tell me that Chris had been to see her at her office at ABT, because he wanted to show her a little photograph he had found of the two of us together. Lucia thought it was an odd thing to do, but of course she didn't say anything. It turned out that Chris had either jumped or fallen out of his apartment window and was instantly killed. Chris's brother called me half an hour later to give me the news, and he explained that it had really been an accident—that Chris did not commit suicide. I cannot presume to know what actually happened. All I know is that I was terribly shaken by this event, because Chris was very dear to me. He was a good friend—someone I could trust, someone I could rely on completely. I miss him to this day."

Although Christopher Allan's death on November 4, 1973, affected Bruhn deeply, he could not fly to New York to attend his friend's funeral. It might have proved ill-advised, because of his own poor state of health, and Bruhn's doctors had told him to stay close to home in case of a possible flareup of his stomach condition.

Under morphine and with the greatest strength of will, Erik Bruhn continued rehearsals of *Rashomon*, which were now being conducted in Copenhagen. During the last week of rehearsal, in December 1973, what he had feared became a reality. Immense stomach pains forced him to consult with a specialist. He was given some injections to ease the pain and told to return the following week. Bruhn managed to continue rehearsing. One evening prior to his second appointment with the specialist, he gave a dinner party for a few friends, including Susse Wold's mother, Marguerite Viby, and an actress friend of hers, Birthe Bachhausen. During the course of the evening he began to feel ill and left the table. He walked into the kitchen, when a terrifying pain assailed him.

Bruhn somehow managed to take himself upstairs and drag himself onto the bed. As he lay there, he felt something bursting in his stomach. With the greatest difficulty he called down to his friends. They came running upstairs and saw that he could not move. Bruhn was curled up in a fetal position and in obvious agony. An ambulance was called and when it came, Bruhn was taken to the Gentofte Hospital. Bruhn remembers that when he got to the hospital the pain was so strong that he passed out.

"I didn't recall anything until the following evening. When I awoke there were six or seven doctors standing around my bed. One doctor said it was appendicitis. Another said it was my liver. The next one said it was my kidney and another said it was my gall bladder. Susse Wold and Bent Mejding were there. Finally the doctors decided to operate on me for appendicitis. They told Bent and Susse to call in in about an hour. When the hour was over, they were told that I was still in surgery. Well, two hours passed, three hours passed, and four hours passed. It was almost five hours before it was over. When I regained consciousness, I was told what my trouble had been all along: it was a perforated ulcer which no X-ray machine had been able to scan. No X ray showed that I even *had* an ulcer. It was only when they operated that they found out what was wrong.

"The specialist told me that the trouble had now been located, but that he would have to perform a corrective operation at a later date. Still, the good news was that I would no longer have those miserable pains, and *that* alone was the greatest gift anybody could give me."

The producers of *Rashomon* postponed the opening of the play for several weeks, in order to give Bruhn time to recover. As soon as he could, he proceeded with the rehearsals. He was feeling much better, but was concerned over the fact that he was not gaining back some of the weight he had lost during his stay in the hospital. He felt oddly weak and one evening, in the middle of rehearsal, he felt nauseated and became sick. The following morning he went to the hospital in Copenhagen, where he was told his corrective operation would take place. The doctors there advised him to have this operation at once, simply to get it over with. Bruhn agreed and told Bent Mejding about this new development. The play, which had already been postponed once, would have to be postponed yet another time. Bruhn felt he could not in all fairness ask Mejding to do this, and told him that it might be best if he were to be replaced by another actor. He did not wish to hold up the production, particularly since so much time had already been lost.

"What happened next was that the entire cast got together and they all decided to postpone the play for six months! They did not want to open *Rashomon* without me, and were willing to make this extremely generous sacrifice. Naturally I told everyone that even with the corrective operation, there was no guarantee that I would be well, but they were willing to take this chance. It was a beautiful thing to do and it gave me courage to face my second operation."

In January 1974 Erik Bruhn entered the Copenhagen Hospital. He was extremely nervous and out of sorts, distressed over the possibility that this second operation might not prove successful after all, and even more distressed to note that the doctors were giving him innumerable new tests. He had thought they were done with all of that, and that the "corrective operation" would be a relatively simple matter. Instead, he had to endure the insertion of countless tubes and be subjected to other discomforts. Finally the surgery took place and when he woke, his doctor smiled down at him. He told Bruhn that everything had gone well and that he would make a complete recovery. Bruhn himself knew in his heart that what the doctor told him was the truth. There would be no more pain and no more suffering. Eleven years of intermittent agony would now be nothing more than a bad memory. The day after his operation, Bruhn was permitted to walk around. He felt so well that instead of walking he did a barre. "I could only do things in second position, because I could not yet bend forward. But the pain had disappeared completely and—knock wood—has not returned to this day!"

(RIGHT) As Madge the Witch in his own production of *La Sylphide* with Nureyev as James, National Ballet of Canada, 1974. Photo: Beverley Gallegos. (BELOW) As Dr. Coppelius in *Coppélia*, National Ballet of Canada, 1975. Photo: Beverley Gallegos.

(ABOVE) As the Saracen in Rudolf Nureyev's production of *Raymonda*, American Ballet Theatre, 1975. Photo: Beverley Gallegos. (OPPOSITE ABOVE) *La Ventana* Pas de Trois with Nureyev and Cynthia Gregory, American Ballet Theatre, 1975. Photo: Jack Vartoogian. (OPPOSITE) Curtain call, *Raymonda*, 1975. Photo: Linda Vartoogian.

(OPPOSITE) With Cynthia Gregory
as Desdemona in *The Moor's Pavane*,
American Ballet Theatre, 1977.
Photo: Martha Swope. (RIGHT) As
Petrouchka, American Ballet Theatre,
1976. Photo: Beverley Gallegos.
(BELOW) As the Moor, *The Moor's
Pavane*, José Limón Company, 1978.
Photo: Martha Swope.

(OPPOSITE) As Rasputin in James Clouser's *Rasputin*, Fort Worth Ballet, 1978.
Photo: Buddy Myers. (ABOVE TOP) Bruhn's production of *Here We Come*,
National Ballet of Canada, 1978. Photo: The National Ballet School. (ABOVE)
Bruhn's *Swan Lake* with Karen Kain and Frank Augustyn, National Ballet of
Canada, 1976. Photo: Andrew Oxenham.

(OPPOSITE ABOVE) With choreographer/dancer Constantin Patsalas, 1975. Photo: Rosemary Winckley. (OPPOSITE BELOW) Bruhn and Betty Oliphant with pupils at the National Ballet School, Canada. Photo: Peter Varley. (BELOW) Bruhn teaching at the National Ballet School, Canada. Photo: Frank Richards.

Photo: Louis Péres.

[CHAPTER 24]

B RUHN SPENT the next weeks regaining his strength and, to that end,
taking class with the Royal Danish Ballet. As *Rashomon* had been
postponed for six months, his immediate plans included a visit to
Toronto, where as "Resident Producer" he would visit the National Ballet
of Canada for his annual stint as a teacher. In addition, he would discuss
the possibility of mounting a new production of *Coppélia*. This would be
the company's fourth major production of a classic by Erik Bruhn, to follow his *La Sylphide, Les Sylphides,* and *Swan Lake.*

As it turned out, the company was preparing for a summer appearance
at the Metropolitan Opera House in New York that August. Rudolf
Nureyev would head the company as guest artist, and the repertoire would
include Bruhn's *Sylphide*. While in Toronto, he was approached with the
tentative suggestion that he portray the role of Madge the Witch—a role
as far removed from his usual classical parts as it would be possible to
imagine. The idea was for Bruhn to make his debut in that role in New
York with Nureyev as James and Nadia Potts as the Sylph. Without hesita-
tion Bruhn accepted. Here would be a new and dramatic challenge which
delighted him.

On August 9, 1974, *La Sylphide* was presented by the Canadians at the
Met, and Bruhn's incarnation of Madge the Witch proved riveting.

"People were horrified," says Bruhn. "They could not believe that I
would take on a role which would make me look positively hideous. They

were used to seeing me as the noble Prince, and here I was . . . a toothless hag, dressed in rags and oozing evil. Well, it was a perfect way to release everything that was evil inside of me. Actually many dancers and actors dislike portraying villainous characters, because the public might feel that it's what they're like offstage. It didn't bother me in the least. After all, I was vicious as Jean in *Miss Julie* and murderously jealous as Don José in *Carmen*!"

Watching the performance that evening was Clive Barnes, who was stunned by Bruhn's interpretation of the Witch. Talking to a friend about the impact of Bruhn's portrayal, he said: "Erik has a way of destroying the opposition just by sitting there. Very few people can live on the stage with him. Later on, Nureyev told me that when Erik lifted that stick above his head, he thought he was actually going to kill him!"

The following week the company returned to Toronto to perform at the open-air Ontario Place Theatre. On August 14 a brand-new James made his debut with the National Ballet of Canada—Mikhail Baryshnikov.

Mikhail Baryshnikov had been touring Canada as a guest artist with a small group from the Bolshoi Ballet in June 1974. He was at the time a member of the Leningrad Kirov Ballet and had already made an extraordinary name for himself in the Soviet Union. When word spread that Baryshnikov would be dancing in Canada, New York dance critics and ballet aficionados flocked to Canada to see an artist who was undoubtedly one of the world's most phenomenal male dancers.

While he danced in Toronto, Baryshnikov made his dramatic decision to remain in the West. He defected from the Bolshoi group on the last night of its tour. Yet another Kirov dancer had made his so-called "leap to freedom" and, as in the case of Nureyev and Makarova before him, the event made world headlines. Baryshnikov went into seclusion with friends, and as soon as he left his country retreat, he was invited to make guest appearances with the National Ballet of Canada. His actual debut with the company was in excerpts from *La Sylphide* for Canadian television in July. Later that month, at the invitation of Natalia Makarova, he made his American debut dancing with American Ballet Theatre in *Giselle*. He danced the work with his former Soviet colleague—it was a debut that made an unforgettable impact on the New York ballet world. With Makarova he also performed in the ballerina's own staging of *La Bayadère* and the *Don Quixote* pas de deux. After these appearances with ABT, Baryshnikov returned to Toronto and made his first stage appearance on August 14 with the National Ballet of Canada dancing with Veronica Tennant as the Sylph in Erik Bruhn's full-length version of *La Sylphide*. On this occasion Bruhn did not dance the Witch but helped the young Russian dancer in the role of James.

Bruhn sat in the audience that evening and watched Baryshnikov give a performance that he considers memorable. "His James was absolutely beautiful. I remember going backstage and telling him that if I had continued dancing the role, I would have liked to have danced it just like that. I was amazed that a Russian dancer who had never before attempted Bournonville could achieve such purity and authenticity of style."

Bruhn and Baryshnikov formed a close professional and personal friendship and the older dancer would later teach Baryshnikov his first full-length *Swan Lake*, which he would dance with the Canadians in 1975. Also in the future, the two dancers would appear together in *La Sylphide*, with Bruhn repeating his role as Madge the Witch.

"Misha may very well be the most dynamic dancer of his time," says Bruhn. "I remember feeling very defensive about him in Canada, when people raved about his *Swan Lake* one day and on the next day said that his James in *La Sylphide* was dull. The point was that Misha was not used to doing one performance after another, because in Russia they might do two performances a month. He had to learn to deliver all the time and, of course, he did. Sometimes he did this at the cost of quality and purity. I have done this myself. My hope for him is that he will continue to keep that essence of stylistic perfection and never merely 'deliver.' The danger for all of us is in thinking that *whatever* we do is good enough for the audience. I'm sure Misha won't fall into that trap.

"I hope also that he will surround himself with people who will have a positive influence on him . . . people he can truly trust."

Baryshnikov himself comments on what Bruhn has meant to him. "Erik Bruhn . . . he was of course one of the international idols of my youth. He had a very big reputation in the Soviet Union. Everyone had seen his photos in books and in magazines. I first saw him in a film of the *Don Quixote* pas de deux taken from ABT's Russian tour in 1961. He had that extraordinary line and he was so beautifully *long* . . . and the cold power he had was so very unusual.

"It was as if he was a new type—like the perfect lithograph but REAL. He was like an Ingres drawing—so fine, but so strong. After the kind of dancer we had seen so often from the forties, he was a herald of a new age. It was always very clear from the pirated movies I saw of Erik how strong his concentration was, how he made an interior power work for him on stage. With most performers, most stars, you expect them to take their imagination outward, directly to the public. With Erik, it is as if he sucks it all into himself and applies that concentration and then lets off an incredible white heat. No audience could ever miss it.

"He was, naturally, the finest example of a pure classical technician and his superb Bournonville training was always there to see. His dancing was very strong, but it never was tricked or 'fancy.'

"I only saw Erik in his great classical roles on film. Roles like Albrecht in *Giselle* with Carla Fracci, his own *Swan Lake, La Sylphide.* Later he worked with me when I first was learning *La Sylphide* and also his *Swan Lake.* His corrections and his help were invaluable. He was extremely generous with his compliments . . . fortifying.

"As Madge he was terrifying (first of all, when he rehearsed me, I couldn't believe he wasn't doing James, because he showed me all the beats and the pirouettes and the tours—everything). But as Madge it was his honesty, his respect for the part and its tradition that made it so great. There was no sense of parody. No exaggeration—no cheap laughs. It was amazing and beautiful!"

Erik Bruhn completed his work with the National Ballet of Canada in late August 1974. He would have to return to Copenhagen, because *Rashomon* would be opening in September. With the play's impending opening, the Danish press was full of stories about Bruhn making his debut as a stage actor.

On September 12, 1974, *Rashomon* opened at the Youth Theatre in Copenhagen. Two days later, *The New York Times* carried a special report on this event:

"Erik Bruhn, who danced his way to world fame in ballet, made his debut as an actor last night, playing a wild-eyed Samurai, in Akiro Kurosawa's *Rashomon*, to generally favorable reviews. 'He demonstrated a powerful personal magnetism,' wrote *Berlingske Tidende*, Copenhagen's largest daily newspaper. 'His glance expressed freezing contempt and petrified wonder . . . a happy comeback for Erik Bruhn.' "

Bruhn gave several interviews relating to his first stage appearance in a straight play. In one, he told an interviewer, "When I am dancing a part, I may spend only three or four minutes with my turns and leaps. What am I doing the rest of the evening? I am acting with my body."

Rashomon completed its run in December 1974. For Bruhn, it was a fulfilling experience, made the more pleasurable by the presence of his co-star and friend Susse Wold.

Miss Wold recalls their sharing the same dressing room in the theater and helping each other with the application of their respective Japanese makeup. "I must admit that the Danish public was a bit confused by *Rashomon*. I mean, we were speaking in Danish and looking Japanese. It was an odd mixture. On top of that, it was Erik's debut in a play and, of course, everybody knew Erik as a dancer and that made it even more curious. Well, Erik and I had lots and lots of fun together. I had a marvelous time performing with him, because he was never dull, but always thoroughly interesting. Nureyev came one night and so did Makarova and Baryshnikov. They seemed to like us very much."

After the play closed, Bruhn received a call from Lucia Chase in New York, telling him that American Ballet Theatre would be celebrating its Thirty-fifth Anniversary on January 11. Would he come and participate? She hoped that he would be a part of this sentimental occasion, even if it meant his merely walking onstage and taking a bow. Bruhn accepted the invitation. A few days later Chase telephoned again, asking him whether he would consider dancing the "kitchen scene" with Cynthia Gregory in *Miss Julie*. Again, Bruhn accepted.

The American Ballet Theatre Thirty-fifth Anniversary Gala was a nostalgic event, with past and present stars of the company taking part in choice excerpts from the company's most famous ballets—works by de Mille, Tudor, Robbins, as well as bravura passages from the classics. There was no question, however, that the highlight of the gala was Erik Bruhn's return to the company with which he had so long been associated. The "kitchen scene" from *Miss Julie* was danced magnificently and it seemed as though time had stood still for Erik Bruhn. The intensity of his dramatic power was as strong as it had been when he had first performed the ballet in 1958, and his dancing had lost none of its former discipline and brilliance.

Cynthia Gregory as Miss Julie was no less magnificent and she remembers the evening with particular pride. "The minute Erik came on we could tell he was in fantastic shape. It was as if he had never stopped dancing. He was as perfect and beautiful as always. We had two days to get it together and only a few hours of actual rehearsal, but it all seemed to fall into place. I'll never forget the ovation he received when first he stepped onstage. I mean, he brought the house down and just stood there letting all that applause wash over him. When we finished the scene, I was reluctant to take a bow with him, because this was Erik's night. I remember looking at him and seeing his expression. It was one of sheer joy. I felt very honored to have danced with Erik on that very special night!"

〖 CHAPTER 25 〗

I T WAS CLEAR that at the age of forty-six Erik Bruhn had made a spectacular comeback as a dancer. Free of his pains, he felt himself a new man.
But with his resolve to return to dance he made several serious deci-
sions regarding the kind of dancer he would henceforth be. "I'm sure that
many people wondered why during the ABT Gala I did not dance something with Fracci or Makarova. They were, after all, two of my most important partners. The reason is simple: If I had danced with either of
them, it would have had to be something from *La Sylphide, Giselle,* or
Coppélia. Well, I was not prepared to do this, because I made up my mind
that I would never again dance the Prince roles. You see, in ballet the idea
is to be young, beautiful, and strong. You have to be eighteen, and if
you're not, you have to look it. For me, this was no longer possible. It
would be a travesty to perform roles one was no longer suited for. One
would look foolish, and that's the last thing I wanted to do. So, when I decided to return to the ballet stage, it would only be in character roles—not,
mind you, that I would stick only to mime roles, but I would avoid those
ballets that stressed the kind of virtuosity with which people had associated me in the past."

Having reached this decision, he let it be known that he was prepared to
perform with American Ballet Theatre, the National Ballet of Canada, and
any other company that could offer him suitable vehicles.

Bruhn had already discussed mounting a new production of *Coppélia*

for the Canadians and immediately after the ABT Gala he went to Toronto, where his new production opened on February 8, 1975, at the
O'Keefe Center. The premiere performance included Veronica Tennant
as Swanilda, Tomas Schramek as Franz, and Jacques Gorrissen as Dr.
Coppélius. The following week Bruhn himself assumed the role of Dr.
Coppélius. Bruhn had once more transformed himself into a character far
removed from the noble image the public remembered. But there was a
new nobility in this Coppélius.

When the company brought this production to London, in the spring
of 1975, Bruhn taught the role of Franz, which he himself had danced so
magnificently only a few years previously, to his friend Rudolf Nureyev.
They appeared together at the London Coliseum and once again the press
was unanimous in its praise.

Oddly enough, Bruhn does not consider his version of *Coppélia* totally
successful. "It's not my dream production. I think it's a bit cutesy—a bit
too Walt Disney for my taste. But since the sets and costumes were in
progress for about six months, I didn't feel I could reverse the plans. It's a
good production, but not a perfect one."

If he deemed his production imperfect, his interpretation of the role of
Dr. Coppélius was considered to be perfection itself. This was a moving
Coppélius—an old man torn by his love for his invented Coppélia—the
doll he thought he had brought to life, only to realize that a cruel hoax had
been played on him, and that the doll was as mechanical as ever—a shattered creature as inanimate as any of his other fabrications. His sorrow at
this discovery was genuinely heartrending, and as he mimed his tentative,
hesitant, and reluctant acceptance of his delusion, audiences were once
more placed in touch with an artist capable of the greatest dramatic depth.

Whenever Bruhn found himself in Toronto, he seldom failed to visit his
sister Benthe, who had settled in Canada in 1951. By this time, Bruhn's
relationship with the rest of his family was not particularly close. He seldom communicated with his half sister Else, nor with Birthe, though he
did see Aase. By the same token, these sisters were not in any large measure concerned with their brother's life, although, to be sure, they were
aware of his stature as a world-renowned artist and no doubt basked in the
reflected glory this gave them. But it was with Benthe that Bruhn maintained a close rapport. This sister had married a Dane and borne him five

children—four girls and one boy, echoing the sequence of children borne to their own mother.

"Unfortunately, Benthe's husband died some years ago, leaving her with all those children," says Bruhn. "So I help her. As with all my sisters, I have left money in trust for all my nephews and nieces—there are nine of them—and that, of course, included Benthe's children. Benthe lives rather far from Toronto, in Prince George, British Columbia—a five-hour plane trip away. But, whenever I am in Canada, I visit her and I consider her the only real family I have. She is an amazing woman. When her husband died, she took a crash course in tax consulting, and is now doing fantastically well. Her kids had practically to raise themselves, because Benthe worked during the day and studied at night. I recently visited her and decided I would invest in a house in the place she lives. She and I drove around for hours and finally found a house we both liked—and I bought it for her. I fixed up the basement for myself, so that when I visit her I can have a place to stay. In a way, Benthe reminds me of our mother. She is a big, enormous woman with a strong personality. She is a real person—a human being I love and respect. Whenever I have the need for family life I always visit Benthe."

Knowing that Erik Bruhn was now fully recovered and indeed eager to continue dancing, albeit in roles suitable to him, Lucia Chase and her associates at American Ballet Theatre put their heads together hoping to come up with appropriate works. As it turned out, ABT would soon be staging a full-length production of *Raymonda,* choreographed after Petipa by Rudolf Nureyev. This would be an elaborate version of a work teeming with dance, some of a highly exotic nature. Set to the lush score by Alexander Glazounov, the work was brought into ABT specifically for Cynthia Gregory, who would dance the role of Raymonda, partnered by Nureyev. Among the many other roles was that of Abdul-Rakhman, a Saracen sheikh, who in Raymonda's dream seduces her in his Moorish harem. Bruhn was invited to undertake this role, in which he would do a sinuous and highly seductive dance in partnership with Gregory. He would be lavishly costumed and his makeup would transform him into an Oriental prince. Bruhn would portray the villain of the ballet—something he had relished doing in the past. It would be a spectacular though not very lengthy role and, at Nureyev's urging, he ultimately agreed to dance the part. The ballet opened on June 26 at the Jones Hall in Houston, Texas, and its New York premiere took place on July 1, at the New York State Theater.

Raymonda's critical reception was mixed. For the most part, the dance press found the ballet cumbersome and the decor by Nicholas Georgiadis dark and heavy-handed. The dancers were praised more for their valiant efforts than for the brilliance of Nureyev's steps. There were those, however, who considered *Raymonda* a superb example of a Petipa reinterpretation, and they were grateful to have a full-length version of a work usually presented in excerpted form. As for Bruhn's portrayal of the Saracen sheikh, it was felt to be unworthy of his talents.

"*Raymonda* did not work for me at all," says Bruhn. "Rudik had promised to make changes for me, and he did. Still, it just didn't work. I suppose it was fun to dance that sort of a role, but I would not call it one of my more memorable dancing experiences."

One week following the New York premiere of *Raymonda*, Bruhn appeared in *Epilogue*, a pas de deux created by John Neumeier for him and Natalia Makarova to music of the Adagietto movement of Mahler's Symphony No. 5. It reunited the two great dancers following their memorable appearances in *Giselle* and other ballets prior to Bruhn's "retirement" in 1971.

The return of Makarova and Bruhn was one of the most anticipated events of that New York season, and their legion of fans were ecstatic seeing them in simple costumes which revealed their flawless line. They were particularly enthralled over Bruhn's pliancy of body—that carriage and mien which recalled the dancer's former roles in the classics. Unfortunately *Epilogue* was not a major work—merely a pas de deux of some six or seven minutes' duration. Too, its content was somewhat arid, showing a relationship that was predominantly brooding and melancholy. There was grace, but not much charm. There was fluency, but none of the seamlessness that these two artists could so easily have imparted. In short, *Epilogue*, despite the presence of Makarova and Bruhn, proved a disappointment. The dance critic Arlene Croce, commenting on the work and its two stars stated: "Middle-aged dancers dance!" Elucidating on Bruhn's stage persona in a more general way, she added: "Bruhn has always been an insular kind of star. Inwardly rigid, absorbed in his own perfection, he has never mated well with any ballerina and his best roles were those that placed barriers between him and women. . . . He remains Erik

Bruhn, possibly the only major male star in ballet who can't walk toward a woman and appear to love her."

Bruhn and Makarova shared a certain dismay over *Epilogue*. Bruhn says: "When we first worked on the pas de deux, we had very little time. John Neumeier redid certain things and, of course, we were in his hands. Once we got the work into our bodies we could translate his ideas more fully. When we danced it again the following season it went much better."

There would be other works for Bruhn, notably a revival of Kenneth MacMillan's *Las Hermanas*, based on Lorca's play *The House of Bernarda Alba*. Here, Bruhn would be seen in a part that distantly echoed Jean in *Miss Julie* and Don José in *Carmen*. It was a role that called for high-voltage sexiness and villainy. Once again, Bruhn transformed himself from golden Dane to fiery Latin.

As it turned out, Bruhn did not find dancing *Las Hermanas* rewarding. "I enjoyed the few performances I did, but I do not miss doing this ballet," he says.

American Ballet Theatre, determined to encourage the American choreographer John Neumeier, brought into the repertoire an especially commissioned work for a stellar cast. This was *Hamlet Connotations*, done to a score by Aaron Copland, based on Shakespeare's play, with Mikhail Baryshnikov as Hamlet, Gelsey Kirkland as Ophelia, Marcia Haydée as Queen Gertrude, William Carter as the Ghost of Hamlet's father, and Erik Bruhn as King Claudius. At its world premiere, held on January 6, 1976, the audience was prepared for a masterpiece. What it got was a numbing work of bodies intertwining and stars rubbing shoulders. Neumeier's concept proved not so much a synopsis of *Hamlet* as a confused mélange of ideas that obscured rather than clarified the subtleties of the play. Erik Bruhn found the experience unchallenging. As for the ballet's critical reception, Walter Terry summed it up amusingly: "In Neumeier's *Hamlet*, and in some other things he has wrought, his policy is to get from one awkward position to another position as awkwardly as possible."

It would seem that Bruhn's return to the dance had not given him the uplifting satisfaction he had anticipated. It was good to be back onstage—but where were the roles? It was not that ABT wasn't trying. Indeed, they next suggested that he appear in Eliot Feld's *At Midnight*. The idea intrigued him. He had liked this choreographer's work and when he saw the ballet performed, felt it a potential vehicle for him.

However, as rehearsals began, the picture altered. "I began to realize that there would have to be changes made for me in order for me to dance the ballet, and I had a feeling that Eliot Feld would not be prepared to make these changes, so I decided to forgo this opportunity.

"It was also suggested that I dance Tudor's *Shadowplay*. Unfortunately, the character I was to portray—Terrestrial—entailed a lot of lifting of other male dancers, and I was not ready to do this, because it would have meant developing a strength I felt I did not possess at that stage of my life. A lot of things were offered to me, but choreographers would either have to change certain steps or my body was not suited for the roles. I did not wish to compromise, although almost everyone was eager to make changes for me. To have compromised would have meant hurting my ego and my ideas about being a dancer. Either I did these works as the choreographer had conceived them or not at all."

During the 1976 ABT season Bruhn was persuaded to appear as The Man She Must Marry in Tudor's *Jardin aux Lilas*. But as in his previous appearances in Tudor ballets, he felt uncomfortable with the choreography, and after a few performances he ceased to dance the role. A staging of Bournonville's *La Ventana*, which Bruhn adapted himself, was offered during an ABT Gala with Bruhn, Cynthia Gregory, and Rudolf Nureyev dancing in this charming pas de trois.

Some months later Erik Bruhn would finally fix on a role that he had long wanted to undertake, yet had inexplicably never attempted during the height of his career. This would be Michel Fokine's masterpiece *Petrouchka*, to the Stravinsky score. "Petrouchka was the kind of role I didn't mind killing myself over. I just had tremendous faith in it, because there aren't many roles like that. Although much younger dancers have done Petrouchka, I came to the realization that it is a ballet which only maturity can bring to full expression. You come to realize that in portraying this role, you are not just a person of this or that age, but a person of any age.

"I remember seeing *Petrouchka* with Børge Ralov when I was an apprentice in the ballet in Denmark and I felt very moved. I don't know what moved me, and I don't recall loving the character Petrouchka. Somehow, I had never wanted to do the role. Then, in 1976, I thought about it again and when I began to rehearse it I tried to think back to my childhood memories of it. Whenever anybody talked about the character of Petrouchka, it was always about the Russian soul. But what is a Russian soul? Is it any different from an American soul or a Danish soul? What is so different about a Russian soul? We all have souls. Well, I thought that if there was to be any soul in Petrouchka, it would have to be an oppressed soul. It is about this clownish puppet who tries to fight for his love but loses out. I think that Fokine didn't have the Russian soul in mind—only the personal suffering of a human being.

"I worked on the role from the point of view of my own personal suffering. I used whatever I had been through in my life, including perhaps that particular time when I was about to stop dancing, and the pain was there, and coming to the realization that I would be alone, lost, and left out. I have often said, 'Thank God for the arts,' because it is through the arts that we can release our emotions on every level. Well, this is how I approached the role of Petrouchka. Of course, I went to other sources— like the Nijinsky photographs. When I saw the expression on Nijinsky's face in the role of Petrouchka, it told me everything. At any rate, when I first appeared in the ballet I immediately injured myself. I had to stop dancing for about two months—but somehow I knew I would return to the role no matter how physically strenuous it might be. Also, the psychological implications of the character are so close to me that I felt I could not drop it."

Petrouchka was without question one of Bruhn's most magnificent conceptions—thought through to the last detail and emotionally direct and piercing. This was a Petrouchka of depth and authority, made the more singular by Bruhn's maturity of years and experience on human terms. Technically demanding as the role is, it did not ultimately play havoc with the dancer's stamina or sense of control. It was a fully realized interpretation, and audiences were thrilled.

With Petrouchka, Erik Bruhn had reached yet another zenith in his distinguished career. Indeed, the years 1975 and 1976 had consolidated his return to the dance and once more firmly established his supremacy among the world's great male dancers. If he had abandoned the Prince roles, he did so without regret. By embracing maturer characterizations, he infused them with a sense of depth and dimension. If the pyrotechnics could no longer be negotiated, they were replaced by carefully modulated dramatic portrayals that contained truth, even when a given role might be wanting in substance. Bruhn's eyes could still speak volumes; the expressiveness of his face revealed endless shades of mood and feeling; his body—pliant, lithe, and elegant—continued to make clear Bruhn's capacity for giving even the subtlest movement an aristocratic intonation. Nearing forty-eight, he had matured with grace. As a dancer, he could still evoke a sense of youth, but youth wedded to experience, high intelligence, and, above all, artistic maturity.

[CHAPTER 26]

THE CRITIC Clive Barnes once made the observation that Erik Bruhn was a man who passes through people's lives like an emblematic figure.

"One thing about Erik is that with almost all of his friends he is much more important to them than they are to Erik. On the other hand, he has this quality of intensity, so that people who don't see him very often feel that he offers a very great deal of himself in a very short span of time."

Patricia Barnes adds: "He is a person of very many different moods. There are times when he doesn't seem to have a trouble in the world and finds joy in everything. At other times, he goes through a kind of melancholia. In some ways, I think Danes are very much like Russians. They emerge and they withdraw."

"I also think that what appeals to people about Erik is that Hamlet-like quality," continues Clive Barnes. "There is something of the lonely, tragic hero about him, and yet it is lit with a Baltic sunshine. If the word charisma had not been around, it would have been invented for Erik. It was something I noticed from the very beginning. It was there in his dancing and in his person."

Bruhn himself is aware of the image he presents to others. But he firmly resents having labels put on him. "Put a label on you and you're dead. I am not a person of mystery. I think one of the truest things I can say about myself is that I am a man of enormous curiosity. My greatest pleasure is to wake up every morning and discover something new—something I have never known or encountered before. If that sense of curiosity is part of the act of being mysterious then I'm being misunderstood."

Curiosity is most decidedly a part of Bruhn's emotional and intellectual makeup, but if his discoveries turn out to be uninteresting or unfulfilling, the span of that curiosity may be quite short-lived. Perhaps people's assessment of Bruhn's all-pervasive quality of the enigmatic may in fact be nothing more than a sense of disappointment—a brooding feeling of letdown that may find the dancer withdrawing. Bruhn is often subjected to moods of depression. This is not necessarily attributable to the cliché of being Danish. His moods are uncategorizable. Bruhn will admit that the Danes are people who settle too easily and too soon into life—that they consider it safer and less hazardous than taking risks. When Bruhn speaks of wanting to discover something new, he generally alludes to those experiences that will enrich his life. For example, he has made a thorough study of Zen Buddhism and has also immersed himself in the writings of the eleventh-century philosopher Meister Eckhardt.

"In a funny way," says Bruhn, "these disciplines and ideas came to me through people who had themselves been helped by these great teachers. Sometimes, in speaking to these people, I garner things that mean even more to me than they do to them. So, I discover things that make life more bearable. What people don't understand is that my so-called moodiness and my desire to be alone is more often than not a time when I am in the process of replenishing myself as a human being. Again, that has seemed to make me out a man of mystery. It is a quality that has at times disturbed my relationship with others. For example, love affairs have been disturbed or stopped because the other person did not understand this need for solitary renewal. They felt that I was not sharing something with them, that I was keeping things from them. But they were wrong. What I was trying to do was to keep myself sane."

The year 1977 found Bruhn continuing to dance with American Ballet Theatre. He had triumphed in *Petrouchka* and would next immerse himself in *Firebird*, originally choreographed by Fokine in 1910 to the famous Stravinsky score. Bruhn's role would be that of Prince Ivan—a role not generally considered penetrating or technically challenging. Not surprisingly, the dancer imbued the character with enormous stature, transforming a pallid role into an altogether riveting characterization. As so many of his colleagues have stated, Bruhn has merely to walk or stand still onstage and every eye is instantly upon him. But Bruhn did more than stand or walk in *Firebird*. In the long pas de deux that opens the ballet, in which the title role was danced by Natalia Makarova, Bruhn elicited awe in his attempt to capture the elusive bird-creature. Every gesture, every choreographic nuance heralded a singular variety of emotions, and throughout the ballet, Prince Ivan emerged as a figure of flesh and blood.

American Ballet Theatre was to make its first European tour in seven years. This would be a long summer tour that would find the company performing in many cities, including Copenhagen. Erik Bruhn was invited to join the tour and he readily accepted. The only problem was repertoire. The company was not taking its productions of *Petrouchka* and *Firebird*. Although they would be performing *Jardin aux Lilas*, Bruhn declined to dance in this Tudor work. Mikhail Baryshnikov, Martine van Hamel, and Kirk Peterson would be dancing one of the company's most successful works, Twyla Tharp's *Push Comes to Shove*; Cynthia Gregory would do several pas de deux with Fernando Bujones and Ivan Nagy and dance in *Giselle* and *La Bayadère*; and there would be other, easily transportable, shorter works. Natalia Makarova would join the tour in various cities and it was thought that she and Bruhn might repeat their *Epilogue*. This, however, was not possible because rehearsal time proved too short. The company's management was eager for Bruhn to appear and tried to come up with suitable vehicles. Finally Daryl Dodson, then ABT's company manager, suggested José Limón's *The Moor's Pavane*.

Bruhn had always been a staunch admirer and champion of Limón's works. Indeed, he had met the choreographer many years earlier and had seen several of his works. As director of the Royal Swedish Ballet, he had invited Limón to come and set several of his works in Stockholm. The idea of dancing the role of the Moor decidedly appealed to Erik Bruhn. Although he had never before attempted a modern-dance work, he felt that this particular ballet, often seen in the repertoires of both modern and classical companies, would prove interesting and appropriate at this stage of his career.

More importantly, Bruhn had not appeared in Denmark for seven years. His last public appearance in Copenhagen was in *Rashomon*, but he had not stepped foot on the ballet stage since November 1970, when he gave his farewell performance there in *La Sylphide*. His return meant a great deal to him and, of course, the Danish public would want to see him dance under the best possible circumstances.

"I had seen *The Moor's Pavane* many times," says Bruhn. "It was also seen at the Royal Danish Ballet, when it was danced by Bruce Marks, Toni Lander, Henning Kronstam, and Vivi Flindt. They were all marvelous in it. Well, that somehow wasn't going to stop me from trying it as well. I had also seen Rudik as the Moor, during his *Nureyev and Friends* a couple of years ago in New York. In fact, Rudik asked me to dance the role of Iago for that occasion, but I didn't like the title of his presentation—I mean, the *Nureyev and Friends* bit. We didn't have an argument, but I said to him, 'Rudik, I cannot be one of your *friends* on that program, because there isn't one person on it who is a real friend, although you're calling it that.' Anyway, I thought it was a bad idea and I couldn't possibly do it. It wasn't that I didn't want to dance with Rudik on the same stage; just didn't like that billing.

"But I saw Rudik do the Moor, and as much as I liked him in other works he danced—especially in Balanchine's *Apollo*—I didn't much care for him as the Moor. Anyway, when Daryl Dodson suggested the Moor to me, I said yes. Right off, I was provided with a wonderful girl, Jennifer Scanlon from the José Limón Company, whom I instantly got on with, and she began to teach me the role. The first rehearsal was awful. I thought, This I cannot do. I'm getting out of here! But Jennifer, somehow realizing how I felt, helped me through those first terrible two or three hours. During the second rehearsal I was already in it. One good thing about my doing *Moor's Pavane* with ABT was that I would get a chance to dance it in Munich before bringing it to Copenhagen—and that was a relief."

Bruhn says that his performance of *The Moor's Pavane* in Munich was like a dress rehearsal. "I was still experimenting with the hair, the color of the face, and trying to remember all the steps, trying to *be* the character, and not to be out of line with the rest of the dancers. It was a good try. Unfortunately, we performed at the Olympic Hall, which is the last place one should see an intimate work like *The Moor*. It's enormous, and I'm sure it was lost on the audience."

From Munich, ABT traveled to Copenhagen, where the company would perform at the Tivoli Theatre. *The Moor's Pavane* would be presented there on the evening of July 15. This would be an important date for Erik Bruhn, and anticipation ran high as the day neared. That July 15 the house was packed. When the curtain rose on Limón's most famous work and the four figures stood in a circular, frozen tableau, an immense roar of applause greeted the dancers. Minutes later, this one-act ballet began and each artist gave their utmost to Limón's tragic unfolding to the Othello story. Cynthia Gregory, Sallie Wilson, and Ivan Nagy entered into their roles with particular passion, for they were aware that the audience was witness to Bruhn's first role as dancer in a modern-dance work. He had chosen to make his Moor light-skinned, although his dark hair and beard and small gold earring made of this Moor as potent a figure as any one had seen in the past.

He sustained the intensity of the role throughout—in fact, he drove the acting to its ultimate pitch. At the same time there was a measured quality to the needed histrionics. A great surge of anguish was expressed through clear, crystal-bright movement. Hands and arms were particularly eloquent and his duets with Ivan Nagy as Iago and Cynthia Gregory as Desdemona contained all the elements of high drama. When it was over, the applause was tumultuous and the curtain calls innumerable. When Bruhn finally took his solo bow there was near pandemonium. Erik Bruhn had reconquered the Danish ballet stage.

There would be other performances of *The Moor's Pavane* when American Ballet Theatre traveled to Paris—performances that were given in the out-of-doors at the Louvre's Cour Carrée. Once more, as in Munich, Limón's intimate work seemed dwarfed on the immense stage and it was only the artists' individual magnetism that saved these concluding European performances.

In Paris, Bruhn met with friends whom he had known for many years—a small enclave of people such as there are in several cities throughout the world. There was Violette Verdy, now director of the Paris Opéra Ballet, with whom Bruhn had danced at ABT during the late fifties. There was Arlette Castagné, a dancer and ballet teacher whom he had befriended during the sixties. There was Pierre Bergé, a director of the Yves Saint Laurent couture house and other enterprises, and there were all the French dancers whom he had partnered on various occasions during his career. Some, like Chauviré and Claude Bessy, had retired from the ballet stage, others, like Christiane Vlassi, were still dancing. But above all,

Paris was a city of memories for Bruhn. It was here that he and Sonia Arova had been young and in love and where each had looked to the future. It was in Paris that Bruhn had made the momentous decision to go to America under the aegis of Blevins Davis to begin his career at Ballet Theatre.

Some of his friends upon meeting him again would reminisce about the young Erik Bruhn and some would speak of him as a man who entered their lives and touched them in ways that left indelible impressions.

Violette Verdy remembers the young Erik Bruhn as someone in a constant state of struggle. "You know, Erik has always been the first one to be amazed at what came out of him. And it was difficult for him to live up to his sense of perfection. He was continually testing himself and also making that pilgrimage toward perfection which has so many built-in dangers. Erik has never been a dreamer, but has walked on the rocks of reality which have wounded him. I feel that he has bled from certain stigmas, of certain realizations which no one could protect him from. The point is, as an artist, Bruhn has always looked for a supreme answer, one that would be higher than anyone could possibly reach. He always has sought a perfection that is bigger than he is. This has hurt him, wounded him. It has made him condemn himself and partially destroy himself. None of us could help him in this respect."

Pierre Bergé had met Erik Bruhn through Roland Petit. He had seen him perform in *Giselle* and in Petit's *Carmen*. He has visited the dancer in Copenhagen or played host to him in Paris. "Erik is a very intelligent man who has a truthful and precise eye for things . . . that does not mean he is always a kind man. Frankly, I don't think one can ever find a man behind the artist, and especially behind a performing artist. Perhaps a man exists behind a writer, but not behind someone in the theater. These are people who are made only to 'represent,' only to perform. I recall Erik best during the time he was very close to Nureyev. I was touched to note the extraordinary admiration that Rudolf always had for Erik. Of course, Rudolf's celebrity has always been greater than Erik's. Rudolf was the big star, although Erik was the great, great dancer. Oddly enough, Erik never achieved Rudolf's stardom. About Erik's dancing: One simply cannot compare him to other dancers. He had a perfection which was a little cold, like the films of Bergman or Robert Bresson or the paintings of Braque. Always, there was total honesty and always an absence of compromise."

To so many of his friends Erik Bruhn represents the perennial wanderer. It is natural for them to assume that a wanderer is a man alone. But like all people who do not delude themselves, Bruhn is well aware that to wander means carrying the weight and responsibility of one's own life on one's own shoulders. There is no escaping who one is.

"Yes, I have friends," he says. "But I somehow move in and out of their lives, because that is what I have always done. I have to move . . . travel. It is part of my life, my physique, my mentality. Wherever I go, I travel with myself. I cannot stand still. I could not bear to stay in one place for too long. It would be so dull! I look at my friends, some of them married. The married ones simply accept their lives. Husband and wife take each other for granted, and in so doing have escaped their own *real* life. They talk about the weather, because there is nothing else to talk about. What I am saying is that for me, *real* life means not escaping what I consider to be my own reality.

"My friends have often said to me, 'Stop being so serious about everything! Why does everything have to have a meaning? Why can't you just talk about nothing? That's important too!' Well, that's very difficult for me to do. If I have nothing to say, then I'd rather not say anything. Even on the stage, whether a role was large or small, I could only dance it if it meant something to me. It may be pedantic, but I must find a reason for everything that I do. If I care for someone, there is a reason behind it. Even when I don't voice that reason, it's there. Silence with someone that you care for can be just as meaningful as making conversation.

"I know that many people think that I'm blasé, but I'm not. Certainly, I don't live *in* my past or *on* my past. I hardly ever think of it. When I am forced to think of it, I wonder whether it was *me*, or just a half-remembered person that I would perhaps like to have been. My ability to live in the present is what makes my future, and therefore my past."

Among all those whose lives have been touched by Erik Bruhn, Sonia Arova is perhaps the only woman whose feelings for him have remained relatively constant. Arova's career continued to be extremely active following her departure from American Ballet Theatre. In 1966 she was invited to head the Norwegian Ballet in Oslo, a post she held until 1970, at which time Rolf Liebermann of the Hamburg State Opera asked the ballerina to become director of the Hamburg Ballet. In the meantime, she had met a young dancer and choreographer, Thor Sutowski, whom she married in 1965. In 1968 Arova gave birth to their child, Ariane. Arova, then living and working in Oslo, wanted Erik Bruhn to be present at the baby's baptism. Bruhn is the child's godfather, but did not attend the christening.

Sonia Arova and Thor Sutowski now live in Birmingham, Alabama, where they are both on the dance faculty of the Alabama School of Fine Arts. In 1975 Arova developed cancer of the colon, which was successfully treated after several operations. Indeed, today, this vivacious and energetic woman continues to retain her glowing ballerina looks. She occasionally performs, but is mainly involved in teaching and choreographing.

Thinking back on her long relationship with Erik Bruhn, Arova turned wistful and somewhat sad. "What can I say? There is no middle-of-the-road for me in trying to analyze Erik. I think he is really a wonderful person and many times he has given of himself and cared for other people. Personally, I feel he could have given more. Perhaps it was a form of self-protection. He did not wish to get hurt himself. I cannot talk about Erik and be cool or objective. He has been part of my life. There were probably a lot of things I should have said to him when we were both young. I might have gotten a better deal for myself! In the back of my mind I felt that he should have understood what it was I wanted from him. It's true we had an instinctive understanding of one another, but somewhere along the line someone has to guide the other person into what instinct tells one to do.

"I *do* believe it would have been a big mistake for us to have gotten married. I am happy the way things turned out. We have a wonderful relationship now. Erik is very fond of my husband, Thor, and I do wish he could meet his godchild, Ariane.

"There is no bitterness, no regrets. Erik is a wanderer. He does not belong to one place or to one person. In a funny way, he is everywhere and nowhere. I like to think that in some way Erik has benefited from his relationship with me. I know *I* have benefited from my relationship with him. Now I consider myself lucky to have people to live for—my husband, my child. Because I am happy, I hope Erik is happy too."

〚 CHAPTER 27 〛

FOLLOWING ITS European tour, American Ballet Theatre returned to New York and after a brief layoff period opened its 1977 fall season at the Metropolitan Opera House. Erik Bruhn was among its principal dancers and on September 27 he appeared as Othello in Limón's *The Moor's Pavane*. His reception as the Moor was as critically dazzling as it had been in Europe.

Completing his Moors with ABT, Bruhn next went to Toronto, where he taught at the National Ballet of Canada School for a period of three months, beginning in October. It was during this period that the Canadian company also honored Bruhn with a special week of his own productions. The National Ballet of Canada was now under the direction of Alexander Grant, a former dancer with London's Royal Ballet, who had taken over the company in 1976. Not only was Bruhn celebrated with performances of his productions of *La Sylphide* and *Coppélia* but he also appeared in both these works. Peter Schaufuss, the young Danish dancer, had just left the New York City Ballet to join the Canadians and performed James in *La Sylphide* and Franz in *Coppélia*. With Bruhn in attendance, Schaufuss could not have had a more eloquent coach during the rehearsals of both ballets.

Bruhn enjoyed the presence of the young Dane in the company and, of course, takes a very special interest in those Danish dancers who, like himself, had risked losing their lifelong pension and security by leaving the

Royal Danish Ballet. He is proud of Schaufuss, Peter Martins, and Adam Lüders, all of whom had followed in his path.

"I must confess that I know Peter Schaufuss better as a dancer than as a person," says Bruhn. "He was devoted to his father and I consider his to be a big talent. In a way, Schaufuss is more like a Russian dancer than a Danish dancer. He has that physicality—that Russian look. Watching him dance, I am never bored. When some of the Danish boys resemble me too much, then I am somewhat less interested—which, of course, doesn't take away from their genuine talent. For example, Peter Martins has some of my own physical traits. But I tell you something. Martins *really* looks like a Prince. I had to *work* at it. As for Adam Lüders, he is a sweet boy. I remember talking with him when he was still very young and growing in size, and nothing seemed to be very coordinated. He was a very hard worker in Denmark and he tried to look very classical, which was somewhat problematic for him. Now that he has matured, and caught up with his physical growth, he is beginning to come into his own. I think he has found a home with the New York City Ballet. I doubt if he would have been too happy with the Danes."

When Erik Bruhn lives in Toronto, he stays with a young Greek-born dancer, Constantin Patsalas, a member of the National Ballet of Canada. Patsalas, who is also a gifted choreographer, has often performed in the character roles made famous by Erik Bruhn. Bruhn has provided Patsalas with the sort of insight that have made his performances studies in viable motivation and artistic refinement.

Bruhn also shares many of his free hours with Betty Oliphant, director of the National Ballet of Canada School. The two have been friends for many years, and when Bruhn was director of the Royal Swedish Ballet, it was Oliphant who was invited to come to Stockholm and restructure the ballet school there.

A woman of great charm, sensitivity, and energy, Betty Oliphant had been aware of Erik Bruhn while still living in her native England. "When I saw Erik, I saw my ideal in terms of artistry and technique. For me, he is the aristocrat of dance. Perfection, but not limited to just technique. It was the thought behind the dancing that deeply moved me. I saw Erik do many different roles, and have always put him on a pedestal.

"Erik is a very private person. When I first met him, he was going through a very troubled phase in his life. It was during his friendship with Nureyev—and he was drinking. I have seen him in agony and it is now so good to see him with so many of his problems resolved. I learned an enormous amount from Erik. I analyzed him technically and I have used what I analyzed in my own teaching, such as the position he holds in the air and the beautiful use of the foot.

"Of course, Erik is very loyal to Celia Franca. She did, after all, bring him to Canada. Personally, however, I feel that Celia does not understand Erik as a person. I also feel that she did not value Erik justly. Erik and I reached an agreement that he would have a separate relationship with Celia and with me, because Celia and I were not getting along. I must say, Erik showed me fantastic loyalty as well. For example, on the Twenty-fifth Anniversary of the National Ballet of Canada, Celia Franca got up on stage and thanked everyone, from secretaries to board members to volunteers. When she got to the end of her list, she had not mentioned me. Erik and I were sitting together and when he realized that Celia has failed to thank me, he took my arm and led me out of the theater."

When Celia Franca retired as director of the National Ballet of Canada in 1974, she was succeeded by David Haber. Betty Oliphant was at that time associate director of the company, but disagreeing with the new policies, she resigned the post. Today, she continues to be director of the school. It is with enormous pride that she points to Erik Bruhn as her most prized guest teacher, for she is aware that through him her ballet students will be in touch with an artist able to impart training at its most refined and rarefied.

When teaching, Erik Bruhn always wears a black top and black leg warmers, white socks, and white ballet slippers. In the classroom he gives a barre notable for its thoroughness and slowness. Soft-spoken, he moves to each student making myriad small corrections, and his eyes take in everyone and everything. His manner is gentle but firm, and he will take special care with those he deems particularly talented. Still, there is no favoritism in the classroom. He is as considerate and helpful to the slower pupils as to the more technically advanced ones. Bruhn will demonstrate, but is careful not to do so "full-out." That is, he will suggest through his own body what the pupil should execute. He then expects the students to make the movements as full as possible. He is always attentive to matters of body placement and line. He will correct details such as a position of the arms, hands, head, the gaze of the eyes, the direction of the shoulders. The keynote is care; and among his greatest contributions as a teacher is his ability to instill a sense of confidence in the student, relieving him or her of strain or tension by suggesting a manner in which control and security can be achieved.

The male pupils of the National Ballet of Canada School eagerly look forward to Bruhn's variation classes, which center on the Bournonville classics. It is here that Bruhn's remarkable knowledge of the style can be observed in greatest detail. In dissecting various variations from *Flower Festival at Genzano* or *La Sylphide*, Bruhn will demonstrate the manner in which difficult passages may be executed with ease and inevitability. In simple and direct language, he will explain the technical means by which the quicksilver flow of the Bournonville steps can be achieved. Because of the clarity of Bruhn's own demonstrations, each of the young male students easily understands what is demanded, although only time and constant practice will achieve the desired effect and accomplishment.

But it is not only in Canada that Bruhn's knowledge of Bournonville is sought after. Wherever he goes, professional dancers seek his advice on technical and stylistic matters. Nureyev, Baryshnikov, Ivan Nagy, Fernando Bujones, among many other male dancers, have benefited from Bruhn's always generous help.

A recently appointed principal dancer of American Ballet Theatre, the talented Kirk Peterson, is especially grateful for Bruhn's advice. "I saw Erik do James in *La Sylphide* and Albrecht in *Giselle*. I was a young corps dancer at ABT and when I watched Erik it was one of the most aesthetically beautiful experiences I've ever had. Not only was he a captivating presence, with his tremendously beautiful bearing, but the technique was so pure, so correct, and classically flawless. It was such an inspiration! He had such tremendous spontaneity—not just in his manner, but in his steps. When he executed a variation, it was as if you knew what the steps were going to be. He made it seem so simple.

"When he coached me in the role of Gurn in *La Sylphide*, he concentrated on purity and cleanness of line—on simplicity. I believe *that* was the formula for his own magnificent dancing. Also, his approach to acting is so wonderful—the motivations, the reasons for responding to things are always so intelligent and logical. I mean, he told me *why* Gurn gives Effie her flowers when he does. *Why* he feels the way he does toward her . . . things like that. Anyway, to have been coached by Erik Bruhn has been my greatest privilege."

Bruhn's regular teaching periods at the National Ballet of Canada School have yielded many rewards for him as well as for his students. In March 1978 he undertook to choreograph a new work, which he set on twelve male students. He entitled it *Here We Come*, and it was set to various American marches. This latest choreographic effort was so successful that it was taken on tour and met with high critical praise.

During the summer of 1977 Erik Bruhn received a most unusual invitation from the Fort Worth Ballet in Texas. They contacted him with the suggestion that he appear in a full-length ballet entitled *Rasputin—The Holy Devil*. Bruhn was offered the title role and told that the work had been created by James Clouser, an American choreographer who had once danced with American Ballet Theatre. Clouser had had considerable success as dancer and ballet master of the Royal Winnipeg Ballet and later freelanced as a choreographer for various companies. He eventually served as ballet master with the Houston Ballet and became its choreographer-in-residence and acting artistic director. In 1976 he formed his own company, Space/Dance/Theater, for which he choreographed a rock ballet, *Caliban*, based on Shakespeare's *The Tempest*.

With members of his own company, as well as the Fort Worth Ballet, Clouser composed his *Rasputin*, a retelling of events surrounding the mad monk Rasputin in Czarist Russia. Bruhn was attracted to the idea, although he was slightly apprehensive when he learned that the music for the ballet would be a rock score, composed and performed by St. Elmo's Fire Band, a well-known Texas rock group. While Bruhn and his friends had frequently enjoyed visits to discos and danced with relish to rock music, he had never quite envisioned himself dancing a full-evening ballet to what he assumed would be the ear-shattering sounds of a wild rock band. Too, the idea of Rasputin's story appended to this sort of music seemed highly unlikely to him. Still, there was something intriguing about it all, and after various conversations with James Clouser, he agreed to give the venture a try.

The ballet would receive a three-week-rehearsal period during the spring of 1978. Bruhn went to Fort Worth to begin work in April. He immediately found this regional company both talented and congenial, and he enjoyed the choreographic sessions with Clouser. As for the music, he soon realized that it would not be of the ear-shattering variety but have a soft-rock sound, which he found appealing. Somehow, the juxtaposition of the dramatic story line with the unexpected music was well realized by Clouser, and within a matter of days the company and its celebrated guest artist were deeply immersed in a ballet in which Bruhn danced one of his most effective and unusual roles.

The premiere of *Rasputin* took place on April 28, at the Tarrant County Convention Center Theater, and Bruhn, bearded and costumed in loose-fitting outfits suggestive of Russian peasant styles, negotiated an extraordinary variety of steps, turns, leaps, and all manner of feats recalling his bravura period. It was an amazing example of a dancer offering the kind of brio and élan of someone half his age.

Bruhn's next assignment took him back to New York City, where he appeared with American Ballet Theatre during May and June at the Metropolitan Opera House. He danced *Petrouchka*, *The Moor's Pavane*, and *La Sylphide*. What made this particular return engagement especially poignant was the reunion with his former great partner Carla Fracci. He danced *The Moor's Pavane*, with Fracci portraying the role of Desdemona, and *La Sylphide*, in which she danced the Sylph and he Madge the Witch.

It was strange and not a little disconcerting for Fracci to see her former partner in the guise of character dancer. The last time she had danced with Bruhn in *La Sylphide*, in 1971, he was her love-smitten James. This time they would be on the same stage, but hardly dance a step together.

"To tell you the truth, it didn't seem real," says Carla Fracci. "It seemed as though I were living in a dream. I thought Erik was magnificent in *The Moor's Pavane* when I danced with him in it. It was almost a bit embarrassing, because all these years had passed and I kept wondering what Erik might be feeling about *me*. I was wondering whether we would find one another again—if we could recapture that incredible feeling we once had together on the stage. When we did *La Sylphide*, the sensation was one of sadness. He had always been my James, and throughout the ballet I kept thinking of the many times we had danced together in this work and what a marvelous feeling there existed between us. My James during the ABT season was Ivan Nagy, and he was of course wonderful. But to see Erik standing there as the Witch gave me the strangest feeling.

Still, it was amazing to see how magnificently he had transformed all his art into this strong character role. He was positively frightening as Madge the Witch!"

Carla Fracci, with whom Bruhn had danced since 1962, continues to value her friendship with the dancer. "I look at Erik and I still see him as this absolutely extraordinary man. There are very few people in life that have truly meant something to me and Erik is one of them. My love for him and my respect for him will continue for the rest of my life."

The recent years have found important ballet stars making forays into modern dance. Rudolf Nureyev lent his body and intelligence to the art of Paul Taylor, Martha Graham, and Murray Louis, to name only the American modern-dance choreographers he has worked with. The José Limón Company, under the direction of one of its dancers, Carla Maxwell, now invited Erik Bruhn to make his first foray as a member of the Limón company. Not surprisingly, Miss Maxwell asked Bruhn to repeat the role of the Moor, but this time with a group of dancers totally imbued with modern-dance techniques.

Although *The Moor's Pavane* is in the repertoire of many classical companies, those who have seen Limón himself perform it in 1949 (together with Lucas Hoving as Iago, Betty Jones as Desdemona, and Pauline Koner as Emilia), have always felt that classically trained dancers could never quite do the work justice. Still, Limón himself adjusted this ballet to suit the movements of ballet dancers, and indeed helped in the staging of ABT's production when Bruce Marks first danced the title role. With Limón's death, in 1972, members of his company kept his repertoire alive and when Bruhn was invited to be a guest artist, Jennifer Scanlon continued to give Bruhn additional help in achieving the modern movements of the Moor, which would have to blend in with his co-dancers—Scanlon as Desdemona, Louis Solino as Iago, and Carla Maxwell as Emilia. Of particular help to Bruhn were two other Limón dancers—Clay Taliaferro and Ryland Jordan—each of whom had danced the role of the Moor in the past.

The José Limón season, with Erik Bruhn as guest artist, took place between June 4 and June 10, 1978, at the Cathedral Church of St. John the Divine in New York. An unusual concession on the part of Bruhn was his dancing in *The Moor* every evening of the run.

These Limón performances were deemed far superior to those Erik

Bruhn had given with ABT. The movements were sharper, more dynamic, and more impassioned than heretofore. Clearly the weeks of rehearsal with the Limón dancers solidified and clarified Bruhn's understanding of the Limón style.

The experience was particularly exhilarating for him, because among the many modern-dance choreographers that Bruhn had come in contact with, José Limón had the greatest impact on him. "I knew José Limón personally and had long admired his work. Back in the fifties, while I was still in the middle of my classical career, I went to see the premiere of his *Missa Brevis*, presented at the Juilliard School. José danced in it, and I was stunned. It was the first time I felt compelled to go backstage to see him. I wanted to thank him for giving me such a powerful experience. From then on we remained friends. Unfortunately I never saw him dance again, but that one impression was indelible."

Commenting on his adjustment to modern-dance techniques, Bruhn says: "It's a question of manipulating your weight. As the movements are generally earthbound, you have to find a different 'center.' You have to feel downward, without looking as if you are digging into the ground. Naturally I received help, and Jennifer Scanlon was wonderful about coaching me in these movements. Little by little, I conquered my fears and relaxed into the style, which, may I add, is by no means easy. I love Limón's work in that he choreographed roles for mature dancers—they are right for a dancer my age."

⟦ CHAPTER 28 ⟧

O N OCTOBER 3, 1978, Erik Bruhn turned fifty. He was in superb physical shape and he continued to radiate a sense of *bien-être*. Time had done little to change his extraordinary appearance. Still fair-haired, clear-eyed, and with barely discernible lines softly etching his handsome, aristocratic face, he quickly becomes the center of attention whenever he makes public or private appearances. At gatherings with fellow dancers, he continues to be a close and respected friend and he will invariably be full of questions about this one or that one, inquiring about someone's latest performance or future plans. When in New York, he has the opportunity of being a house guest of various friends, but since the death of Christopher Allan, he prefers the flexibility of hotel living. Bruhn also has a home in Spain; in 1969 he purchased a triplex apartment on the island of Ibiza. He has also bought a tract of land there, upon which he will eventually build a house. Thus it is that Bruhn's life is divided among several cities and continents. It is as he prefers it, for he cherishes his independence. He knows that wherever he happens to be, there will be friends to greet him, entertain him, amuse him, or comfort him. His working schedule is carefully planned in advance, and Bruhn has become extremely selective about projects that come his way.

As a world-famous figure of the dance, he is constantly asked to perform, to teach, to hold seminars, or to make television appearances. A celebrity whose mode of living has always been understated, he neither seeks nor enjoys the sort of spotlight allotted to dancers such as Nureyev or Baryshnikov. A man of many moods, and still thought to be an enigma, Bruhn holds his own counsel. As a man alone, cherishing his privacy, he does not lend himself to the artificialities often forced upon stars. Fiercely loyal to his friends, he will appear in their lives at unpredictable intervals and it will seem as if no break in time had taken place. There will be a telephone call and a relationship will resume.

When he is in New York, he will invariably be in touch with his friends at American Ballet Theatre—Lucia Chase, her assistant, Florence Pettan, and the various dancers and choreographers he has known for years. There will be dinners with Peter Martins and his friend Heather Watts, a soloist with the New York City Ballet. Bruhn will call his good friend Marit Gentele, now married to Sydney Gruson, a vice-president of *The New York Times*. Clive and Patricia Barnes will also be telephoned and the three will sit and reminisce for hours. Bruhn never fails to attend ballet performances when he himself is not dancing. He likes to keep up—see how the younger dancers are doing, spot this or that corps girl or boy, and perhaps seek out their names and mention them for possible advancement. Bruhn enjoys going to the theater and will occasionally be persuaded to go and dance at a disco. Best of all, he enjoys the intimate moment—the quiet drink or dinner with people he cares for.

For their part, these friends are continually astonished at Bruhn's intense interest in them and he never fails to bring out the best in them. During a recent visit to New York, he met with Peter Martins and Heather Watts.

Reflecting on Erik Bruhn, Martins and Miss Watts spoke about their friend. "To me Erik Bruhn stands alone," says Martins. "He is a loner, and no one is an heir to his throne. Nobody takes over where he left off. Nobody ever competes with Erik Bruhn. Great dancers have come along, since and before Erik and they all have contributed to the history of ballet, but for some strange reason, Erik's contribution is very mysterious. It is an enormous contribution, not in a public sense but in a truly historical sense. He is untouchable."

"Erik has always made me feel comfortable," says Heather Watts. "He was always incredibly glamorous to me. I think there is a great love between Erik and Peter. At the same time, there is a fierce denial of it. Maybe it's a Danish thing. Erik has always told me that he is waiting for

Peter to finally commit himself as an artist. I think he misses in Peter the thing that *he* has so strongly—that commitment and ability to really let go onstage. At the same time, I know that he is very proud of Peter."

Cynthia Gregory and her husband, John Hemminger, also value Erik Bruhn's friendship. Says Gregory: "Erik is a gentleman and very sophisticated—well traveled. Underneath it all, though, I think he is an insecure man. Of course, I think most artists are insecure. But Erik knows his worth. He is not overly egotistical as a lot of great artists are. There are paradoxes in him. I think Erik likes to shock people sometimes. There are moments when I don't know whether to take him seriously or not. I believe Erik wants to maintain a kind of mystery about himself. Personally, I think he's right to do this, because when people get to know artists too well, they tend to think less of them. You need to maintain some kind of distance, and Erik manages to do that.

"I can't think of any specific time when I have seen him angry. I believe he holds in an awful lot. But he can be cutting when he wants to be. Mostly he is very warm, loving, and giving, especially when you work with him. Erik has gotten more beautiful as he got older. I've seen pictures of him as a young man, but as he grew older he became more handsome and appealing. I think it's a shame that Erik somehow missed out on the tremendous publicity and fame that came to people like Nureyev and Baryshnikov—I mean, they are practically household names by now. Well, I feel that Erik is just as great a dancer—maybe even greater than either of them. You see, Erik was around at a time when ballet had not yet boomed, and so he lost out on all that publicity and all that stardom he could have had. The fact is, Erik is a legend."

Legend or not, Erik Bruhn looks upon himself as a human being first. While well aware of his stature as an artist, he is not a man given to dwelling on his legend, his genius, or his greatness as one of this century's foremost male dancers. In short, he is not someone who likes living in the past.

"I don't look back too much," he says. "I seldom think about my past, unless someone starts reminding me of it. In a strange way I was always frightened of my responsibility. At fifteen, it was announced that I was something incredible, and at nineteen, it was demonstrated that I was. Always I carried around with me the fear of being unable to fulfill what was expected of me . . . like being a rosebud that never bloomed. Some people suck up to that kind of ego satisfaction, but it was like poison for me. I suffered from hearing that. When fantastic reviews started to be written about me, I felt like running away. In later years I always waited three or four months before reading my reviews. In that way I could place some distance between myself and what the critics thought about me—good or bad. Of course, reviews are important, because they tell you where you stand. I have had my share of good reviews and bad reviews, but they always seemed unreal to me.

"The most important thing for a dancer is to mature into a human being. When I teach, I don't give messages. I am not a Bible. I give students what they need, but what interests me most is the personal relationship between a student and a teacher and that, of course, varies from student to student. I try to reach each one of my students on a level that they can relate to. Sometimes it's through humor. Sometimes it's by listening to their problems.

"What I can say to boys who are studying the dance is that they should be proud to be male dancers—and that they should show that pride. Coming from Denmark, I could always be openly proud of being a dancer. We have a tradition, and when you tell somebody in Denmark that you are a dancer nobody thinks twice about it—they accept it. Unfortunately, when I came to America in 1949, telling somebody that I danced for a living was looked upon as something very peculiar. Happily this is becoming less so—at least in the larger American cities."

Again and again, Erik Bruhn has been called a loner. The fact is that being a loner has never meant that Bruhn walks through life as a lonely, solitary figure in search of some unattainable fulfillment.

"If I am a loner, then I can tell you that I was a loner even in the happiest moments of my life. To me being a loner equals having freedom. I need to be allowed to have this freedom—to walk by myself. I assure you it does not mean being lonely. I cannot be with someone one hundred percent of the time. People don't understand that about me. If they let me go and let me be with myself, I will return and be able to give more of myself to them. I assure you, I do not shun people. It's just that I'm very selective. I am attracted to those people who have something to offer on an intellectual level—or someone who is simply amusing or fun to be with. Like everyone else, there are certain people to whom I am drawn physically, but it has seldom happened that I have come across that special combination where someone means something to me both physically *and* intellectually.

In fact, I have never come across that combination and I dare anyone to say that they have."

If Erik Bruhn has not met that individual who would totally fulfill his needs, he takes comfort and joy in his friends. Those who are closest to him in Denmark are his housekeeper, Ella Schram, Susse Wold, Ingrid Glindemann, and Lennart Passborg. There are, of course, many other people whom he knows and sees in Copenhagen—his lawyer, Esther Tonsgaard, Niels Bjørn Larsen and his wife, Elvi, the critic Svend Kragh-Jacobsen, and many dancers at the Royal Danish Ballet. His friendship with Rudolf Nureyev, complex though it is, continues to hold an important place in his life. There is the former dancer Ray Barra, whom he sees when he visits Ibiza.

Bruhn has strong opinions and strong feelings about all these individuals. "I see a great deal of Ingrid and Lennart. Ingrid has had a very turbulent past. Her father got into very serious business trouble when Ingrid was a teenager, and it left a mark on her. She suffered a great deal and built a wall around herself. Many people came to dislike her. But she worked very hard at the Royal Danish Ballet and developed into a good dancer. Ingrid and Lennart were very good to me during the time of my illness and I will not forget this. My friendship with Ingrid is based on the fact that she revealed herself to me. She broke down the barriers and we have a very honest and very warm relationship.

"As for Lennart, I know him less well, although I will say that I know him as well as he knows himself—and that is not enough. I like to think that I have helped him to understand himself better. He is a very beautiful person, and, as a doctor, he tries to be understanding of everyone's problems. In a sense, I feel that this great understanding of others somehow obscures a confrontation with himself. Perhaps in time this will come about.

"I have spoken about Ella Schram and Susse Wold. Ella is my family. I am very, very attached to her. Susse is a good and loyal friend. I can always depend on her. I have known Esther Tonsgaard, my lawyer, for twenty-five years. She has handled all my legal affairs in Denmark and most of my contracts. She is in charge of my estate. She pays all my bills. I have to ask her for money when I need it. She has invested some of my money, not always with my consent, but she has such a good nose for investments that

I have always made a profit. I trust her completely. At any rate, I would say that I am considerably well-off in Denmark. Esther is very warm toward me and when we are together we usually talk about business for half an hour and the rest of the time we just laugh and enjoy ourselves!

"There is Ray Barra. He was in my life. We became very great friends when I met him at Ballet Theatre many years ago, and I still love and adore that man to this day. He's done incredibly well for himself, first as a dancer and later as a ballet master and regisseur. Ray was and is a wonderful person.

"I think Rudik will always be in my life. You know, he was in Copenhagen recently and we celebrated his fortieth birthday together. Time is catching up with us both! Anyway, he was in Denmark with his *Nureyev and Friends*, and his performances created a whole new impact there. He had not danced in Denmark for some time and he was in wonderful shape. In fact, he was a different person—much more relaxed and easygoing.

"In thinking back on my friendship with Rudik, I would say that it has been intense, stormy, and at times very, very beautiful. I have probably done plenty of things to him that may have hurt or upset him. Well, he has done the same to me. And still we are very close. He has enjoyed, and still enjoys incredible fame. I remember years ago telling Rudik that I would never want to change places with him. I would never want to put up with the kind of things and people that he has to put up with in order to maintain that kind of stardom. But Rudik told me then that it was what he wanted and that he was willing to pay the price for it. I suppose I am paying my own price for *not* having gone after all that publicity, but I have never wanted it. I don't think I would have survived that. Rudik enjoys being a public person. I don't. At any rate, I don't believe that my friendship with Rudik can ever be lost—it will be there for all our lives."

Erik Bruhn is unafraid to speak about the strongest emotion of all—love. "I don't fall in love with love. When love is offered to me, I do not always respond well. I do not like for love to be something possessive. I find it smothering. For me, loving does not mean owning. Of course, one wants a response. Sometimes there is none. There were times when I fell in love, and I was not loved back. But I do not regret having felt something for someone. It's not that I am of the school which says it is better to give than to receive. But at least when I loved someone the emotion was valuable. It is important to love. We all need to give love and to receive love. I was privileged to have had at least a few affairs that were mutually satisfying. Those which failed were the ones when someone tried to possess me. *That* I could never abide, and when a relationship turned in that direction it became destructive. It burned me out as a person and as a dancer."

Erik Bruhn once said, "The perfect dancer has not yet been born." This statement reflects both his humility and his sense of self-awareness. He realizes that perfection is an abstraction—a goal, something ideal, perhaps something unattainable. And yet there is no question that for thirty years Erik Bruhn has represented the distillation of pure classical dance. As an artist he existed within a circumference of unmatched creative eloquence. No male dancer of his generation could approximate his singular gifts and no male dancer since has risen to prominence without somehow having been touched or inspired by him. Bruhn transformed control into freedom. He transmuted technique into expressivity. Through his body the difficult became the inevitable; the complex became radiantly effortless. His was an all-giving vision of movement at its most exalted, and the art of male dancing in the twentieth century was enriched by his presence.

But Bruhn's art has moved forward. He is perhaps the only male dancer to have masterfully bridged the gap between the danseur noble and the character dancer. Miraculously, and without apparent strain, he has moved from prince to wise king. In his maturity he has reached deep within himself and brought forth a new and shining nobility.

As a man, Erik Bruhn does not presume to have found wisdom. And yet he has reached a plateau on which to build a meaningful life. All artists are condemned to an insoluble duality. Bruhn's art exists only on the stage. Away from it, he is but another man. But as a man he has also moved forward. Through years of physical pain and through private anguish he has come to understand and be compassionate of the suffering of others and he is deeply moved by those who are able to face themselves with honesty, for he has done as much himself.

Being considered a legend, a man of mystery, an enigma, or an oracle holds little meaning for Erik Bruhn. "I strive to be a human being. I've never wanted to just move *through* life but go deeply into it even at the cost of complete personal fulfillment. If I have left some small mark in my profession, then I am content. But what ultimately means most to me is having matured as a man and perhaps reached some sort of inner strength to keep me alive and alert to everything and everyone around me."

⟦ Appendix ⟧

BRUHN: ROLES DANCED

(Titles of ballets in which Bruhn created roles appear in upper-case letters and give available production credits: *ch* = choreography; *m* = music; *arr* = arrangement; *b* = book; *d* = decor; *c* = costume; *l* = lighting)

1942
Napoli (*ch* A. Bournonville; *m* H. S. Paulli, E. Helsted, N. W. Gade, & H. C. Lumbye)
    Royal Danish Ballet School

1946
Far from Denmark (*ch* A. Bournonville; *m* J. Glaeser & H. C. Lumbye)
    Royal Danish Ballet
    (Indian Dance)
The Whims of Cupid and the Ballet Master (*ch* V. Galeotti; *m* J. Lolle)
    Royal Danish Ballet
    (Greek Dance)
Torvaldsen (*ch* H. Lander; *m* J. Hye-Knudsen)
    Royal Danish Ballet
    (Adonis)

1947
LOVERS' GALLERY
(*ch* F. Staff; *m* L. Berkeley; *b* & *d* G. Kirsta)
    Metropolitan Ballet, Royal Opera House, Blackpool, England
    October 10

1947–48
Swan Lake, Act II (*ch* L. Ivanov; *m* P. I. Tchaikovsky)
    Metropolitan Ballet
    (Siegfried)
Bluebird, Pas de Deux (*ch* M. Petipa; *m* P. I. Tchaikovsky)
    Metropolitan Ballet
Sleeping Beauty, Act III, Pas de Deux (*ch* M. Petipa; *m* P. I. Tchaikovsky)
    Metropolitan Ballet
    Ballet Theatre, 1950
Les Sylphides (*ch* M. Fokine; *m* F. Chopin)
    Metropolitan Ballet
    Royal Ballet, 1962
    (Poet)
Le Spectre de la Rose (*ch* M. Fokine; *m* C. M. von Weber)
    Metropolitan Ballet
Dances of Galatea and Pygmalion (*ch* V. Gsovsky; *m* Z. Kodaly)
    Metropolitan Ballet
Designs with Strings (*ch* J. Taras; *m* P. I. Tchaikovsky)
    Metropolitan Ballet
    Ballet Theatre, 1950
Swan Lake, Act I (*ch* M. Petipa; *m* P. I. Tchaikovsky)
    Metropolitan Ballet
    (Pas de Trois)

1948
THE PILGRIM'S PROGRESS
(*ch* A. Howard; *m* J. S. Bach, C. W. Gluck, & G. Handel; *arr* Sir M. Sargent;
    d & *c* J. Carl)
    Metropolitan Ballet, Royal Opera House, London, England
    June 19

1948–49
Conservatoriet (*ch* A. Bournonville; *m* H. S. Paulli)
    Royal Danish Ballet
    (Soloist)
Napoli (*ch* A. Bournonville; *m* H. S. Paulli et al.)
    Royal Danish Ballet
Le Beau Danube (*ch* L. Massine; *m* J. Strauss)
    Royal Danish Ballet
    (Hussar; Dandy)
Symphonie Fantastique (*ch* L. Massine; *m* H. Berlioz)
    Royal Danish Ballet
    (Shepherd)

Etudes (*ch* H. Lander; *m* K. Czerny; *arr* K. Riisager)
    Royal Danish Ballet
    (Corps de ballet)
The Widow in the Mirror (*ch* B. Ralov; *m* B. Christensen)
    Royal Danish Ballet
    (Officer; Adagio Dancer)
La Sylphide, Act II (*ch* A. Bournonville; *m* H. von Løvenskjold)
    Royal Danish Ballet
    (James)
Coppélia (*ch* H. Lander, after A. Saint-Léon; *m* L. Delibes)
    Royal Danish Ballet
    (Czardas)

1949
RHAPSODIE
(*ch* H. Lander; *m* F. Liszt; *d* & *c* S. Chaney)
    Royal Danish Ballet, Royal Opera House, Copenhagen
    March 5
Helen of Troy (*ch* D. Lichine; *m* J. Offenbach)
    Ballet Theatre
    (Orestes)
Romeo and Juliet (*ch* A. Tudor; *m* F. Delius)
    Ballet Theatre
    (Paris)

1950
Nutcracker, Pas de Deux (*ch* L. Ivanov; *m* P. I. Tchaikovsky)
    Metropolitan Ballet
    Ballet Theatre

1951
SCHUMANN CONCERTO
(*ch* B. Nijinska; *m* R. Schumann; *d* & *c* S. Chaney)
    Ballet Theatre, Metropolitan Opera House, New York
    September 27
Concerto (*Constantia*) (*ch* W. Dollar; *m* F. Chopin; *arr* A. Schmid)
    Ballet Theatre
Bluebeard (*ch* M. Fokine; *m* J. Offenbach; *arr* A. Dorati)
    Ballet Theatre
    (Prince Sapphire)
Don Quixote, Pas de Deux (*ch* A. Oboukhoff, after M. Petipa; *m* L. Minkus)
    Ballet Theatre
Les Patineurs (*ch* F. Ashton; *m* G. Meyerbeer; *arr* C. Lambert)
    Ballet Theatre
    (Lover)

La Sylphide (*ch* A. Bournonville; *m* H. von Løvenskjold)
 Royal Danish Ballet
 National Ballet of Canada, 1964
 (James)
Etudes (*ch* H. Lander; *m* K. Czerny; *arr* K. Riisager)
 Royal Danish Ballet
 (Solo dancer)
Romeo and Juliet (*ch* B. Bartholin; *m* P. I. Tchaikovsky)
 Royal Danish Ballet
 (Romeo)

1952
IDOLON
(*ch* F. Schaufuss; *m* P. I. Tchaikovsky; *d & c* H. Refn)
 Royal Danish Ballet, Royal Opera House, Copenhagen
 December 21
Symphony in C (*ch* G. Balanchine; *m* G. Bizet)
 Royal Danish Ballet
 (Third Movement)
A Folk Tale (*ch* A. Bournonville; *m* N. W. Gade, J. Peder, & E. Hartman)
 Royal Danish Ballet
 (Ove)

1953
LA COURTISANE
(*ch* B. Ralov; *m* N. Viggo Bentzon; *d* H. Bloch)
 Royal Danish Ballet, Royal Opera House, Copenhagen
 December 19
 (Prince)
PARISIANA
(*ch* B. Bartholin; *m* G. Tailleferre; *d* J.-L. de Rudder)
 December 19
 (A Student)

1954–55
Jardin aux Lilas (*ch* A. Tudor; *m* E. Chausson)
 Ballet Theatre
Black Swan, Pas de Deux (*ch* M. Petipa; *m* P. I. Tchaikovsky)
 Ballet Theatre
Aleko (*ch* L. Massine; *m* P. I. Tchaikovsky)
 Ballet Theatre
 (Aleko)
Theme and Variations (*ch* G. Balanchine; *m* P. I. Tchaikovsky)
 Ballet Theatre

Graduation Ball (*ch* D. Lichine; *m* J. Strauss; *arr* A. Dorati)
 Ballet Theatre
 (Pas de deux)
Helen of Troy (*ch* D. Lichine; *m* J. Offenbach)
 Ballet Theatre
 (Paris)
Mam'zelle Angot (*ch* L. Massine; *m* C. Lecocq)
 Ballet Theatre
 (Caricaturist)
Giselle (*ch* Coralli & J. Perrot; *m* A. Adam)
 Ballet Theatre;
 Royal Ballet, London, 1962
 Houston Ballet, 1967
 (Albrecht)

1955
Romeo and Juliet (*ch* F. Ashton; *m* S. Prokofiev)
 Royal Danish Ballet
 (Romeo)

1956
Pas des Déesses (*ch* R. Joffrey; *m* J. Field; *arr* J. Wilson)
 American Ballet Theatre
 (Saint-Léon)

1957
JOURNEY
(*ch* K. MacMillan; *m* B. Bartok; *d* N. Georgiadis)
 American Ballet Theatre, Phoenix Theatre, New York
 May 6
LA MUERTE ENAMORADA
 (*ch* E. Martinez; *m* J. Turina)
 American Ballet Theatre, Phoenix Theatre, New York
 May 20
 (The Youth)
THE CARELESS BURGHERS
(*ch* J. Sanders; *m* D. Marsh)
 American Ballet Theatre, Phoenix Theatre, New York
 May 27
 (The Troubador)
PAQUITA
(*ch* A. Fedorova; *m* L. Minkus)
 American Ballet Theatre, Carter Barron Amphitheatre, Washington, D. C.
 August 6

Blood Wedding (*ch* A. Rodrigues; *m* D. ApIvor)
American Ballet Theatre
(Bridegroom)
Graduation Ball (*ch* D. Lichine; *m* J. Strauss)
American Ballet Theatre
(Junior Cadet)

1958
CONCERTO
(*ch* H. Ross; *m* P. I. Tchaikovsky; *d* & *c* R. Bezombes)
American Ballet Theatre, Metropolitan Opera House, New York
September 16
TRISTAN
(*ch* H. Ross; *m* R. Wagner; *d* O. Smith; *c* M. White)
American Ballet Theatre, Metropolitan Opera House, New York
September 23
Miss Julie (*ch* B. Cullberg; *m* T. Rangström; *arr* H. Grossman)
American Ballet Theatre
(Jean)
Variations for Four (*ch* A. Dolin; *m* M. Keogh)
American Ballet Theatre

1959
DUET
(*ch* E. Bruhn; *m* A. Beriot)
With Violette Verdy, Bellas Artes, Guatemala City, Guatemala
June
Swan Lake, Act II (*ch* G. Balanchine; *m* P. I. Tchaikovsky)
New York City Ballet
(Prince Siegfried)
Divertimento No. 15 (*ch* G. Balanchine; *m* W. A. Mozart)
New York City Ballet
Pas de Dix (*ch* G. Balanchine; *m* A. Glazounov)
New York City Ballet
Nutcracker (*ch* G. Balanchine; *m* P. I. Tchaikovsky)
New York City Ballet
(Prince)

1960
PRELUDIOS PARA PERCUSIÓN from PANAMERICA
(*ch* G. Balanchine; *m* L. Escobar; *d* D. Hays; *s* B. Karinska & E. Francés)
New York City Ballet, City Center, New York
January 20

HELIOS
(*ch* E. M. Von Rosen; *m* C. Nielsen)
  Danish Television, December 31
  (The Young Man)
Night Shadow (*ch* G. Balanchine; *m* V. Rieti, after V. Bellini)
  New York City Ballet
  (The Poet)
Lady From the Sea (*ch* B. Cullberg; *m* K. Riisager)
  American Ballet Theatre
  (Seaman)
Carmen (*ch* R. Petit; *m* G. Bizet)
  Royal Danish Ballet
  (Don José)

1961
LA CHALOUPÉE
(*ch* R. Petit; *m* M. Thiriet)
  Royal Danish Ballet, Royal Opera House, Copenhagen
  February 18
  (The Gangster)
Grand Pas Glazounov from *Raymonda* (*ch* G. Balanchine; *m* A. Glazounov)
  American Ballet Theatre
Flower Festival at Genzano, Pas de Deux (*ch* A. Bournonville;
    m E. Helsted & H. S. Paulli)
  Jacob's Pillow Dance Festival
  Royal Ballet, London, 1962
Swan Lake (*ch* M. Petipa–L. Ivanov; *m* P. I. Tchaikovsky)
  Munich Ballet
  Royal Ballet, London, 1962
  Australian Ballet, 1962
  (Prince Siegfried)

1962
FANTAISIE
(*ch* E. Bruhn; *m* traditional Spanish; *d* J. Robin)
  Théâtre du Casino Municipale, Cannes, France
  January 6
TOCCATA AND FUGUE
(*ch* E. Bruhn; *m* J. S. Bach; *d* J. Robin)
  January 6
SERENADE
(*ch* E. Bruhn; *m* O. Olsen)
  Munich Ballet, Opera House, Munich, Germany
  June 19

DAPHNIS AND CHLOË
(*ch* J. Cranko; *m* M. Ravel; *d* N. Georgiadis)
    Stuttgart Ballet, Würtembergische Staatstheater, Stuttgart, Germany
    July 15
    (Daphnis)
PAS DE DEUX (Celebrating 100th Anniversary of Tivoli Gardens)
    (*ch* E. Bruhn)
    With Sonia Arova, Tivoli Gardens, Copenhagen, Denmark
    September
Sleeping Beauty (*ch* M. Petipa; *m* P. I. Tchaikovsky)
    Royal Ballet, London
    (Prince Florimund)
Coppélia (*ch* P. Van Praagh, after A. Saint-Léon; *m* L. Delibes)
    Australian Ballet
    American Ballet Theatre, 1968
    (Franz)

1964
Daphnis and Chloë (*ch* G. Skibine; *m* M. Ravel)
    Paris Opera Ballet
    (Daphnis)

1965
SCOTTISH FANTASY
(*ch* E. Bruhn; *m* G. Crum; *d* A. Delfau)
    Harkness Ballet, Théâtre du Casino Municipale, Cannes, France
    February 19
THE ABYSS
(*ch* S. Hodes; *m* M. Richter; *d* & *c* A. Delfau)
    Harkness Ballet, Théâtre du Casino Municipale, Cannes, France
    February 21

1966
ROMEO AND JULIET, Pas de Deux
(*ch* E. Bruhn; *m* S. Prokofiev; *d* E. D'Assia)
    Rome Opera Ballet, Teatro dell'Opera, Rome, Italy
    March 24

1967
MORNING, NOON, AND NIGHT
(*ch* B. Åkesson & K. Gundersen; *m* B. Hallberg)
    Swedish Television
    April 9
    (Solo)

1971

THE RIVER

(*ch* A. Ailey; *m* D. Ellington)
  American Ballet Theatre, New York State Theater, New York
  June 20
  (Additional pas de deux created for Bruhn and Natalia Makarova, after original premiere, June 1970)
The Miraculous Mandarin (*ch* U. Gadd; *m* B. Bartok)
  American Ballet Theatre
  (The Mandarin)

1974

RASHOMON (Play)

(Written by A. Kurosawa; directed by B. Mejding; *d* J. Voigt)
  Allescenen Theatre, Copenhagen, Denmark
  September 12
  (The Samurai)
La Sylphide (*ch* E. Bruhn, after A. Bournonville; *m* H. von Løvenskjold)
  National Ballet of Canada
  American Ballet Theatre, 1976
  (Madge the Witch)

1975

EPILOGUE

(*ch* J. Neumeier; *m* G. Mahler; *c* Michel)
  American Ballet Theatre, New York State Theater, New York
  July 8
Coppélia (*ch* E. Bruhn; *m* L. Delibes)
  National Ballet of Canada
  (Dr. Coppelius)
Raymonda (*ch* R. Nureyev, after M. Petipa; *m* A. Glazounov)
  American Ballet Theatre
  (Abdul-Rakhman)
La Ventana, Pas de Trois (*ch* E. Bruhn, after A. Bournonville; *m* H. C. Lumbye)
  American Ballet Theatre
Las Hermanas (*ch* K. MacMillan; *m* F. Martin)
  American Ballet Theatre
  (The Man)

1976

HAMLET CONNOTATIONS

(*ch* J. Neumeier; *m* A. Copland; *d* R. Wagner; *c* T. Aldredge)
  American Ballet Theatre, Uris Theatre, New York
  January 6
  (Claudius)

Jardin aux Lilas (*ch* A. Tudor; *m* E. Chausson)
  American Ballet Theatre
  (The Man She Must Marry)
Petrouchka (*ch* M. Fokine; *m* I. Stravinsky)
  American Ballet Theatre
  (Petrouchka)

1977
The Moor's Pavane (*ch* J. Limón; *m* H. Purcell)
  American Ballet Theatre
  José Limón Company, 1978
  (The Moor)

1978
RASPUTIN—THE HOLY DEVIL
(*ch* J. Clouser; *m* St. Elmo's Fire Band; *c* S. Zarek; *l* J. E. Salberg)
  Fort Worth Ballet and James Clouser's Space/Dance/Theater, Tarrant
    County Convention Center, Fort Worth, Texas
  April 28
  (Rasputin)

1979
THE MIST
(*ch* C. Patsalas; *m* L. Janáček)
  Pas de deux, with Karen Tessmer, Wolf Trap, Virginia
  June 12

BRUHN: PRODUCTIONS

CONCERTETTE
  (*m* M. Gould; *d* J. Espen-Hansen)
  Royal Danish Ballet, Royal Theatre, Copenhagen
  May 18, 1953

FESTA
  (*m* G. Rossini)
  American Ballet Theatre, Phoenix Theatre, New York
  May 6, 1957

DUET
  (*m* A. Beriot)
  Erik Bruhn and Violette Verdy, Bellas Artes, Guatemala City, Guatemala
  June 1959

FESTA (New version)
Royal Danish Ballet, Royal Theatre, Copenhagen
October 1, 1959

NAPOLI, Pas de Six
(after A. Bournonville; m H. S. Paulli et al.)
Royal Ballet, Royal Opera House, London
May 3, 1962

FLOWER FESTIVAL AT GENZANO
(after A. Bournonville; m E. Helsted & H. S. Paulli)
May 3, 1962

TOCCATA AND FUGUE
(m J. S. Bach; d J. Robin)
Théâtre du Casino Municipale, Cannes, France
January 6, 1962

FANTAISIE
(m traditional Spanish; d J. Robin)
January 6, 1962

SERENADE
(m O. Olsen)
Munich Ballet, Opera House, Munich, Germany
June 19, 1962

PAS DE DEUX (Celebrating 100th Anniversary of Tivoli Gardens)
Erik Bruhn and Sonia Arova, Tivoli Gardens, Copenhagen
September 1962

GISELLE
(after Coralli and Perrot; m A. Adam)
Royal Danish Ballet, Royal Opera House, Copenhagen
1964
(with d D. Heeley)
Royal Swedish Ballet, Opera House, Stockholm
February 28, 1969

LA SYLPHIDE
(after A. Bournonville; m H. Løvenskjold)
National Ballet of Canada, O'Keefe Center, Toronto
December 31, 1964
(with d E. D'Assia)
Rome Opera Ballet, Rome Opera House, Rome, Italy
March 24, 1966
Royal Swedish Ballet, Opera House, Stockholm
June 1, 1968

(with *d* R. O'Hearn)
American Ballet Theatre, New York State Theater, New York
July 7, 1971

SCOTTISH FANTASY
(*m* G. Crum; *d* A. Delfau)
Harkness Ballet, Théâtre du Casino Municipale, Cannes, France
February 21, 1965

SWAN LAKE, Act II
(after L. Ivanov; *d* E. D'Assia; *m* P. I. Tchaikovsky)
Rome Opera Ballet, Rome Opera House, Rome, Italy
March 24, 1966

ROMEO AND JULIET, Pas de Deux
(*m* S. Prokofiev; *d* E. D'Assia)
March 24, 1966

SWAN LAKE
(after L. Ivanov & M. Petipa, *Mazurka* and *Spanish Dance*
   by permission of Bolshoi Ballet)
National Ballet of Canada, O'Keefe Center, Toronto
March 27, 1967

LES SYLPHIDES
(after M. Fokine; *m* F. Chopin; *d* P. Farmer)
Royal Danish Ballet, Royal Theatre, Copenhagen
   1972
National Ballet of Canada, O'Keefe Center, Toronto, Canada
   1973

COPPÉLIA
(*m* L. Delibes; *d* M. Strike)
National Ballet of Canada, O'Keefe Center, Toronto
February 8, 1975

LA VENTANA, Pas de Trois
(after A. Bournonville; *m* H. C. Lumbye)
American Ballet Theatre, New York State Theater, New York
July 28, 1975

HERE WE COME
(*m* American marches)
National Ballet of Canada School, St. Lawrence Center, Toronto
April 28, 1978

[[Filmography]]

Symphonie Fantastique
Royal Danish Ballet
Filmed in Copenhagen
April 1948

Hans Christian Andersen
Samuel Goldwyn Productions
1952
With Danny Kaye, Zizi Jeanmaire,
and Roland Petit
Choreography by Roland Petit

Don Quixote, Pas de Deux
Filmed at Jacob's Pillow by
Carol Lynn
1955
With Mary Ellen Moylan

Giselle, Act II, Pas de Deux
Filmed at Jacob's Pillow by
Carol Lynn
1955
With Alicia Alonso

The Nutcracker, Act II, Pas de Deux
Filmed at Jacob's Pillow by
Carol Lynn

1955
With Mary Ellen Moylan

Swan Lake, Act III, Black Swan
Pas de Deux
Filmed at Jacob's Pillow by
Carol Lynn
1955
With Alicia Alonso

Swan Lake, Act III, Black Swan
Pas de Deux
Ed Sullivan Show, CBS-TV
August 25, 1957
With Nora Kaye

Don Quixote, Pas de Deux
Bell Telephone Hour, NBC-TV
January 6, 1961
With Maria Tallchief

La Sylphide, Act II
Bell Telephone Hour, NBC-TV
October 22, 1962
With Carla Fracci

Swan Lake, Act III, Black Swan
  Pas de Deux
Bell Telephone Hour, NBC-TV
February 4, 1963
With Sonia Arova

Coppélia, Act III, Pas de Deux
Bell Telephone Hour, NBC-TV
November 11, 1963
With Sonia Arova

Many Faces of Romeo and Juliet
Bell Telephone Hour, NBC-TV
September 22, 1967
With Carla Fracci
Choreography by Erik Bruhn

Swan Lake
WNET-TV/13
Telecast of
Canadian Broadcasting Corporation
  1967 broadcast
November 27, 1970
With National Ballet of Canada

Swan Lake
Live From Lincoln Center,
  WNEW-TV/13
June 30, 1976
American Ballet Theatre
With Natalia Makarova and
  Ivan Nagy
Intermission interview with
  Erik Bruhn

⟦ Selected Bibliography ⟧

Åschengreen, Erik. "Forsvinder Bournonville-Ballettern." *Perspektiv*, Copenhagen, March 1962, pp. 53–55.

Barnes, Clive. "Bruhn and Fracci in 'Sylph of the Highlands.'" *New York Times*, July 18, 1968.

———. "A Star, But Not Overnight." *New York Times*, January 19, 1969.

———. "'The Miraculous Mandarin.'" *New York Times*, July 31, 1971.

———. "Bruhn—A Great Dancer Retires." *New York Times*, January 16, 1972.

———. "Men Are the Most Exciting Dancers." *New York Times*, August 18, 1974.

———. "Bruhn Gives 'Coppélia' a New Look." *New York Times*, March 2, 1975.

———. "Bruhn's Career Is Set to Enter New Phase." *New York Post*, May 26, 1978.

Barnes, Patricia. "American Ballet Theatre at State Theater, New York. Line-Up of Stars." *Dance and Dancers*, London, January 1976, pp. 31–33.

———. "New York: American Ballet Theatre at the Uris Theatre & Metropolitan Opera House: The Year in Retrospect." *Dance and Dancers*, London, December 1976, pp. 38–40.

Barzel, Ann. "Looking at Television." *Dance Magazine*, New York, December 1962, pp. 28–29.

Bivona, Elena. "Bruhn: Star Trip." *Ballet Review*, Brooklyn, N.Y., v. 2, no. 3, September–October, 1968, pp. 15ff.

Bruhn, Erik. *Beyond Technique*. New York: Dance Perspectives Foundation, 1968, 50 pp.

———. "Ballon and the Bournonville Style," with Lillian Moore, *The Dancing Times*, London, November 1961, pp. 89–95.

————, and Moore, Lillian. *Bournonville and Ballet Technique: Studies and Comments on August Bournonville's Études Chorégraphiques.* London: A. & C. Black, 1961, 70 pp.

"Bruhn, Bournonville, and Ballet." *Dance Magazine*, New York, February 1962, pp. 38–42.

"The Bruhn-Fracci 'Romeo and Juliet' on NBC-TV, September 22, 1967." *Dance News*, New York, September 1967, p. 13.

"Bruhn Leaves Royal Danish Ballet to Join Ballet Theatre." *Dance News*, New York, December 1955, p. 1.

Cohen, Nathan. " 'La Sylphide' in Toronto: Erik Bruhn Triumphs and Rudolf Nureyev Does Well with the Canadian National Ballet." *The Dancing Times*, London, February 1965, pp. 236–37.

————. "For Sheer Humor It's Hard to Beat the National 'Swan Lake.' " *Toronto Daily Star*, April 23, 1968.

Croce, Arlene. "A Brief Against Bruhn, Critics, and Miss Farrell." *Ballet Review*, Brooklyn, N.Y., v. 2, no. 3, September–October 1968, pp. 3–9.

Crowle, Pigeon. "Erik Bruhn." *Ballet Today*, London, October 1956, pp. 14–15, 20.

"Dunham, Bruhn, Fracci Receive 1969 Dance Magazine Awards." *Dance Magazine*, New York, July 1969, pp. 44–46.

"Erik Bruhn Joins Hightower in Cannes, Tallchief in Lisbon." *Dance News*, New York, May 1963, p. 6.

"Erik Bruhn Talks to Dance and Dancers." *Dance and Dancers*, London, June 1962, pp. 28–29.

Flage, Percy. "Bruhn Made a Knight of the Order of Dannebrog. . . ." *Dance News*, New York, September 1963, p. 8.

Franks, A. H. "Erik Bruhn with the Royal Ballet." *The Dancing Times*, London, May 1962, pp. 470–72.

————. "The Press and the Dance: Bruhn, Nerina, and Fonteyn." *The Dancing Times*, London, May 1962, p. 485.

————. "Dancer and Teacher: A Very Special Guest." *The Dancing Times*, London, June 1962, p. 551.

Fridericia, Allan. "Ballet in Denmark." *The Dancing Times*, London, February 1951, pp. 269–70, 281.

"Froken Julie 25 ar-nagra minnesbilder," in: *Dans; Tidskrift for Dansvetenskap*, Stockholm, no. 6, February 1975, pp. 1–13.

Goldner, Nancy. "American Ballet Theatre, Gala 35th Anniversary Performance, New York City Center, January 11, 1975." *Dance News*, New York, February 1975, pp. 5, 10.

————. "National Ballet of Canada, Metropolitan Opera House, July 22–August 10." *Dance News*, New York, November 1975, pp. 12–13.

Goodman, Saul. "Brief Biographies: Erik Bruhn." *Dance Magazine*, New York, May 1955, pp. 40–41.

Gruen, John. "Observing Dance: Carla Fracci." *Dance Magazine*, New York, October 1974, p. 34.

———. "Erik Bruhn." *The Private World of Ballet*. New York: The Viking Press, 1975, pp. 268–77.

———. "Erik Bruhn Returns to Dance." *New York Times*, Sunday, June 4, 1978, Section D, pp. 17, 30.

Harriton, Maria. "Giselle on Film with Fracci and Bruhn." *Dance Magazine*, New York, December, 1969, pp. 24–27.

Hering, Doris. "Maria Tallchief, Erik Bruhn and assisting artists. . . ." *Dance Magazine*, New York, August 1961, p. 57.

Hodgson, Moira. "Cynthia Gregory: In Search of Siegfried." *Dance News*, New York, March 1975, pp. 1–4.

———. "Erik Bruhn: A New Dimension." *Dance News*, New York, December 1975, pp. 3, 7.

Joel, Lydia. "Erik Bruhn and Stockholm." *Dance Magazine*, New York, September 1968, p. 45.

Kragh-Jacobsen, Svend. *Aereskunstneren Erik Bruhn*. Copenhagen, 1965, 38 pp.

Macdonald, Fraser. "Canadian Sylphide Triumph for Bruhn and Nureyev." *Dance News*, New York, February 1965, p. 11.

Manchester, P. W. " 'Hans Christian Andersen' with Ballets by Roland Petit." *Dance News*, New York, March 1953, pp. 9, 12.

———. "The Matinee That Made History." *Dance News*, New York, June 1955, p. 8.

———. "Bruhn to Return to Copenhagen." *Dance News*, New York, June 1958, p. 6.

Martin, John. "Another Link in the History of 'Giselle.' " *Dance Magazine*, New York, July 1955, pp. 14–21.

Maynard, Olga. "Erik Bruhn Talks to Olga Maynard." *Dance Magazine*, New York, January 1966, pp. 22–23.

———. "On Tour with a King, Two Queens, and Four Aces." *Dance Magazine*, New York, May 1971, pp. 44–46.

———. "Peter Schaufuss Far from Denmark." *Dance Magazine*, New York, September 1974, pp. 36–39.

———. "Conversations with Cynthia Gregory." *Dance Magazine*, New York, April 1975, pp. 36–46.

Monahan, James. "The Royal Academy of Dancing Gala Matinee." *The Dancing Times*, London, January 1961, p. 233.

Moore, Lillian. "New York: Bruhn and Arova." *The Dancing Times*, London, January 1964, p. 201.

———. "Erik Bruhn: Profile." *The Dancing Times*, London, May 1964, pp. 410–11.

———. "Barre Exercises by Erik Bruhn." *The Dancing Times*, London, April 1966, p. 356.

————. "Soft Frappé: A Barre Exercise with Erik Bruhn." *The Dancing Times*, London, May 1966, p. 421.

Pepys, Tom. "Curtain Up!" *Dance and Dancers*. London, October 1974, p. 12.

Percival, John. "Assembly of Stars for American Ballet Theatre's 35th Anniversary Season." *Dance and Dancers*. London, March 1975, pp. 18–20, 25–27, 34, 36, 38.

"Personality of the Month: Erik Bruhn." *Dance and Dancers*, London, July 1953, p. 3.

"Personality of the Month: Erik Bruhn." *Dance and Dancers*, London, March 1962, p. 5.

"Royal Dane." *The Dancing Times*, London, June 1975, pp. 473–75.

Siegel, Marcia B. "One Thousand Roses." *The Hudson Review*, January 1975, pp. 583–88.

Ståhle, Anna Greta. "Cunningham, Bruhn, Flindt Score in Scandinavia." *Dance News*, New York, November 1964, p. 5.

————. "Erik Bruhn Accepts Post as Swedish Ballet Director." *Dance News*, New York, February 1967, p. 7.

Svedin, Lulli. "Dance in Sweden." *Dance Magazine*, New York, May 1971, pp. 50–61.

Terry, Walter. "Erik Bruhn: Rare Artistry." New York *Herald Tribune*, June 24, 1960.

————. "Teen-age Squeals for Two Ballet Stars." New York *Herald Tribune*, June 10, 1962.

————. "World of Dance: A Newcomer Plus Two Top Stars." *Saturday Review*, New York, June 10, 1967.

————. "Beyond Technique." *Saturday Review*, New York, February 22, 1969.

————. "An Era's End: A Pioneer, A King and a Dancing Prince." *Saturday Review*, February 12, 1972.

Tobias, Tobi. "Erik Bruhn's New Career: 'I am Not Finished as a Dancer.' " *New York Times*, June 29, 1975.

————. "Peter Martins." *Dance Magazine*, June 1977, pp. 36–46.

————. "Works and Progress: American Ballet Theatre, July 1–August 9, 1975, New York State Theater." *Dance Magazine*, New York, October 1975, pp. 39–59.

"Toronto Excitement; Bruhn and Nureyev Share the National Ballet of Canada's Debut of 'La Sylphide.' " *Dance Magazine*, New York, February 1965, pp. 22–23.

Williams, Peter, and John Percival. "Upholding the Traditions." *Dance and Dancers*, London, July 1975, pp. 14–19, 38, 40.

Wilson, G. B. L. "Erik Bruhn's First Festival; Ballet in Stockholm and Drottningholm." *The Dancing Times*, London, August 1968, p. 580.

⟦ Index ⟧